WILLIAM OF SHERWOOD'S

Introduction to Logic

translated with an
introduction and notes by
NORMAN KRETZMANN

UNIVERSITY OF MINNESOTA PRESS
Minneapolis

Printed in the United States of America at the
North Central Publishing Company, St. Paul

Library of Congress Catalog Card Number: 66-16468

PUBLISHED IN GREAT BRITAIN, INDIA, AND PAKISTAN BY THE OXFORD
UNIVERSITY PRESS, LONDON, BOMBAY, AND KARACHI, AND IN CANADA
BY THE COPP CLARK PUBLISHING CO. LIMITED, TORONTO

To Anita

Preface

Among philosophers there is more interest in medieval logic now than at any other time since the middle ages. Nevertheless, only two or three specialized treatises or portions of treatises have been translated — by Mullally and Boehner, for example — and no general medieval treatise on logic has been available in a complete English translation. The present volume constitutes a first step toward filling that gap in the literature. The reasons why William of Sherwood's *Introductiones in logicam* seemed a good choice for that purpose are set forth in the introduction to the translation. I have provided some of the background necessary for an understanding of medieval logic in the notes to the translation, but they are, of course, oriented specifically around Sherwood's treatise. For presentations of the broader theoretical and historical background I recommend Boehner's *Medieval Logic*, Bocheński's *History of Formal Logic*, and especially Kneale's *Development of Logic*.

In preparing the translation I made use of Martin Grabmann's edition, published as "Die Introductiones in logicam des Wilhelm von Shyreswood (†nach 1267)" in *Sitzungsberichte der Bayerischen Akademie der Wissenschaften*, Philosophisch-historische Klasse, Jahrgang 1937, Heft 10. I am grateful to the Bayerische Akademie der Wissenschaften for granting permission to publish this translation.

Professor Gareth B. Matthews of the University of Minnesota first encouraged me to undertake this project and has helped immeasurably at every stage of its development, not only with the interpretation of the text but even with the practical details of publication. Whatever value the book has was greatly enhanced by his efforts, for which I am deeply indebted to him. I am grateful also to the members of my seminars in medieval philosophy, particularly Mr. Gerald W. Lilje and Miss Marilyn McCord, for their many careful criticisms; and to Mrs. Sally Ginet, who corrected or clarified many passages in the text and the notes in the course of typing the final draft; and to my wife, Barbara, who helped in countless ways with the preparation of the book. Finally, I wish to thank the administration of the Bibliothèque Nationale for permitting the microfilming of the Sherwood manuscript, the University of Illinois Library for providing me with the microfilm, and the editorial staff of the University of Minnesota Press for their many helpful suggestions.

NORMAN KRETZMANN

University of Illinois
October 1965

Table of Contents

WILLIAM OF SHERWOOD'S
Introduction to Logic

Introduction

William of Sherwood [1] was an English logician of the thirteenth century whose works constitute an important stage in the development of medieval logic. His career can now be traced with some confidence, but there are several reasons why it is difficult to be certain about his life and his influence on others. To begin with, for Sherwood (as for many other medieval philosophers) documentary evidence is scanty, and some of the documents we do have are puzzling. Moreover, thirteenth-century philosophers (with the notable exception of Roger Bacon) rarely referred to their contemporaries at all and almost never acknowledged intellectual debts except to the standard authorities, e.g., Aristotle, Augustine, Boethius. Finally, until quite recently the treatment of Sherwood by historians has been misleading because he has so often been confused with other thirteenth-century Williams. [2]

Judging by his appellative and the later definite dates we have for him, he was probably born in Nottinghamshire between 1200 and 1210. It is virtually certain that, like other learned Englishmen of the time, he studied at Oxford or Paris or both. [3] Whether or not he was a student

---

[1] Like most medieval names, this one is spelled in several different ways, paralleling the spellings of the English place-name "Sherwood." All the following versions are found in references to William of Sherwood in medieval and modern sources: Schirewode, Schirwood, Schyrwode, Schyrwodus, Schyrwood, Scirwood, Scurwod, Scurwood, Sherwood, Shireswoodus, Shirewode, Shirovodus, Shirvodius, Shirwood, Shirwoode, Shyreswod, Shyreswode, Shyreswood, Shyrewode, Shyrowode, Shyrwode, Shyrwood, Sirewode, Sirwode, Skirwodde, Syrewode, Syrewude, Syrwode. Medieval versions of his first name are Guilelmus, Gulielmus, Guillielmus, Wilhelmus, Willelmus, Williamus, Willielmus.

[2] E.g., William of Leicester (d. 1213) and William of Durham (d. 1249). See Martin Grabmann, "Einleitung" to his edition of Sherwood's *Introductiones in logicam* (hereafter cited as "Einleitung"), pp. 11–13. This essay of Grabmann's is by far the most extensive historical study of Sherwood to date.

[3] John Leland (ca. 1506–1552) says in his *Commentarii de Scriptoribus Britannicis* (hereafter cited as *Commentarii*), 2.260, that Sherwood began his studies at Oxford and received most of his education at Paris; however, he gives no source for this and is provably mistaken in most of his short chapter (2.260–262) on Sherwood.

at the University of Paris, we have several reasons for believing that he was a master there. In the first place, he lived at a time when "scholars were, indeed, to a degree which is hardly intelligible in modern times, citizens of the world" and when "almost all the greatest schoolmen . . . taught at Paris at one period or other of their lives." [4] Secondly, in each of his two main works Sherwood uses an example with a Parisian setting: in one case the Seine, and in another the University.[5] Finally, all the philosophers who show signs of having been influenced directly by Sherwood or his writings were at Paris at some time during a span of years when he certainly could have been lecturing there, given what is known of his later life.

All the books that have been reliably ascribed to Sherwood are logical treatises (see pp. 12–16 below), and the period when he is likely to have been at Paris is one in which logic formed "the main subject of instruction." "The old and new dialectic of Aristotle, i.e. the whole Organon together with the *Isagoge* of Porphyry, are to be read *ordinarie* [as the prescribed curriculum]; rhetoric and philosophy [i.e., the first three books of Aristotle's *Ethics* and the subjects of the quadrivium: arithmetic, geometry, music, and astronomy] are reserved by way of a treat for festivals." [6] Naturally, then, Sherwood had his greatest influence on other logicians. Benefiting most directly from his work were Peter of Spain, who studied and lectured at Paris before he left for Siena in 1245,[7] and Lambert of Auxerre, who taught logic at Paris around 1250.[8] Peter of Spain's *Summulae logicales* [9] became the stand-

---

[4] Hastings Rashdall, *The Universities of Europe in the Middle Ages* (hereafter cited as *Universities*), 1.540.

[5] *Introductiones in logicam* (hereafter cited as *Introductiones*), p. 87: "whatever runs has feet, the Seine runs; therefore the Seine has feet" (p. 136 below); *Syncategoremata*, p. 82: "no man lectures at Paris unless he is an ass." On place-names in medieval examples see Grabmann, "Einleitung," p. 17, and Étienne Gilson, *History of Christian Philosophy in the Middle Ages* (hereafter cited as *History*), pp. 679–680.

[6] Rashdall, *Universities*, 1.440–441.

[7] Peter of Spain, later Pope John XXI, was born sometime between 1210 and 1220 and died May 20, 1277; see Innocentius M. Bocheński, "Introductio" to his edition of Peter of Spain's *Summulae logicales* (hereafter cited as "Introductio"), p. xii, and Gilson, *History*, pp. 319–323, 680.

[8] Not much is known of Lambert of Auxerre. His *Summulae logicales* has sometimes been placed between Sherwood's and Peter of Spain's, sometimes after both. It has not yet been printed. As evidence that these three treatises "belong together," Martin Grabmann ("Forschungen über die lateinischen Aristotelesübersetzungen des XIII. Jahrhunderts" (hereafter cited as "Forschungen"), pp. 40–41) cites a late thirteenth-century commentary on Aristotle's Organon "based on the

4

ard logic text of the later middle ages and the renaissance.[10] Since the nature and organization of its contents owes much to Sherwood's work, his influence continued to be felt, though not directly,[11] throughout the period of greatest development in medieval logic, culminating in the work of William of Ockham (1280/90–1347/49).

Apparently metaphysicians as well as logicians learned from Sherwood at Paris. Albert the Great began lecturing there in 1240, and his pupil, Thomas Aquinas, arrived at Paris in 1245 and stayed until he and Albert left together in 1248.[12] In his commentary on Aristotle's *Prior Analytics*, Albert treats the notion of "appellation" (see p. 106 below) as Sherwood does rather than as Peter of Spain does; and Aquinas seems to be using Sherwood's analysis of modal propositions in his own short treatise *De propositionibus modalibus*.[13]

Sherwood's importance among his contemporaries seems to have gone unacknowledged except by Roger Bacon, whose opinion of most of the philosophers of his time verged on disgust. Bacon must have been a Parisian master before 1245, and he went back to Oxford about 1247;[14] he might very well have known Sherwood at both universities. In his *Opus tertium*, written in 1267 in response to a mandate from Pope Clement IV in 1266, he addressed the Pope as follows:

And since I considered that nothing ought to be presented to your Highness except something magnificent, to your Beatitude something unsurpassed, to your Wisdom something most beautiful, it is no wonder if I put off undertaking the treatise — which you might measure against the more famous wise men in Christendom, one of whom is brother Albert of the order of the Preachers [i.e., Albert the Great, a Domini-

---

writings of these three logicians." On Lambert see Fernand van Steenberghen, *Aristotle in the West* (hereafter cited as *Aristotle*), pp. 103–104; Gilson, *History*, pp. 318–319, 680; Grabmann, "Forschungen," pp. 35–36, 41–58.

[9] Edited by Bocheński, partially translated by Mullally.

[10] In his bibliography, pp. 133–158, Mullally describes one hundred and sixty-six editions of the book, one hundred and fifteen of them including a commentary on it. In *Paradiso*, Canto XII, Dante places Peter of Spain in the second circle of lights: ". . . Pietro Ispano, who giveth light below in twelve booklets . . ." See Grabmann, "Forschungen," pp. 81–85, for a discussion of the place of the *Summulae logicales* in the curriculum of the medieval and renaissance Arts Faculty.

[11] During the late middle ages, Peter of Spain was considered the *originator* of the *logica moderna* (see p. 19 below), which he certainly was not. See Lambertus Maria de Rijk, *Logica modernorum*, Vol. I, p. 15.

[12] Gilson, *History*, p. 277.

[13] Grabmann, "Einleitung," pp. 28–29.

[14] Gilson, *History*, p. 294.

5

can], another of whom is master William of Sherwood, the treasurer of the church of Lincoln in England, who is much wiser than Albert; for in *philosophia communis* no one is greater than he.

Therefore let your Wisdom write to them the points I have treated in the works I have sent and which I touch on in this third writing, and you will see that ten years will go by before they send you the sort of thing I have written. Surely you will find a hundred passages (on subjects which, in a way, they know) that they will not match during their whole lifetime. For I know the state of their knowledge better than anyone else, and I know that at any rate they are not presenting you with the sort of thing I have written in *less* time than has elapsed since your mandate, Albert no more than William (*sicut nec ab ultimo, sic nec a primo*).[15]

The *"philosophia communis"* in which no one was greater than Sherwood must have been logic;[16] Bacon himself later wrote logic books of the same sort as Sherwood's.[17] As for the comparison of Albert with Sherwood, it may have been partly motivated by the fact that Bacon was a Franciscan while Albert was a Dominican, but Albert's philosophy and theology do seem to have been distasteful to Bacon on other grounds.[18] Soon afterwards Albert was honored by the epithets *"doctor universalis"* and "the Great," and his works were circulated everywhere in many manuscripts. Sherwood, on the other hand, seems to have been forgotten; of his principal works one survived in only two manuscripts, the other in only one.[19]

Bacon's praise of Sherwood in the *Opus tertium* may seem to be an

---

[15] Brewer ed., pp. 13–14, my translation.

[16] On *"philosophia communis,"* an unusual term, cf. Grabmann, "Einleitung," p. 15; *Opera hactenus inedita Rogeri Baconi* (hereafter cited as *Opera Baconi*) XV, Robert Steele's "Introduction," p. xix.

[17] *Sumule dialectices* (in *Opera Baconi*, XV), which has been dated 1250. Regarding this work of Bacon's, Steele says, "It cannot be said that Bacon owed much to his predecessors, though it is probable that he knew the work of Hispanus [Peter of Spain] . . . There does not seem to be any trace of acquaintance with the work of Shirewood, though Bacon must have known of his work by more than repute" (Steele's "Introduction," p. xx. For the date, see p. xiv). J. S. Brewer ("Preface" to his edition of Bacon's *Opus tertium* (hereafter cited as "Preface"), p. lxix) ascribes a *Syncategorematica fratris Roberti* to Bacon; this same treatise was ascribed to Grosseteste by Carl Prantl (*Geschichte der Logik im Abendlande* (hereafter cited as *Geschichte*), 3.121, n. 558; cf. Philotheus Boehner, *Medieval Logic*, p. 7), but it is actually the work of Robert Kilwardby (d. 1279). See S. Harrison Thomson, *The Writings of Robert Grosseteste*, p. 266.

[18] See J. H. Bridges's "Preface" to his edition of Bacon's *Opus majus*, p. xxxiv, n. 6; Gilson, *History*, p. 295. Cf. William and Martha Kneale, *The Development of Logic* (hereafter cited as *Development*), p. 234.

[19] See Grabmann, "Einleitung," p. 15; see p. 13 below.

effort on his part to inflate the reputation of a rival only in order to make his own talents loom larger in the eyes of the Pope, and of course he does conclude by ranking himself considerably higher than Sherwood, at least in the subject matter of the *Opus tertium*. But in that connection it is essential to note that the subject matter of the *Opus tertium*, like that of his *Opus majus* and *Opus minus* which preceded it, is *"with the exception of logic,* the whole range of science, as science was then understood."[20] His evaluation of Sherwood as a first-rate logician is in no way affected by the fact that he invited comparison with him in all the other branches of science.

Further evidence that Bacon's praise of Sherwood was sincere can be found in the following passage from his *Compendium studii philosophiae*, written in 1271, in which he is discussing the origin of the Franciscan and Dominican orders of friars.

The third cause of the appearance of the orders is the fact that for forty years the secular clergy neglected the study of theology and philosophy along the true paths of those studies, having been possessed with the desire for pleasure, riches, and honors, and corrupted by the above-mentioned causes of ignorance to such an extent that they completely left the paths of the wise *antiqui,* some of whom we have seen in our own time — namely, the lord Robert [Grosseteste], formerly bishop of Lincoln, of holy memory, the lord Thomas, bishop of St. David in Wallia, brother Adam Marsh, master Robert Marsh, masters William Lupus and William of Sherwood, and others like them. The seculars who are *moderni* (*moderni saeculares*) have totally abandoned their footsteps, as will be abundantly proved below in the appropriate places.[21]

By *"antiqui"* and *"moderni"* Bacon may have meant no more than a distinction between the solid philosophers and theologians of the older generation and the young upstarts; but there is a medieval use of these designations for those (*antiqui*) who, like Bacon (or Sherwood), retain the Aristotelian doctrine of universals and those (*moderni*) who reject it in favor of the view that, for example, there is no Aristotelian form of man but only discrete individual men.[22]

---

[20] Brewer, "Preface," p. xxviii; italics added.

[21] Brewer ed., p. 428, my translation. This passage seems to have been overlooked by recent writers on Sherwood. It appears in Anthony à Wood's *The History and Antiquities of the University of Oxford,* 1.296, and it is noted in D. A. Callus, ed., *Robert Grosseteste, Scholar and Bishop* (hereafter cited as *Grosseteste*), p. 37, particularly as a reference to Grosseteste.

[22] On *"antiqui"* and *"moderni"* see De Rijk, *Logica modernorum,* Vol. I, pp. 16–17; also Kneale, *Development,* p. 200; but especially M.-D. Chenu, "Notes de

Because of Sherwood's influence over logicians and metaphysicians known to have been at Paris in the years 1240–1248, it seems reasonable to suppose that he was a master in the Arts Faculty there during all or most of that period.[23] He had returned to England, however, and had probably become a master at Oxford sometime before January 27, 1249, when "magister Willielmus de Shirwood" was one of the witnesses to the foundation deed of the Nunnery of Marham.[24] He certainly was at Oxford by 1252. In that year, "a great disturbance having taken place between the Northern and the Irish scholars," several persons on each side — "rich men, whether Regents or otherwise" — swore an oath "not to disturb the peace of the University themselves, not to comfort others in doing so, and to give secret information to the Chancellor if they shall hear of any other person thus transgressing." "Magister Wilhelmus de Skirwodde" was the seventh of the twenty-one who swore "on behalf of the Northerners."[25]

All the remaining documentary information about Sherwood connects him with one or another ecclesiastical position, but that need not and probably does not mean that he retired from academic life.[26] Bacon would hardly have referred to him as he did in the *Opus tertium* of 1267 (see pp. 5–6 above) if Sherwood had been philosophically inactive for a decade or more.

Sherwood next appears as the treasurer of the cathedral church of

---

lexicographie médiévale — ANTIQUI, MODERNI," *Revue des sciences philosophiques et théologiques*, 17.82–94.

[23] Van Steenberghen (*Aristotle*, pp. 101–103) suggests that Sherwood "must have been teaching at Paris at more or less the same time as William of St. Amour," who was there from 1236 to 1247. Josiah Cox Russell (*Dictionary of Writers of Thirteenth Century England* (hereafter cited as *Dictionary*), p. 200) says that he "probably spent his life teaching at Paris," which seems clearly mistaken even in the light of the data presented by Russell on Sherwood's career.

[24] William Dugdale's *Monasticon anglicanum*, 5.744; see also Francis Blomefield's *An Essay Towards a Topographical History of the County of Norfolk* (hereafter cited as *Top. Hist.*), 7.384–385. The nunnery was founded by Isabel Countess of Arundel, who was patron of Attleborough when Sherwood became rector there; see n. 32 below.

[25] Henry Anstey, ed., *Munimenta academica*, 1.20–22; cf. Rashdall, *Universities*, 3.50–51. The oath was to be administered to "absent masters" as well, but Sherwood is one of those who swore "at the time of the settlement." Since his name appears seventh in the list he may have been one of the "twelve persons chosen from each party to draw up conditions of peace." Russell (*Dictionary*, p. 200) considers this a doubtful reference but gives no reason for doubting it.

[26] See Kathleen Edwards, *The English Secular Cathedrals in the Middle Ages* (hereafter cited as *Cathedrals*), pp. 20–21, 37–38, 88–89, 329.

Lincoln.[27] Robert Grosseteste, the great philosopher-scientist, had been bishop of Lincoln from 1235 until his death in 1253.[28] The vacancy of the see during the following months gave King Henry III the opportunity, in March 1254, to appoint his favorite, Peter Chaceporc, treasurer of Lincoln. After Chaceporc's death in December of that year[29] there seems to be no record of a treasurer of Lincoln until "Willelmus de Syrwode" witnessed a document as treasurer sometime in the period December 1254 to November 1258.[30]

On January 2, 1258, Pope Alexander IV granted a special dispensation

---

[27] "The treasurer [one of the four principal officers] of the English medieval secular cathedrals was in no sense a financial or business officer . . . His first duty . . . was to keep the treasures of the church, the gold and silver vessels, the ornaments, relics, jewels, embroidered silk copes, and altar cloths, while at the same time he provided the lights, bread, wine, incense and other material necessaries for the services." "His personal residence in the close was held to be very necessary." On the other hand, he was provided with a deputy, or subtreasurer, and a large staff of officers, so that he could be absent frequently as long as he returned to perform the duties he could not delegate to his staff. "The most elaborate system of treasury officers was at Lincoln." Edwards, *Cathedrals*, pp. 220–221, 226, 230.

[28] Callus, *Grosseteste*, pp. 251–252. Writers on Grosseteste frequently remark on a supposed friendship between Grosseteste and Sherwood. A highly speculative account appears in A. C. Crombie (*Robert Grosseteste and the Origins of Experimental Science*, 1953, p. 190, n. 3), who got the gist of it from Francis Seymour Stevenson (*Robert Grosseteste, Bishop of Lincoln*, 1899, p. 42, n. 1) and Samuel Pegge (*The Life of Robert Grosseteste*, 1793, p. 237), Pegge having got it from Thomas Tanner's reprinting (*Bibliotheca britannica-hibernica* (hereafter cited as *Bibliotheca*), p. 545) of Leland's chapter on Nicholas the Greek (*Commentarii*, p. 263): ". . . Robert Grosseteste, bishop of Lincoln, though in no way erudite himself, was in his day an untiring supporter and patron of all men of letters. As a result he enjoyed the closest friendship with the foremost men of the English school, such as Bacon, Basingo (?), Fishacre, Sherwood, Adam Marsh, Blund, Belloclivo (?), and Fernamio (?)." Of all these only Adam Marsh and Roger Blund seem certainly to have been members of Grosseteste's *familia* (see Kathleen Major, "The *Familia* of Robert Grosseteste" (hereafter cited as "*Familia*"), in Callus, *Grosseteste*, pp. 216–241). Perhaps Leland's evaluation of Grosseteste, who was the leading intellectual figure of his time, provides an index to the reliability of the rest of this passage. Sherwood and Grosseteste *are* very likely to have known and thought well of each other, but whatever documentary evidence Leland may have had for this list seems to have vanished.

[29] On Chaceporc, see the *Dictionary of National Biography* (hereafter cited as *DNB*), also John Le Neve, *Fasti ecclesiae anglicanae* (hereafter cited as *Fasti*), 2.87–88. Chaceporc seems to have spent his ten months as treasurer entirely in France (where he died), which is further evidence that Sherwood might have spent considerable time at Oxford or even at Paris while he was treasurer of Lincoln. See n. 27 above.

[30] Document in Charles W. Foster and Kathleen Major, eds., *The Registrum antiquissimum of the Cathedral Church of Lincoln* (hereafter cited as *Reg. antiquiss.*), 6.61–62. Since Richard (Gravesend) is named in it as dean, it must be dated before November 3, 1258, when Gravesend was consecrated bishop

to William of Sherwood, treasurer of Lincoln, to hold an additional benefice with cure of souls.[31] That additional benefice could have been either Attleborough or Aylesbury, both of which Sherwood held.[32]

There are several documents involving the treasurer of Lincoln, the earliest of which presents a minor difficulty. Henry of Lexington, Grosseteste's successor as bishop of Lincoln, died in August 1258, and the news of his death was brought to King Henry's court by four (or five)

---

of Lincoln (F. N. Davis, ed., *Rotuli Ricardi Gravesend* (hereafter cited as *Rot. Ric. Gra.*), pp. vii–viii), and it cannot be earlier than December 24, 1254, when Chaceporc died. (Gravesend became dean in 1254.)

[31] *Calendar of Entries in the Papal Register Relating to Great Britain and Ireland*, 1.355. "By a decree of the Lateran council of 1215, which was enforced in England, no clerk can hold two benefices with cure of souls, and if a beneficed clerk shall take a second benefice with cure of souls, he vacates *ipso facto* his first benefice. Dispensations, however, could easily be obtained from Rome, before the reformation of the Church of England, to enable a clerk to hold several ecclesiastical dignities or benefices at the same time . . ." (*Encyclopaedia Britannica*, 11th ed., 3.726, "Benefice"). Treasurers "were bound to be priests, and, unlike the simple canons, were generally prohibited from holding other benefices with cure of souls" (Edwards, *Cathedrals*, pp. 136–137).

[32] In his list of "rectors of the greater part" of "Atleburgh" Blomefield gives the following: "In King *Henry* the Third's time [1216–1272] the four following persons were rectors, viz.

"*Godfrey Giffard*. Hugh de Albany [d. 1243; patron].

"*Peter Giffard*, clerk. Hugh de Albany [patron].

"*Master William de Shirewood*. Isabel, widow of *Hugh de Albany*, in right of Plasset's manor, which she holds in dower [patron].

"*Haman de Warren*, on *Shirewood's* death. The same Isabell, who holds it in dower, remainder to Sir *Robert de Tateshale*" (*Top. Hist.*, 1.523).

Peter Giffard secured exemption from assizes at the instance of Robert de Tateshale on September 15, 1257 (*Calendar of the Patent Rolls Preserved in the Public Record Office* (hereafter cited as *CPR*), 1247–1258, p. 579), and was evidently then still rector. Sherwood probably held Attleborough no earlier than 1257 and must have died before 1272.

Le Neve (*Fasti*, 2.95) lists Sherwood as succeeding Roger de Weseham as prebendary of Aylesbury in the diocese of Lincoln in 1245. He gives no documentary evidence for this, however, and Matthew Paris (*Chronica maiora*, 4.425) reports that Grosseteste, as the bishop of Lincoln, conferred the prebend of Aylesbury on Robert Marsh at that time. Thus there are good grounds for rejecting Le Neve's date. On the other hand, even so early a date need not conflict with the probable dates of Sherwood's stay in Paris, since he could have received the income without residing in the diocese or even in England (see Edwards, *Cathedrals*, pp. 20–21, 37–38, 88–89, 329). Moreover, in 1252 Sherwood seemed to be included among "rich men" at Oxford (see p. 8 above), and the prebend of Aylesbury was especially lucrative: "The value of the prebend — 75 marks [50 pounds] — shows his [Sherwood's] importance" (Steele's "Introduction," p. xix).

As the contemporary source, Matthew Paris is more likely to be correct, and his account suits Sherwood's other dates very well. Robert Marsh became dean of Lincoln in 1258 or 1259 (*Rot. Ric. Gra.*, p. xxxv; *Reg. antiquiss.*, 4.274–275; cf. Major, "*Familia*" in Callus, *Grosseteste*, p. 231, and Le Neve, *Fasti*, 2.95), and it is likely that Sherwood succeeded him as prebendary of Aylesbury then.

members of the Lincoln chapter beginning with "master R. the treasurer." [33] But, as has been suggested,[34] this is almost certainly a scribe's
error for "master R[ichard Gravesend] the dean and master W[illiam
of Sherwood] the treasurer." In 1259 he is named as treasurer in a charter issued by the dean and chapter of Lincoln.[35]

As treasurer Sherwood had charge of a number of lay servants of
the cathedral, and in Easter week of 1263 he figured prominently in the
settlement "of a long-standing dispute [with the City of Lincoln] con-
cerning the rights and liberties of the same mother church of Lincoln
with respect to four of its servants who customarily bear the wand . . .
Now in token of the consummation of peace and fellowship, the lord
the Treasurer of Lincoln and the Mayor of the city openly gave each
other kisses of peace." [36]

The latest document providing direct evidence of Sherwood's serving
as treasurer is a grant witnessed by him in that capacity which "probably can be dated Michaelmas [September 29] 1264 — May 1265." [37]
As we have seen (pp. 5–6 above), in 1267 Roger Bacon believed that
Sherwood was still living and still treasurer of Lincoln, but Bacon himself was living in France at the time [38] and could easily have been
mistaken.

Sherwood certainly was still living in October 1266 and was then
still (or again) rector of Aylesbury,[39] but it is certain that he had been

---

[33] *CPR*, 1247–1258, p. 651; *Rot. Ric. Gra.*, p. vii.

[34] By Russell, *Dictionary*, p. 200.

[35] Cited by Anthony à Wood, *Historia et antiquitates universitatis oxoniensis*,
2.61: "Anno CDCCLIX. in vivis agebat, ac Thesaurarius *Lincolniensis* tunc
temporis erat, quemadmodum e charta quadam Decani & Capituli *Lincolniensis*
constat, Ecclesiam S. *Georgii* in Castro *Oxoniensi, Osneiensibus* eodem anno
confirmante . . ."

[36] Document in *Reg. antiquiss.*, 3.300–304. William of Sherwood, treasurer, is
named among those present at the ceremony, Saturday, April 7, 1263.

[37] Document in *Reg. antiquiss.*, 8.24–25.

[38] See Ch. III of *Opus tertium*, p. 15, where he speaks of having had to spend
more than sixty French livres (*libras Parisienses*) on the preparation of the work;
also p. 16, where he says that he has written to his brother "*in terra mea.*" Cf.
Brewer's "Preface," pp. xiv, xxviii, xlv.

[39] *CPR*, 1313–1317, p. 304 (July 1, 1315): "*Inspeximus* and confirmation of an
inspeximus" of an original "charter sealed with bishop's seal and the seal of Master
William de Shirewode, dated the Nones of October 1266, by which the bishop
granted, with the consent of Master William de Shirewode, rector of the pre-
bendal church of Eylesbyry, to the dean and chapter of Lincoln, to enable them
to bear their charges . . . [certain chapels] belonging to the prebend of Eylesbyry
. . . " See also William Page, ed., *The Victoria County History of the County of
Buckingham*, 2.326. For an earlier reference to the charter of October 1266 see n.
40 below.

replaced as rector of Aylesbury sometime before November 1267.[40] Sometime in the period 1269–1272 Richard of Battle became treasurer of Lincoln, probably as Sherwood's immediate successor.[41] Finally, Roger Bacon, writing in 1271, again referred to Sherwood and others in terms of high praise in a passage (see p. 7 above) that seems to indicate that the men referred to had all died rather recently, and of the five he names besides Sherwood, four certainly were dead in 1271.[42] In all probability, then, Sherwood died sometime in the period 1266–1271.[43]

The difficulties historians have had with the life and even with the identity of William of Sherwood are naturally accompanied by special difficulties in identifying writings as his.[44] In the sixteenth century John Leland saw a commentary on the *Sentences* of Peter Lombard in the library of the Dominicans at Exeter entitled "*Shirovodus super sententias.*"[45] It seems to be lost now, and in any case it would have been mainly a theological work, quite unlike the logical treatises that can be definitely ascribed to Sherwood. Another theological work, *Distinctiones theologicae*, is attributed to him by Leland.[46] In the *Dictionary of*

---

[40] Document in *Reg. antiquiss.*, 3.334–335. "Memorandum of a mandate of bishop Richard Gravesend to the Dean and Chapter" dated November 18, 1267. In it the bishop announces that he has "conferred the prebend of Aylesbury, vacant by the resignation of Master John of Scharested, who was last rector of Aylesbury, on Percival of Lavagna," and refers to the grant of certain chapels of Aylesbury to the dean and chapter [see n. 39 above] made "with the consent of Master William of Schirewode, then rector of Aylesbury . . ."

[41] *Reg. antiquiss.*, 8.25, note.

[42] Robert Grosseteste died in 1253, Thomas Wallensis in 1255, Adam Marsh in 1257 or 1258, Robert Marsh in 1262. A William Lupus was named as an heir in the will of Bishop Hugh II of Lincoln in 1233 (document in *Reg. antiquiss.*, 2.72), which might mean that Lupus was then a canon of Lincoln and therefore at least twenty-two years old. He would then have been at least sixty years old, if still living, at the time Bacon wrote the passage mentioned above.

[43] He was certainly dead in 1272 (see n. 32 above). Grabmann gives "after 1267" as a death date, relying on Roger Bacon's reference to William in that year, but see page 11 above. Russell says, "He held this [prebend of Aylesbury] on his death in 1279 or earlier" and gives this reference: "Public Record Office, Exchequer, 7 Edw. I, E. 13/7; *cf.* also E. 13/8, mm. 4, 12b, 15." Neither Grabmann nor Russell mentions Bacon's reference in the *Compendium philosophiae* of 1271.

[44] Grabmann's "Einleitung," pp. 11–13, contains a review and critique of the question of Sherwood's works as treated by historians.

[45] Leland, *Commentarii*, 2.262; *De rebus Britannicis collectanea*, 4.151.

[46] *Commentarii*, 2.262: "Vidi etiam *Grantae* in publica bibliotheca *Distinctiones Theologicas*, ejusdem *Gulielmi* opus." Grabmann believes this is the work of William of Leicester, whose *Distinctiones theologicae* were widely circulated in manuscript.

National Biography C. L. Kingsford lists these two plus a *Conciones* as all of Sherwood's works.[47]

William of Sherwood's *Introduction to Logic* survives in only one manuscript of the late thirteenth or early fourteenth century.[48] The scribe's hand is neat, and the text is frequently corrected by two other hands, one of which has added occasional titles in the margins of the parchment manuscript. (In the translation below the titles preceded by an asterisk are by this hand; the others have been added by the translator.) The work appears under the heading "*Introductiones Magistri Guilli. de Shyreswode in logicam,*"[49] and occupies folios 1^r–23^r in the manuscript.

Folios 23^r–46^r are taken up by the only other work unquestionably written by William of Sherwood, a more advanced logical treatise on the semantical and logical properties of the "syncategoremata," words that have special logical or semantic effects on subjects, predicates, or combinations of subjects and predicates. The words treated by Sherwood are '*omnis,*' '*totum,*' *dictiones numerales,* '*infinita*' *in plurali,* '*uterque,*' '*qualelibet,*' '*nullus,*' '*nihil,*' '*neutrum,*' '*praeter,*' '*solus,*' '*tantum,*' '*est,*' '*non,*' '*necessario,*' '*contingenter,*' '*incipit,*' '*desinit,*' '*si,*' '*nisi,*' '*quin,*' '*et,*' '*vel,*' '*an,*' '*ne,*' *and* '*sive.*'[50] In the right-hand margin of folio 23^r the work is entitled "*Sincategoreumata Magistri Guilli. de Shireswode*"; it has also survived in a second manuscript[51] in the margin of which it is described as "*Sincategoreumata Magistri Willielmi de Sire-*

---

[47] *DNB*, "Shirwood, William of." I can find no earlier reference to the *Conciones* than Tanner's *Bibliotheca* (p. 669, n.), where the following list is given: "Scripsit *Lecturam Sententiarum,* lib. iv. Ms. Lel. Trin. *Distinctiones theologicae,* lib. iv. Ms. Lel. Trin. *Conciones aliquot,* Ms. lib. i." "*Conciones*" is a standard designation for a collection of sermons.

[48] Bibliothèque Nationale MS. Lat. 16, 617; formerly Sorbonne 1797, under which designation it is cited (frequently) by Prantl. Technical descriptions of the manuscript are to be found in Leopold Victor Delisle, *Inventaire général et méthodique des manuscrits français de la Bibliothèque nationale,* 70; Grabmann, "Einleitung," pp. 15ff; J. R. O'Donnell, "Foreword" to his edition of *Syncategoremata,* p. 46; Steele, "Introduction," p. xvii. I have had access to a microfilm of the manuscript supplied by the Bibliothèque Nationale through the Library of the University of Illinois.

[49] Russell, who says (*Dictionary,* p. 200), "William's authorship of the '*Introductiones*' is very doubtful," cannot have seen the manuscript, since he also describes it as "entitled 'G. de Lincoln.'"

[50] Sherwood does not consider all these to be genuine syncategoremata. For example, he says that he is considering '*est*' "not because it *is* a syncategorema, but because many take it to be one" (p. 70). In a note to this passage O'Donnell names Abelard as one of those many and cites a reference.

[51] Bodleian MS. Digby 55, ff. 206–225.

wode."[52] This treatise, which deserves translation and further study, begins with the following general introduction (my translation):

In order to understand anything one must understand its parts, and so in order that the statement may be fully understood, one must understand the parts of it. Now its parts are of two kinds: principal and secondary. The principal parts are the substantival name and the verb, for they are necessary for an understanding of the statement. The secondary parts are the adjectival name, the adverb, and conjunctions and prepositions, for a statement can exist without them.

Some secondary parts are determinations of principal parts with respect to the things belonging to them (*ratione suarum rerum*) [i.e., the things bearing the forms signified by the principal part — see p. 111 below]; these are *not* syncategoremata. For example, when I say, 'white man,' the 'white' signifies that some thing belonging to 'man' is white.[53]

Other [secondary parts] are determinations of principal parts insofar as they are subjects or predicates. For example, when I say, 'every man runs,' the 'every,' which is a universal sign [see p. 28 below], does not signify that some thing belonging to 'man' is universal, but that 'man' is a universal subject. [Secondary parts] of this sort are called syncategoremata. They cause a great deal of difficulty in discourse and for that reason they are to be investigated.

The word 'syncategorema' comes from 'syn-' — i.e., 'con-' — and 'categoreuma' — i.e., 'significative' or 'predicative' — as if to say 'compredicative,' for a syncategorema is always joined with something else in discourse. But since some of them are determinations of the subject, why do they all derive their name from the predicate? The answer is that the predicate is the completive part of the statement, but every syncategorema affects both the subject and the predicate in some way, and so the syncategoremata derive their name from the predicate as from the completing and more important (*dignior*) part.

The first to be investigated, however, are those that are associated with the subject — i.e., [distributive] signs and certain others.

Neither Sherwood's *Introductiones* nor his *Syncategoremata* appeared in print until the twentieth century,[54] and no other works that could be ascribed to him have ever been printed.

---

[52] Regarding the many thirteenth- and fourteenth-century treatises on syncategoremata, see Prantl, especially Vol. III; Grabmann, "Bearbeitungen und Auslegungen der aristotelischen Logik aus der Zeit von Peter Abaelard bis Petrus Hispanus . . ." (hereafter cited as "Bearbeitungen"), p. 7.

[53] Parts of these opening paragraphs are translated in Innocentius M. Bocheński, *A History of Formal Logic* (hereafter cited as *History*), p. 157 (26.09), where the sense of this essential distinction is badly mangled.

[54] In Grabmann's edition of the *Introductiones* (1937) and O'Donnell's edition

Following the *Syncategoremata* in the Paris manuscript are three short logical treatises: *De insolubilibus* (ff. 46ᵛ–54ᵛ), on the paradoxes of self-reference — e.g., 'What I am saying is false' — which were considered not strictly insoluble but uniquely difficult;[55] *Obligationes* (ff. 54ᵛ–62ᵛ), on the rules of argument under which formal disputations were to be conducted;[56] and *Petitiones contrariorum* (ff. 62ᵛ–64ᵛ), on the solution of sophismata (logical puzzles) that arise from hidden contrariety in the premisses. These three treatises closely resemble the *Introductiones* and especially the *Syncategoremata* in the authorities cited, in the examples chosen, and in their terse, clear style. Moreover, they appear immediately after the two certifiably genuine works in a single manuscript by the same hand, there seems to be an explicit reference to the *De insolubilibus* in the *Syncategoremata*,[57] and the *Obligationes* closes with the formula *"Expliciunt obligationes Magistri W."*[58] It seems very likely, then, that the manuscript contains not just two but five logical treatises by William of Sherwood.[59]

Immediately following the *Petitiones* the Paris manuscript contains, in a different hand, the *Summulae logicales* of Lambert of Auxerre (see p. 4 above) (ff. 64ʳ–131ʳ); following it is another logical treatise, a rather long anonymous *Ars opponendi et respondendi* (ff. 131ʳ–164ᵛ) which, especially because of the authorities cited in it, is almost surely not Sherwood's, although it does contain a passage in which the author describes himself as having taught logic at Paris and in England.[60]

Two more logical treatises deserve mention as just possibly the works

---

of the *Syncategoremata* (1941). Portions of each had been printed in the notes to Prantl's Vol. III.

[55] On *insolubilia* generally and Sherwood's treatment of them in particular see Kneale, *Development*, pp. 227–229.

[56] On *obligationes* generally, see Kneale, *Development*, p. 234.

[57] *Syncategoremata* (ed. O'Donnell), p. 58: "Certain difficulties pertaining to the treatise on *insolubilia*, which are being set aside until the others [are treated], could be mentioned here." Grabmann does not cite this reference.

[58] It is worth noting that this closing formula is written in the same hand that wrote the manuscript itself, not in the hand that supplied the titles in the margins, since the latter used a form of William's name beginning with a "G" rather than a "W."

[59] Grabmann discusses the authorship of these last three in detail ("Einleitung," pp. 20–24). They have never been printed, but Grabmann (*loc. cit.*) gives the *initium* (opening sentences) of each.

[60] See Grabmann's discussion of it, "Einleitung," pp. 24–26. There are four further treatises in the Paris manuscript; no one has suggested that any of them is the work of Sherwood.

of Sherwood. One is an *Insolubilia* with a colophon attributing it to master "Ricardus de Schirwode." [61] No such person is known of, and confusion of first names is by no means rare in medieval manuscripts; but the treatise is markedly different, at least in its opening sentences, from the *De insolubilibus* associated with Sherwood's works in the Paris manuscript. The other candidate for inclusion is a *Fallaciae magistri Willelmi* which, if genuine, is another treatment of the material in the last chapter of Sherwood's *Introduction*.[62] Neither the *Insolubilia* nor the *Fallaciae* has yet been carefully compared with the treatises that definitely belong to Sherwood.

Sherwood's *Introduction to Logic* is discussed in detail in the notes to the translation below, and the analytical table of contents above provides a fairly complete summary of its six chapters, or treatises.[63] Broadly speaking, five of the six chapters correspond to five of Aristotle's logical works: Chapter One, "Statements," to the treatise *On Interpretation*; Chapter Two, "The Predicables," to the *Categories*; Chapter Three, "Syllogism," to the *Prior Analytics*; Chapter Four, "Dialectical Reasoning," to the *Topics*; and Chapter Six, "Sophistical Reasoning," to the *Sophistical Refutations*. Of course, this is not to say that those five chapters contain in some form or other everything in those Aristotelian treatises; moreover, some of what they contain cannot be found anywhere in Aristotle.

But the most interesting and distinctively medieval innovations are concentrated in Chapter Five, "Properties of Terms." To what extent are they *Sherwood's* innovations? Historians of logic are still in the early stages of uncovering the relations of this part of medieval logic to the logic of Aristotle and the earlier middle ages,[64] and so no precise an-

---

[61] MS. 100, St. John's College, Cambridge (Russell, *Dictionary*, p. 200). Grabmann discusses it briefly ("Einleitung," p. 26) and rejects it, apparently on the grounds that Sherwood is much more likely to have written the *De insolubilibus* in the Paris manuscript and unlikely to have written twice on the same subject.

[62] Beginning on f. 227ʳ of MS. 9 E XII of the King's Library in the British Museum (Grabmann, "Einleitung," p. 26).

[63] The plural *"introductiones"* in the Latin title, like the plural in *"summulae logicales,"* seems to indicate that each of the six main divisions of the book was taken as a relatively independent introduction to one part of logic. As a result, the book is a little more like a collection of monographs than like a modern organized textbook.

[64] The most important work in this area is that of L. M. de Rijk in the introductions to his editions of Abelard and Garland and especially in his *Logica modernorum*. See also Minio-Paluello's volumes of texts and studies under the general

swer can be given to that question now. We can make a start in the right direction, however, by describing the background against which Sherwood's work made its appearance.

Until about the middle of the twelfth century the only parts of Aristotle's logic — in fact, the only works of Aristotle — available in western Europe were Boethius's translations of the *Categories* and the treatise *On Interpretation*. The remainder of the logic of the early middle ages consisted of a set of books centering more or less closely around those two; namely, translations by Boethius and Marius Victorinus of Porphyry's *Isagoge* (Introduction) to the *Categories*, Boethius's commentary on the *Isagoge* (in two editions), his own commentary on the *Categories* (also in two editions), his commentary on the treatise *On Interpretation*, his commentary on Cicero's *Topica*, and the following relatively original treatises by Boethius: *Introductio ad syllogismos categoricos, De syllogismis categoricis, De syllogismis hypotheticis, De differentiis topicis,* and *De divisionibus.*[65] Later in the middle ages this collection of books, or the kind of logic these books contained, became known as the *ars vetus* or *logica vetus,* the "old logic."[66] The first four chapters of Sherwood's *Introduction,* then, are devoted to the subject matter of the *logica vetus,* and any innovations in them (there are some, as we shall see) are bound to be relatively minor.

The most important work done largely if not wholly in the framework of the *logica vetus* was that of Abelard (ca. 1079–1142), who produced nearly 2,000 pages of logical writings.[67] He seems to have anticipated at least the outlines of many of the developments of thirteenth-century logic, and a thorough evaluation of Sherwood's logic (as well as that of

title *Twelfth Century Logic* and the pioneering work of Grabmann in, e.g., his "Bearbeitungen," "Kommentare zur aristotelischen Logik aus dem 12. und 13. Jahrhundert . . .," "Die Sophismatenliteratur des 12. und 13. Jahrhunderts . . .," and "Aristoteles im zwölften Jahrhundert." Cf. Kneale, *Development,* pp. 224–225.

[65] See De Rijk, "Introduction" to Garland's *Dialectica,* p. xlvi. De Rijk does not mention the commentary on Cicero's *Topica,* but cf. Kneale, *Development,* pp. 189 and 199. On Boethius's logical writings see Kneale, *Development,* pp. 189–198; also Karl Dürr, *The Propositional Logic of Boethius.*

[66] On the distinctions *logica vetus, nova, antiqua, moderna,* see De Rijk, *Logica modernorum,* Vol. I, pp. 14–15. About 1200 another book on the *Categories,* Gilbert de la Porrée's *Liber de sex principiis* (written about 1150), was included in the *logica vetus* (De Rijk, *loc. cit.*). For a discussion of this work see Gilson, *History,* pp. 140–141.

[67] See editions by Geyer, De Rijk, and Minio-Paluello.

treatise that, from its title, seems to deal with appellation, one of the properties of terms discussed by Sherwood.[75] In fact, several of the properties of terms in Sherwood's Chapter Five had already been mentioned in a more or less rudimentary way, usually in isolated passages, in late twelfth-century treatises on fallacies.[76] But, as far as I have been able to discover, no one has yet turned up an attempt earlier than Sherwood's to develop the notions of the *logica moderna* in an organized way, in the way that became characteristic of medieval logic after Sherwood. No doubt more and more ingredients of Sherwood's work on the properties of terms and syncategoremata will be uncovered as the research in twelfth- and early thirteenth-century logic proceeds,[77] but it would be very surprising indeed if an earlier synthesis of those ingredients were to be found. Whatever exactly it was that Roger Bacon had in mind when he said that no one was greater than Sherwood in *philosophia communis*, those are surely not words in which one would describe a man who produced no more than textbooks in subjects that had already been opened to investigation. Sherwood's *Introduction to Logic* is unmistakably a textbook, but like other first-rate textbooks it made a substantial contribution to its subject and very likely opened up a new branch of that subject; in his *Syncategoremata* the atmosphere of the textbook is less evident and the presentation of what must be largely original research is correspondingly enhanced.

The logic of William of Sherwood must be studied by everyone who wants to understand those developments in medieval logic and philosophy of language that are perhaps most interesting from a twentieth-century point of view. Luckily, the study of his work turns out to be intriguing in its own right as well.

---

[75] See Van Steenberghen, *Aristotle*, pp. 100–101; also Gilson, *History*, pp. 316 and 677.

[76] See De Rijk, *Logica modernorum, passim*. Specific passages are cited below at the appropriate places in the notes to the translation.

[77] See especially the projected second volume of De Rijk's *Logica modernorum*, which is to deal specifically with the twelfth-century sources of these inquiries.

CHAPTER ONE

Statements

1. THE NATURE OF LOGIC

Since there are two sources (*principia*) of things, namely nature and the soul, there will be two kinds of things. Some are the things whose source is nature, and they are the concern of what is generally called natural science. The others, whose source is the soul, are of two sorts. For since the soul is created without virtues or knowledge, it performs certain operations by means of which it attains to the virtues, and these are the concern of ethics; it also performs other operations by means of which it attains to knowledge, and these are the concern of the science of discourse (*sermocinalis scientia*).[1] This science has three parts: grammar, which teaches one how to speak correctly; rhetoric, which teaches one how to speak elegantly; and logic, which teaches one how to speak truly. Logic is principally concerned with the syllogism, the understanding of which requires an understanding of the proposition; and, because every proposition is made up of terms, an understanding of the term is necessary.

2. STATEMENTS AND PROPOSITIONS

A proposition and a statement (*enuntiatio*) are the same considered as entities (*secundum rem*), but they differ in that a statement signi-

---

[1] The term '*scientia sermocinalis*' seems to have come into use in the late twelfth or early thirteenth century. Sherwood is using it in its original sense, as an uncontroversial general designation for the disciplines making up the *trivium*. The fact that the notion of logic as a science of discourse was universally accepted during that period is, no doubt, among the reasons why medieval logic developed its distinctive logico-semantic inquiries into the properties of terms and the signification and function of syncategorematic words. Around the time Sherwood was writing, however, this view of logic was expressly challenged for the first time during the middle ages by Albert the Great (1193–1280), who based his opposition on the teaching of Avicenna (980–1037) that logic was a science of mental entities (*intentiones*), concerned with discourse only incidentally, if at all. During the remainder of the middle ages the controversy continued over the status of logic as *scientia sermocinalis* or *scientia rationalis*, but it seems to have begun too late

fies something absolutely while a proposition signifies something in relation to something else. It is clear from the very name 'proposition' that a proposition signifies in relation to something else, for a proposition is a *positing for* something, namely, the conclusion that is to be drawn. Thus, what is a statement considered in itself is a proposition considered as it is [a premiss] in a syllogism.[2] Our first consideration, therefore, is the statement, for understanding something in itself is prior to understanding it in relation to something else.[3]

3. THE PARTS OF A STATEMENT

Now, since we are to consider the statement, the first thing we have to consider is its parts, the noun and the verb. These are called the parts of the statement because it is possible for a statement to be made up of them and of nothing else. For even if a statement is made up of a pronoun and a verb, or a participle and a verb, this still is a result of the noun-character (*natura nominis*) possessed by the pronoun and the participle, and so to the extent that they share in the noun-character, [30][4] they are included under the noun.

4. UTTERANCES

The noun ought to be considered before the verb because it is a more important (*principalior*) part than the verb,[5] and so we must begin with it. And since every noun is an utterance (*vox*) and every utterance is a sound, we must begin with sound.

Sound is the property to which the ears are sensitive; it is divided into vocal and nonvocal. Vocal sound is an utterance such as is made by an animal's mouth. Nonvocal sound is footsteps, the crashing of trees, and the like.

---

to have had much effect on the development of the *"logica moderna."* (See "Semantics, History of," Section *"Scientia sermocinalis,"* in Paul Edwards, ed., *Encyclopedia of Philosophy* (forthcoming).)

[2] Later in the treatise Sherwood tends to relax this distinction and to use 'proposition' where the distinction calls for 'statement.' See, e.g., pp. 40–41.

[3] In G (Grabmann's edition) this sentence occurs immediately after the first sentence of this paragraph.

[4] The numbers in brackets throughout the text are the numbers of the corresponding pages in G and appear at points corresponding to the *conclusions* of pages in G.

[5] Cf. *Syncategoremata*, p. 48 (quoted in Introduction, p. 14), where Sherwood describes the predicate as the more important (*dignior*) part of the statement.

Utterances are divided into significant and nonsignificant. A significant utterance is one that signifies something; a nonsignificant one signifies nothing; e.g., 'buba blictrix.' Some significant utterances signify naturally, some by convention (*ad placitum*). The kind that signifies naturally is the kind produced by nature and significant of something, such as the groans of the sick; the kind that signifies by convention is the kind that acquires its signification as the result of some human custom (*humana institutione*). Nouns and verbs, then, are of this latter kind.

An utterance significant by convention is either complex (in the case of an expression[6] (*oratio*)) or simple (*incomplexa*) (in the case of a word (*dictio*)). Some of the simple kind signify [something] together with time (i.e., the verb) and others apart from time (i.e., the noun). Each of these is divided into finite and infinite, direct and oblique.[7]

5. NOUNS[8]

A noun is an utterance significant by convention, apart from time, finite and direct, no part of which taken by itself signifies anything.

It is called "an utterance" because of its difference from a nonvocal sound like the crashing of trees; "significant" because of its difference from a nonsignificant utterance; "[significant] by convention" because of its difference from a naturally significant utterance; "[significant] apart from time" because of its difference from the verb and participle, which signify [something] together with time. The clause "no part of which taken by itself [signifies anything]" is added because of the difference between a noun and an expression, parts of which taken by themselves do signify, as we shall see;[9] "finite" because of its difference from the infinite noun, which is, strictly speaking, not a noun — for example, the word 'non-man,' which is called infinite because it signifies [indefinitely];[10] "direct" because of its difference from the oblique

---

[6] See p. 25. Cf. Priscian, *Institutionum grammaticarum libri XVII* (hereafter cited as *Inst. gram.*), 2.2.3: "Dictio est pars minima orationis constructae, id est in ordine compositae . . ."; also 2.2.4: "Oratio est ordinatio dictionum congrua sententiam perfectam demonstrans . . ."

[7] On these distinctions see pp. 23 and 24.

[8] Compare this section with Aristotle's *De interpretatione* (hereafter cited as *De int.*), Ch. 2. The heading "Definition of a Noun" appears in the margin of the manuscript at this point.

[29] P. 25.

[10] The scribe has omitted the end of this explanation. Grabmann interpolates '*indeterminate.*'

noun, which is not a noun from the logician's point of view because a statement cannot be made up of it and a verb (although it is a noun from the viewpoint of the grammarian).[11]

Notice, by the way, that some nouns do signify time, although not by means of tense (*per modum temporis*) — e.g., 'year,' 'month,' 'day.' [31]

6. VERBS [12]

A verb is an utterance significant by convention, together with time, finite and direct, no part of which taken by itself signifies anything.

It should be noted that several parts of this definition are doing the same work here as they did in the previous definition. However, "together with time" is set down because of the difference from a noun, which signifies apart from time; "finite" because of the difference from an infinite verb, such as 'does not run,' 'does not work'; "direct," of course, because of the difference from an oblique verb. One ought to know that a verb in the indicative mood is called direct, and a verb in any other mood is called an oblique verb. More strictly, however, only a verb in the present indicative mood is called direct. Verbs of any other tense "lean on" the present tense and are thus made oblique[13] (*ad hoc inclinant et obliquantur*).

7. INDECLINABLES

It should be noted that in both definitions all the indeclinable parts [of speech] are ruled out in virtue of the word "significant," since, speaking strictly, they do not signify but consignify; that is, they signify together with another [word]. For what they signify they signify insofar as they are dispositions (*dispositiones*) of something else.[14]

---

[11] The nominative, vocative (and sometimes accusative) cases are "direct," the others "oblique."

[12] Compare this section with *De int.*, Ch. 3. The heading "Definition of a Verb" appears in the margin of the manuscript at this point.

[13] Sherwood seems to be suggesting not that the other tenses depend grammatically on the present tense but that their temporal range is dependent on the central position of the present tense.

[14] Conjunctions, adverbs, prepositions, and interjections are the parts of speech traditionally classified as indeclinable. Approximately half the words discussed by Sherwood in his *Syncategoremata* are indeclinables (conjunctions and adverbs), the other half being adjectives and verbs. There he speaks quite freely of the signification (rather than consignification) of the syncategorematic words, de-

8. EXPRESSIONS [15]

Since an understanding of the expression is required for an understanding of the statement, we have to see what an expression is. An expression, then, is an utterance significant by convention, parts of which taken by themselves do signify.

The words "utterance significant by convention" are doing the same work here as they did in the preceding definitions. But the words "parts of which," etc., are added because of the difference between an expression and a word, the parts of which do not signify.

9. COMPLETE AND INCOMPLETE EXPRESSIONS

Expressions are divided into the following kinds. Some expressions are complete (*perfecta*), others incomplete (*imperfecta*). A complete expression is one that establishes a complete thought (*intellectum*) in the hearer's mind — e.g., 'the man is white.' An incomplete expression is one that establishes an incomplete thought in the hearer's mind — e.g., 'white man.' Complete expressions are of course further divided. One kind is indicative and is produced by means of the indicative mood — e.g., 'a man is running.' [16] Another kind is imperative (or entreating) and takes place through the imperative (or entreating) mood — e.g., 'come to read' (*veni lectum*). Another kind is optative — e.g., 'if only I were reading.' Another kind is conjunctive — e.g., 'when I am reading.' Another kind is infinitive — e.g., 'that Socrates is reading.' [17] Another kind is interrogative — e.g., 'which man is running?'.

---

clinable and indeclinable alike. Cf. his introduction to that treatise (quoted in Introduction, p. 14), where he evidently used 'determination' in the sense in which he uses 'disposition' here; cf. also his discussion of '*est*' in that treatise, where he distinguishes between consignification as introduced here and what Aristotle has to say about the copula in *De int.*, Ch. 3 (16b24). See also p. 27 and Chapter Five, Section 16.4, p. 129 below.

[15] Compare this section with *De int.*, Ch. 4. The heading "Definition of an Expression" appears in the margin of the manuscript at this point.

[16] The Latin example is '*homo currit*,' which is ordinarily translated, as here, using the English progressive present — 'is running.' But the absence of the verb 'to be' in the Latin construction sometimes makes a difference in Sherwood's discussion (as on p. 26), and then '*currit*' will be translated simply as 'runs.'

[17] This is the Latin construction known as the infinitive with subject accusative, which usually occurs as the subject or object of another verb, often as a clause in indirect discourse — e.g., 'Plato says that Socrates is reading' ('*Plato ait Sortem legere*').

10. STATEMENTS AND EXPRESSIONS

But among all these moods only the indicative expression signifies the true and the false (*verum et falsum*) as has been said,[18] since the response [32] "either it is true or it is false" is appropriate only to it. Therefore it is only the indicative expression that is a statement; for Boethius says that a proposition is an expression signifying the true or the false (and thus at that point he does [not] distinguish between a proposition and a statement).[19] Aristotle, however, defines a statement as follows: a statement is an expression signifying something of something else or something apart from something else (*aliquid de aliquo vel aliquid ab aliquo*).[20] When he says "of something else" he means the inherence of the predicate in the subject; and when he says "apart from something else" he means the separation (*remotio*) of the predicate from the subject.

11. INTEGRAL AND SUBJECTIVE PARTS OF STATEMENTS[21]

Now that we understand the statement through its definition and in itself, we have still to understand it through a division [of its kinds] and in its parts.

There are two kinds of parts, either integral or subjective.[22] Integral parts are those making up an integral whole (*totum secundum integritatem*); the whole is never predicated of such parts. Subjective parts are those making up a whole in its generality (*in sua communitate*); but the whole *is* predicated of these.

The integral parts of the statement are, therefore, the subject and the predicate. The subject is what the discourse (*sermo*) is about. The predicate, however, is what is proclaimed (or predicated) about something other than itself (*illud, quod de alio predicatur*). For example, in 'Socrates runs' the term 'Socrates' is the subject, because the discourse is about him,[23] and the predicate is 'runs,' because it is said about something other than itself.

---

[18] Apparently a reference to Section 9 above.

[19] Boethius, *In librum de interpretatione*, 2nd ed. Migne, *P.L.*, 64.454 (M.G.).

[20] *De int.*, Ch. 5 (17a20).

[21] Compare sections 11–14 with *De int.*, Chs. 5 and 6. The heading "Division of the Statement" appears in the margin of the manuscript at this point.

[22] Cf. Aristotle, *Metaphysics* (hereafter cited as *Met.*), Bk. 5, Chs. 25 and 26. Cf. also Chapter Four, Section 3.2.3, below.

[23] The Latin '*de eo*' admits of the translation 'about *it*' — i.e., the term. Moreover, Sherwood says the term is the subject and the subject is what the discourse

Some say that the word 'is' is a third part, the copula. But that is not the case; for since it is a verb it signifies that which is said[24] of something other than itself, and thus it is a predicate. But it does *consignify* composition, which is [the function of] the copula (*que est copula*). And every other verb by its very nature consignifies in this respect.[25]

The statement is divided into subjective parts as follows, depending on the nature of the subject or the predicate. Some statements are single (*una*), others multiple (*plures*). A single statement is one in which one thing is predicated of one thing. A multiple statement is one in which one thing is predicated of many things, or many of one, or many of many.

12. THE SUBSTANCE OF STATEMENTS

Statements are divided also with respect to their *substance*, as follows. Some statements are categorical, others hypothetical. A categorical statement is one whose substance consists of a subject and a predicate; and it gets the name 'categorical' from 'καθηγορίζω, -ζας' — i.e., '*predico, -cas*'[26] — because such a statement is completed by the predicate. A statement whose substance consists of two categorical statements con-

---

is about. But of course in 'Socrates runs' nothing is being said about the term 'Socrates.' This kind of vagueness about the status of subjects and predicates has been surprisingly common in the history of logic. Cf. Peter Geach, *Reference and Generality* (hereafter cited as *Reference*), Ch. 2, "Subject and Predicate."

[24] G has '*predicatur*'; '*dicitur*' in manuscript.

[25] The difficulty of this paragraph is partly the result of its telegraphic style, and it should be compared with the longer treatment of 'is' in Sherwood's *Syncategoremata*, pp. 70–71. There he discusses three sorts of occurrences of 'is': (1) alone with a noun, as in 'a man is,' in which case it indicates *being*, either the actual being of an individual (as in the example above) or the conditional being of a nature, form, or species — as in 'man is'; (2) as the composition (the relation between the subject and the predicate of a statement) of two nouns, as in 'man is an animal,' in which case it is genuinely a "third part," which may be considered part of the predicate; (3) as an element in every (singular direct) verb (see p. 24 above), since when another verb is the predicate, as in 'a man runs,' it can always be resolved into its participle and the verb 'is,' as in 'a man is running,' in which case the 'is' "becomes different predicates" through association with different participles. On consignification see pp. 24 and 129.

[26] The Greek verb should be 'κατηγορέω'; Sherwood has his version of it in Roman characters: 'cathegorizo.' The Latin verb may be translated here as 'I predicate.' For both verbs Sherwood gives second-person singular endings after the first-person form (mistaken in the case of the Greek). This passage occurs in G as follows: "Et dicitur cathegorica a cathegorizo zas, quod est predico cas eo, quod talis perficitur per predicatum." The manuscript has commas between the first- and second-person forms and following '*cas*' and no comma between '*eo*' and '*quod*.' G's punctuation obscures the sense.

joined is called hypothetical. It gets its name from 'ὑπό,' which [in Latin] is *'sub,'* and 'θέσις,' which [in Latin] is *'positio,'* so that it might be called "suppositive"[27] (*quasi suppositiva*), for one categorical statement is *put under* another,[28] as in 'Socrates [33] is running and Plato is arguing.'

So the question "what kind [of statement]?" since it is a question of substance, is to be answered "categorical" or "hypothetical."

13. THE QUALITY OF CATEGORICAL STATEMENTS

[Categorical] statements are divided with respect to *quality* into affirmative and negative. An affirmative statement is one whose predicate is said to be in the subject — e.g., 'a man is running.' A negative statement is one whose predicate is said to be separated from the subject — e.g., 'a man is not running.' So the question "what quality [of statement]?" is to be answered "affirmative" or "negative."

14. THE QUANTITY OF CATEGORICAL STATEMENTS

Categorical statements are divided with respect to *quantity* into universal, particular, indefinite, and singular.[29] A universal statement is one in which the subject is a common term determined by a universal sign — e.g., 'every man is running.' A common term is a term naturally suited to be predicated of many things.[30] A universal sign is that which signifies that the predicate is said of or separated from the subject uni-

---

[27] See p. 43, n. 74.

[28] The Greek words are in Roman characters. This use of 'hypothetical' does originate with Greek writers on logic. In the *Introduction to Dialectic* of Galen (ca. 129–199 A.D.), "we find the word 'hypothetical' firmly established . . . as a generic name for complex statements, whether conditional, disjunctive, or conjunctive" (Kneale, *Development*, p. 182). In the twelfth century "the word 'hypothetical' was still used to cover both conditional and disjunctive propositions, and for purposes of contrast under the general heading the former were sometimes called conjunctive" (*ibid.*, p. 221). *'Suppositiva'* may be no more than Sherwood's attempt at a Latin equivalent to 'hypothetical'; however, Aquinas seems to use *'oratio suppositiva'* as roughly synonymous with *'oratio indicativa'* or *'oratio iudicativa'* (see "oratio" in Roy Joseph Deferrari, *A Lexicon of St. Thomas Aquinas* (hereafter cited as *Lexicon*). See especially p. 34.

[29] The notions of the quality and quantity of statements are not Aristotelian but seem to have originated in the logic of the twelfth century. See, e.g., Abelard, *Super periermenias* in *Abaelardiana inedita* (ed. Minio-Paluello), p. 23. Cf. Bocheński's mistaken suggestion (*History*, p. 211) that they may have occurred first in Peter of Spain.

[30] Cf. *De int.*, Ch. 7 (17a37ff).

versally, that is, for any and every part.[31] Such are 'every,' 'all,' 'no,' 'each,' 'both,' 'however many,' 'any,' and the like.[32]

A particular statement, on the other hand, is one in which the subject is a common term determinated by a particular sign — e.g., 'some man is running.' A particular sign is that which signifies that the predicate is said of or separated from the subject for some part or other. Of this sort are 'some,' 'a certain,' 'another,' 'a certain amount of,' 'several,' 'some sort of,' and the like. [Both kinds of signs] are called "signs" because they signify whether the discourse is about the whole [of the subject] or about a part.

An indefinite statement is one in which the subject is a common term not determinated by any sign. Such statements are called indefinite because they do not determine whether the discourse is about the whole [of the subject] or about a part.

A singular statement is one in which the subject is a discrete term, which can be either a proper name or a determinate pronoun — e.g., 'Socrates is running' or 'that one is running.'

Since this division is based on quantity, the question 'what quantity [of statement]?' is to be answered with one of the above.

15. THE OPPOSITION OF STATEMENTS [33]

There is still another division of statements, one that arises in case one statement is organized relative to another (*que accidit ei sicut una ordinatur ad aliam*). In order to have that division, however, we must begin with another division, as follows.

Some statements have one or the other term in common — e.g., 'a man is an animal,' 'an ass is an animal' — and others have none in common — e.g., 'a man is an animal,' 'an ass is running.' Again, of those that share a term, some share only one or the other, as in the first example just

---

[31] According to the long section on the universal sign '*omnis*' in the *Syncategoremata*, a universal sign "divides the subject with respect to the predicate" (p. 48), the result of the division being "parts" of the subject — either "specific parts" or "numerical parts" (*ibid.*). The "division" produced by the universal sign seems to be what is more often called "distribution," even by Sherwood.

[32] Sherwood's *Syncategoremata* contains discussions of all these universal signs.

[33] Compare this section with *De int.*, Ch. 7. Sherwood does not use the word '*oppositio*' here although it had been established as the standard technical term for this relation among statements by its occurrence in Boethius's translation of *De interpretatione*. Cf., however, Sherwood's use of '*oppositio*' and related words in this connection — e.g., on pp. 48 and 65.

above, and others share both — e.g., 'every man is an animal,' 'some man is an animal.' Likewise, of those that share both terms, some share them in [34] the same order, as in the last example; others in the converse order — e.g., 'every man is an animal,' 'some animal is a man.'

[As for those that share both terms] in the same order, either both [statements] are universal, or both are particular, or one is universal and the other particular. If both are universal, then they will be of different quality; otherwise they would be identical. For since they agree in both terms in the same order and are also of the same quantity, they must be of different quality. In this case they will be contraries — e.g., 'every man is running,' 'no man is running.'

If both statements are particular, then, by the above reasoning, they will be of different quality, and in that case they will be subcontraries — e.g., 'some man is running,' 'some man is not running.'

If either the one statement or the other is particular, then either they [i.e., the particular statement and the universal statement] are of the same quality, and in that case subalterns [34] (*subalterne*) — e.g., 'every man is running,' 'some man is running'; 'no man is running,' 'some man is not running' — or they are of different quality, in which case they are contradictories — e.g., 'every man is running,' 'some man is not running'; 'no man is running,' 'some man is running.'

Note that it is unnecessary to add the indefinite class [of statements] to this last division, because indefinite judgment (*iudicium*) is like particular [35] judgment.[36] The addition of the singular class is likewise

---

[34] According to Kneale (*Development*, p. 56), "the two particular statements have been said by later logicians [i.e., later than Aristotle] to be *subaltern* to the universal statements under which they occur in the figure" (see p. 32 below). Sherwood, however, uses 'subaltern' as a generic term for both the universal and the particular (of the same quality and with the same terms in the same order), as do logicians long after the middle ages — e.g., Isaac Watts in his *Logick* of 1725: "Both particular and universal Propositions which agree in Quality but not in Quantity are called *Subaltern*"; Archbishop Whately in his *Elements of Logic* of 1826: "in the Subalterns, the truth of the particular (which is called the *subalternate*) follows from the truth of the universal (*subalternans*)"; H. W. B. Joseph in his *Introduction to Logic* of 1906: "A and I, E and O are called subaltern, because in each pair one is subordinated to the other." The explicit introduction of 'subalternant' and 'subalternate' as technical terms is scarcely necessary for the medieval logician, to whom the appropriate use of the present active and perfect passive participles (*subalternans, subalternata*) would occur quite naturally. See, for example, p. 33 and especially p. 49.

[35] G has '*particulariter*'; '*particulare*' in manuscript.

[36] Cf. *Analytica Priora* (hereafter cited as *An. pr.*), Bk. 1, Ch. 7 (29a27), and Kneale, *Development*, p. 55. Sherwood is summarizing Aristotle's rather subtle dis-

unnecessary by the same reasoning, except that [singular statements] differ [from particular statements] in this respect: if two statements are singular and of different quality they are not subcontraries but, in accordance with the theory, contradictories (*sed ratione contradictorie*) — e.g., 'Socrates is running,' 'Socrates is not running.'

Note, moreover, that a universal affirmative and a singular negative, as well as a universal negative and a singular affirmative, are mutually contrary (at least as far as the law goes (*ad minus quantum ad legem*)),[37] because they can be false at the same time and cannot be true at the same time. Suppose that Socrates is running and no one else; in that case these statements are false: 'every man is running,' 'Socrates is not running.' Again, suppose that Socrates is not running but everyone except him [is running]; then these statements are false: 'no man is running,' 'Socrates is running.'[38]

This, then, is the division of statements arising from the arrangement

---

missal of the indefinite statement for syllogistic purposes, but he does it so hastily as to produce a doctrine as untenable for Latin as it is for English. The indefinite statement '*homo currit*' ('a man is running') is "particular," but the indefinite statement '*homo est animal*' ('a man is an animal') is "universal." Moreover, these two indefinites happen to be Sherwood's favorite examples and appear frequently throughout the book.

[37] Sherwood is referring to "the law of contraries" given on p. 32, and he says "*at least* as far as *the law* goes" because it is only one of two characterizations he gives of contrariety, the other being the definition in terms of universal statements given on p. 30.

[38] I do not know of any logician earlier than Sherwood who made this observation. (Peter of Spain omits it, and, perhaps as a result, it is not a regular feature of treatments of traditional logic.) Sherwood has already pointed out (on p. 31) one respect in which singular and particular statements differ, one that Aristotle had already recognized (cf. *De int.*, Ch. 7 (17b28, 18a2)). In this paragraph he points out a second difference. The universal affirmative 'every man is running' and the particular negative 'some man is not running' are contradictories; when one is true the other must be false and vice versa. On the other hand, that same universal affirmative and the *singular* negative 'Socrates is not running' are not contradictories but *contraries*; obviously when one is true the other must be false, but they can both be false at once, just in case Socrates is running and there is at least one other man who is not running. (Sherwood stipulates more than he needs when he says "no one else" is running.) And he goes on to make the same sort of observation about the universal negative and the singular affirmative (again stipulating more than he needs). The result of his discussion of singular statements is that they are like particulars (with respect to the forms of opposition) only in that a universal and a corresponding singular of the same quality will be subalterns. (By a "corresponding" singular I mean one having the subject of the universal together with a demonstrative pronoun or definite description — e.g., 'this man,' 'the man in the iron mask' — or one having as its subject a proper name accepted as belonging to an individual of the kind mentioned in the subject of the universal — e.g., 'Socrates,' 'G. E. Moore.')

(*ordinatio*) or relation (*comparatio*) of one statement with another —
viz., some are contraries, some subcontraries, some subalterns, and some
contradictories, as in the figure below.[39]

16. THE LAWS OF OPPOSITION [40]

The law of contraries, it should be noted, is that they can never be
true at the same time but can be false at the same time — e.g., 'every
animal is a man,' 'no animal is a man,' both of which [35] are false.

The law of subcontraries, on the other hand, is that they can never be

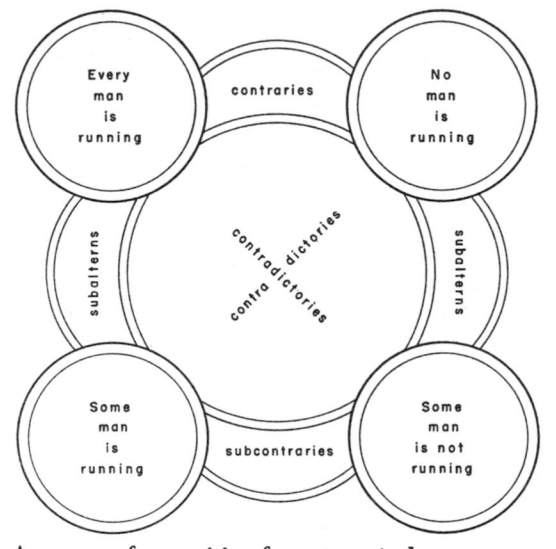

A square of opposition for categorical statements

false at the same time but can be true at the same time — e.g., 'some
animal is a man,' which is true, and 'some animal is not a man,' which
is likewise true. But in case 'some animal is a man' is false, that predicate cannot be in any singular belonging to that subject, since if it were
so the particular affirmative would be true, for truth in [the case of]
any singular produces truth in the particular [statement]. If, however,

---

[39] The "square of opposition" has some remote ancestors in the tables to be
found in *De int.*, Ch. 10, but it occurred in this traditional form as early as the
second century A.D. in the logic manual of Apuleius of Madaura. See Bocheński,
History, pp. 140–141. Combining what seem to be Sherwood's own observations
with those he derives from Aristotle, one may construct a "hexagon of opposition"
(see the opposite page). (I owe this suggestion to Mr. Gerald W. Lilje.)

[40] Compare this section with *De int.*, 17b23–18a12, 18a27–18a33.

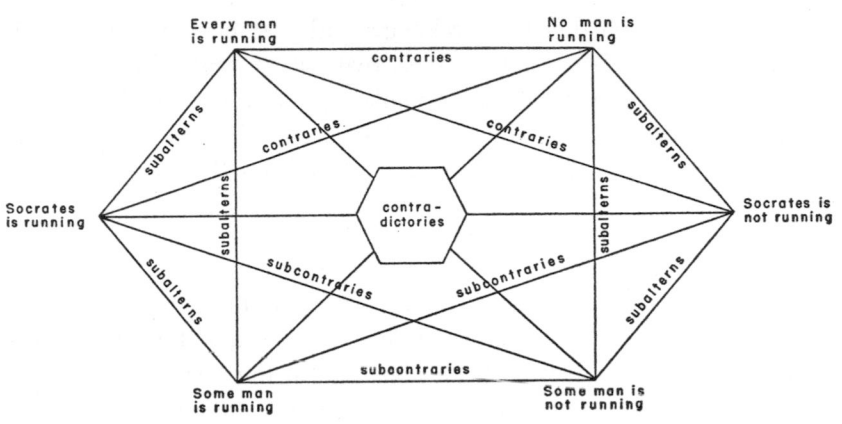

A "hexagon of opposition" combining what seem to be Sherwood's own observations with those he derives from Aristotle

[the predicate] is in no singular [belonging to that subject], then 'some animal is not a man' is not false. Thus it is clear that if the [particular] affirmative is false, the [particular] negative is not false, and vice versa.

The law of subalterns is that if the universal is true the particular is true, but not vice versa. Similarly, if the particular is false, then the universal is also false, but not vice versa.

The law of contradictories is that they can be neither true at the same time nor false at the same time, as is clear enough.

17. THE MATTER OF STATEMENTS [41]

It should also be noted that the matter of statements is of three kinds, viz., natural, contingent, and separate. The matter is natural in case the subject receives the predicate by its very nature, as in 'a man is an animal.' It is contingent in case the subject receives the predicate contingently, as in [36] 'a man is running.' It is separate in case the predicate is naturally separated from the subject, as in 'a man is an ass.'

Notice that whenever a particular statement is true in natural matter its subcontrary cannot be true, because whatever is in one particular in natural matter is in all. Similarly, whatever is separated from one in separate matter is separated from all. Moreover, in natural matter and in

---

[41] The doctrine of the matter of statements dates back at least to the *Dialectica* of Garland the Computist (eleventh century) (see De Rijk's edition, pp. 54–55); and it can be found frequently both before and after Sherwood — e.g., in Abelard, Peter of Spain, Aquinas, and Albert of Saxony.

separate matter a particular interchanges with (*convertitur cum*) a universal. Therefore subcontraries in these two matters cannot be true at the same time, and the truth of the particular subaltern entails (*infert*) the truth of the subalternant universal. These truths do not, however, depend on the nature of the particular but only on the nature of [its] matter.[42]

18. HYPOTHETICAL STATEMENTS

Everything that has been said so far pertains to the categorical statement; thus it now remains for us to deal with the hypothetical. An explanation of the name was given above;[43] on the basis of it we can construct the following definition: a hypothetical statement is one that is conjoined out of two categoricals. This can occur in three different ways: either through a copulative conjunction, in which case it is called a copulative — e.g., 'Socrates is running and Plato is arguing'; or through a disjunctive conjunction, in which case it is called a disjunctive — e.g., 'Socrates is a man or an ass'; or through a consecutive [conjunction], in which case it is called a conditional — e.g., 'if Socrates is a man, Socrates is an animal.'[44] This [last] is called hypothetical in the strict sense because of the stated hypothesis — i.e., the condition.

In order that a copulative be true, then, it is necessary that both parts be true. But in order that a disjunctive be true, the truth of one or the other part is sufficient. In order that a conditional be true the truth of its parts is not required, but only that whenever the antecedent is

---

[42] Sherwood's argument here seems to be founded on the recognition that there is something peculiar about *particular* statements the terms of which are naturally associated (or dissociated) — i.e., about particular statements that could and should be *universal*. For example, if it is true that *some* member of the species man is a member of the genus animal, then it is true that *every* member of the species man is a member of the genus animal, statements about genus-species relations being (at least one instance of) statements "in natural matter." But if 'some man is an animal' entails 'every man is an animal,' subalternation is transformed into a kind of equivalence; moreover, since 'every man is an animal' is the contradictory of 'some man is not an animal,' subcontrariety is transformed into a kind of contradiction. If Sherwood's argument does nothing else, it indicates the wisdom of using statements "in contingent matter," as he does, to illustrate the forms of opposition. This application of the old doctrine of the three kinds of statemental matter may be Sherwood's own contribution; at any rate it was clearly ignored by Peter of Spain, whose model square of opposition is built on 'every man is an animal,' 'some man is an animal,' etc. (*Summulae logicales*, ed. Bocheński (hereafter cited as *Sum. log.*), p. 5).

[43] See p. 28.

[44] On this use of "hypothetical" see Kneale, *Development*, pp. 182–183.

[true], the consequent is [true].[45] (The antecedent is the part that immediately follows the consecutive conjunction, and the consequent is the other part.)

19. EQUIPOLLENT SIGNS [46]

It was said above that a statement ought to be judged universal or particular according to the nature of the sign added to its subject.[47] But since it is the case that a universal sign acquires the force (*virtus*) of the other sign through the addition of a negation and acquires other forces through other additions, it remains to be seen just what force is produced in a sign by the addition of a negation.

It is important to know, then, that if a negation is added following a universal affirmative sign — as in 'every man is not-running' — or preceding a particular [sign], it causes either one to be equipollent (*equipollere*) to a universal negative sign.[48] This can be clarified in the following way. The sign [37] 'every' signifies that the predicate (together with its dispositions) belongs to each part of the subject;[49] therefore whenever the predicate follows with a negation it will signify

---

[45] Consider the following examples: (1) (Copulative) It is raining and the streets are slippery. (2) (Disjunctive) Either it is raining or the streets are slippery. (3) (Conditional) If it is raining, the streets are slippery. Sherwood's point about the conditional is that it is unlike (1) and (2) in that in order to determine the truth of either (1) or (2) we must know that one or the other or both parts of those "hypotheticals" are true, while in determining the truth of (3) we need not know whether it is in fact raining or whether the streets are in fact slippery but only that it is never the case that it is raining while the streets are not slippery — i.e., that the first part is never true while the second part is false. Peter of Spain goes further along this line: "The truth of the conditional requires that the antecedent cannot be true without the consequent, as in 'if it is a man, it is an animal'; thus every true conditional is necessary and every false conditional is impossible. For the falsity of the conditional it is sufficient that the antecedent can be true without the consequent, as in 'if it is a man, it is white' " (*Sum. log.*, ed. Bocheński, p. 8, 1.23). For Boethius's broader view, see Bocheński, *History*, pp. 137–138. For Abelard's view of necessary connection in conditional statements, see Kneale, *Development*, pp. 217–218.

[46] The heading in the top margin of the manuscript at this point is "*De Equipollentiis.*" Compare this section with *De int.*, Ch. 10 (19b5ff).

[47] See pp. 28–29.

[48] That is, 'every man is not-running' may be rewritten for logical purposes as 'no man is running'; likewise 'not some man is running' or 'it is not the case that some man is running.' (Sherwood neglects to point out that a negation before a particular sign has this effect only if the particular statement is affirmative.)

[49] On "parts" of the subject see n. 31, this chapter. Negation and other adverbial modifications of the predicate are at least part of what is meant by "its dispositions." Cf. pp. 43 and 46.

that the negated predicate belongs to each part of the subject and thus that the predicate as such is separated from every part; therefore it is equipollent to a universal negative sign. Thus if one says 'every man is not-running,' it is clear that this is universal, on account of the sign, and negative; and therefore it is as described above. It is also clear that 'not some' is equipollent to 'no' (*nullus*), because 'any' (*ullus*) and 'some' are equipollent.[50] Therefore the results of adding [negation] to each of these will be equipollent — e.g., 'not some,' 'not any'; therefore 'no.' Again, 'some' is contradicted both by 'not some' and by 'no.' Therefore they are the same, since two different things do not contradict one and the same thing (*quia duo eidem non contradicunt*). Likewise, if 'not some man is running' is true, then 'some man is running' is false; and if that is the case, then the predicate is separated from every individual, as is clear from what has been said. Therefore ['not some'] is equipollent to a universal negative [sign].

On the other hand, a universal negative sign with a following negation or a particular sign with two negations — one preceding and the other following — is equipollent to a universal affirmative [sign]. The proof of this is as follows. A universal negative sign signifies that the predicate (together with its dispositions) is separated from every part of the subject. Therefore, whenever a negation follows and negates the predicate, the negated predicate, or the negation of the predicate, must be separated from every part of the subject, and thus the affirmed predicate, or the affirmation of the predicate, goes together with (*convenire*) every part of the subject, and so [the universal negative sign with a following negation] is equipollent to a universal affirmative sign. Again, the first negation falls on (*cadit supra*) the negated predicate; therefore it separates it from every part; therefore it signifies its opposite, viz., that the affirmative predicate goes together with the subject for every part. Therefore the third [combination][51] is equipollent to a universal affirmative [sign]. From what has already been said,[52] it is

---

[50] This remark seems to depend partly on the fact that in Latin '*nullus*' is as obviously a negative of '*ullus*' as in English 'none' is a negative of 'one.' '*Ullus*' and '*aliquis*' seem no more nearly equipollent in Latin than do 'any' and 'some' in English.

[51] I.e., the universal negative sign with a following negation, the third combination he has investigated, the first two being the universal affirmative sign with a following negation and the particular sign with a preceding negation.

[52] On p. 36.

also clear that a particular sign with a preceding negation is equipollent to a universal negative sign. Therefore, if another negation is added to each of them they will still be equipollent, because when equals are added to equals (*eidem eodem apposito*) the whole remains the same. Therefore, since a universal negative [sign] with a following negation is equipollent to a universal affirmative [sign], it is clear that a particular [sign] with negation preceding and following it will be equipollent to it [also]. Furthermore, 'some . . . not' and 'every' are contradictory, and so are 'some . . . not' and 'not some . . . not.' Therefore 'every' and 'not some . . . not' are really (*secundum rem*) the same, since whatever things contradict the same thing are themselves the same.

Next, a universal negative [sign] with a [38] preceding negation is equipollent to a particular affirmative [sign]. The reason for this is the following. 'No' and 'some' are contradictory; similarly 'no' and 'not no.' Therefore 'not no' and 'some' are the same, since they contradict the same thing. For the same reason 'some' and 'not every . . . not' are the same, for they contradict the same thing, viz., 'every . . . not.' And since the sign 'some' contradicts 'every . . . not,' it is clear that 'every . . . not' and 'no' are the same.

Finally, a universal affirmative sign with a preceding negation or a [universal] negative [sign] with negation preceding and following is equipollent to a particular negative sign of this sort — 'some . . . not.' The reason for this is the following. 'Not every' contradicts 'every'; so does 'some . . . not.' Therefore, 'not every' and 'some . . . not' are the same. Again, 'not no' and 'some' are equipollent; therefore if the same thing is added [to each] they will [continue to] be equipollent. Therefore 'not no . . . not' and 'some . . . not' are the same.

It should be noted, then, that each sign is equipollent to its contradictory with a preceding negation. Similarly, each sign is equipollent to its subaltern with negation preceding and following. Similarly, every universal sign is equipollent to its contrary with a following negation.[53]

Everything said so far can be retained in these verses:

> 'Every,' 'no . . . not,' 'not some . . . not' are equivalent;
> 'No,' 'not some,' 'every . . . not' are equal;

---

[53] Note that Sherwood does not go on to say that each particular sign is equipollent to its subcontrary with a following negation, perhaps because 'some' with a following negation just *is* the particular negative sign.

'Some,' 'not no,' 'not every . . . not' are associated;
'Some . . . not,' 'not no . . . not,' 'not every' stick together.[54]

Or in this verse:

Pre[-negation] produces the contradictory;
Post[-negation] produces the contrary;
Pre- and post[-negation] produce the subaltern

(*Pre contradicit, post contrariatur, pre postque subalternantur*).

20. STATEMENTS CONTAINING TWO SIGNS

Notice that if there are two signs in a single locution, the first of which is universal, then the first is equipollent to [its] contrary and the second to its contradictory; and I say this in case the first extends to (*extendit se ad*) the second. The reason for this is the following. If the first is a universal affirmative [sign] it will signify that the predicate together with the other sign goes together with every part of the subject. Thus it will signify that the predicate together with the contradictory of the following sign is separated from every part of the subject.

---

[54] The Latin mnemonic verse reads as follows:

Equivalent omnis, nullus non, non aliquis non.
Nullus, non aliquis, omnis non equiparantur.
Quidam, non nullus, non omnis non sociantur.
Quidam non, non nullus non, non omnis adherent.

(In the third and fourth lines (and elsewhere in the preceding paragraphs) G has '*ullus*' where the manuscript has '*nullus*.') As Kneale suggests, one reason for the greater popularity of Peter of Spain's *Summulae logicales* may be "the fact that it contains more and better mnemonic verses than William of Shyreswood's work" (*Development*, p. 234). At the end of his much shorter and simpler treatment of equipollence Peter gives (in addition to a modified square of opposition for equipollent signs) the following two sets of verses corresponding to Sherwood's here:

Non omnis — quidam non; omnis non, quasi nullus;
Non nullus — quidam; sed nullus non valet omnis;
Non aliquis — nullus; non quidam non valet omnis;
Non alter — neuter; neuter non praestat uterque.

Prae contradicit contraria post tibi mansit
Eritque subalterna si postponatur et ante.

(ed. Bocheński, p. 9, where the verses are differently punctuated). Already in the twelfth century the use of metrical devices in textbooks had become a fad, for, as one grammarian of the period put it, "the metrical form can be more easily comprehended, is more elegant, is briefer, and can be remembered more easily." (See Louis John Paetow, *The Arts Course at Medieval Universities with Special Reference to Grammar and Rhetoric*, pp. 34–35: "A veritable craze for versifying [particularly in grammar textbooks] prevailed during the twelfth and thirteenth centuries.")

For example, 'every man is no ass' is equipollent to 'no man is some ass.' Similarly, 'every man is some animal' is equipollent to 'no man is no animal'; and 'every man is not some animal' is equipollent to 'no man is every animal.'

Likewise if the first sign is a universal negative; for then it will signify that the predicate itself together with its sign [39] is separated from every part of the subject and thus that the predicate itself together with the opposite [sign] goes together with every part of the subject; but in that case it will be equipollent to a universal affirmative sign. For example, 'no man is some ass' is equipollent to 'every man is no ass.' Similarly, 'no man is every animal' is equipollent to 'every man is not some animal'; and 'no man is not some risible being' is equipollent to 'every man is every risible being.'[55]

So, then, the equipollence of signs is clear in both kinds of cases — whether they occur in the same sentence (*sermo*) or in different ones.[56]

21. ASSERTORIC AND MODAL STATEMENTS[57]

Since our treatment of statements is oriented toward syllogism (*cum intentio sit de enuntiatione propter syllogismum*), we have to consider them under those differences that make a difference in syllogism. These are such differences as affirmative, negative; universal, particular; modal, assertoric (*de inesse*); and others of that sort. For one syllogism differs from another as a result of those differences.[58]

---

[55] Cf. *De int.*, Ch. 7 (17b12ff). For Sherwood's later view on the occurrence of signs in the predicate see his *Syncategoremata*, ed. O'Donnell, p. 50.

[56] Sherwood's generally creditable struggles with multiple quantification were so modified as to be virtually abandoned by Peter of Spain, whose corresponding discussion reads as follows: ". . . If two universal negative signs occur in the same locution so that one is in the subject and the other in the predicate, the first is equipollent to its contrary, the other to its contradictory. Thus these [statements] are equipollent: 'nothing is nothing,' 'everything is something,' by the second rule — i.e., 'everything . . . not' and 'nothing' are equipollent because 'every . . . not' and 'no' are equipollent by the second rule, and so 'everything . . . not' and 'nothing.' But by the first rule 'not no' and 'some' are equipollent. Thus 'nothing is nothing' is equipollent to 'everything is something,' since 'not nothing' and 'some' are equipollent. Likewise, 'no man is no animal' and 'every man is some animal,' or 'neither is neither,' 'either is some.'" (*Sum. log.*, ed. Bocheński, p. 9.)

[57] Compare this section with *De int.*, Chs. 12–13 (21a34–23a26).

[58] On these differences among syllogisms cf. *An. pr.*, Bk. I, Ch. 8 (29b29ff). In spite of this remark, which seems to promise a consideration of the modal/assertoric difference as it relates to the syllogism, there is no treatment of modal syllogisms in any of the works that have been ascribed to Sherwood. Cf. Kneale, *Development*, p. 233.

Let us then consider statements under the division assertoric/modal. This division depends on the nature of the composition.[59]

An assertoric statement, then, is one that simply signifies the inherence of the predicate in the subject — i.e., without determinating *how* it inheres. A modal statement, on the other hand, is one that does determinate the inherence of the predicate in the subject — i.e., one that says how the predicate inheres in the subject. And because the latter member of the division contains more difficulties it must be considered separately, first considering [the modal statement] as such, then relating one modal [statement] to another. Considering it as such, the first thing to consider is the substance of the modal statement, then its dispositions.[60]

22. THE NATURE OF A MODE

In order to understand its substance it is necessary to know what a mode is and how a mode produces a modal proposition. The word 'mode' is used both broadly (*communiter*) and strictly. Broadly speaking, a mode is the determination of an act, and in this respect it goes together with every adverb. Strictly speaking, a mode is the determination of [the inherence of] the predicate in the subject, as may be seen in 'a man is necessarily an animal,' for in this case the way in which the predicate inheres in the subject is determinated. But if one says 'the man is running swiftly,' all that is determinated is the action of the verb as such, and not the inherence [of that action] in the subject, and so that sort is not called a modal proposition.

23. THE SIX MODES

There are six modes — viz., true, false, possible, impossible, contingent,[61] necessary. However, since the first two do not distinguish [40] a

---

[59] The composition is the relation between the subject and the predicate. See n. 25, this chapter. In the original text this sentence follows the two sentences describing assertoric and modal statements.

[60] For the "dispositions" of modal statements see p. 46.

[61] Twelfth-century logicians distinguished between 'possible' and 'contingent,' using the former somewhat as 'logically possible' and the latter as 'really possible.' John of Salisbury says in his *Metalogicon* (1159), "the word 'contingent' today has a somewhat different sense from that in which Aristotle employed it. At present, we by no means consider 'contingent' equivalent to 'possible,' although this is the meaning Aristotle gave it in his treatise on modals [see *De int.*, Chs. 12–13]. While it is possible for the Ethiopian race to become white, and the species we know as swans to become black, neither of these is contingent" (tr. McGarry, Book III,

modal proposition from an assertoric statement, they are omitted; for it is the same thing to say 'Socrates is running' and 'it is true that Socrates is running,' for if it is false that Socrates is running, then Socrates is not running.

The following adverbial modes are grouped together with the other four modes: possibly, impossibly, contingently, and necessarily. Furthermore, a proposition with an inflected form (*suo casuali*) in place of the mode *necessary* is grouped together with the mode — e.g., 'a man is of necessity an animal.'

Thus there are four principal modes. Notice, however, that 'impossible' is used in two ways. It is used in one way of whatever cannot be true now or in the future or in the past (*quod non potest nec poterit nec potuit esse verum*); and this is "impossible *per se*" — e.g., 'a man is an ass.' It is used in the other way of whatever cannot be true now or in the future although it could have been true in the past, as if I were to say 'I have not walked'; and this is "impossible *per accidens.*" Similarly, in case something cannot be false now or in the future or in the past it is said to be "necessary *per se*" — e.g., 'God is.' But it is "necessary *per accidens*" in case something cannot be false now or in the future although it could have been [false] in the past — e.g., 'I have walked.' Both 'possible' and 'contingent' are also used in two ways. They are used in one way only of what can have both truth and falsity, and in that case strictly. In the other way they are used broadly and used of everything that can have truth, whether it is necessary or not; [62] and it is in this latter way that they are used here.

24. THE EFFECTS OF ADVERBIAL MODES

Now that these things have been considered it remains to be seen how a mode produces a modal proposition. It should be noted, then, that adverbial modes can occur in discourse in two ways — viz., by determinating either the action itself of the verb or the inherence of the predicate in the subject. Take, for example, 'Socrates is running contingently.' Here the word 'contingently' can determinate the action as such, in

---

pp. 168–169). Sherwood retains the two words as indicative of two different modes, but he tends to lump them together in discussion. See, e.g., p. 41 and especially pp. 47 and 50.

[62] Cf. *An. pr.*, Bk. 1, Ch. 3 (25a36–40), Ch. 13 (32a15ff), Ch. 14 (33b17–24).

which case the sense is 'Socrates's running is contingent' (*cursus contingens est Sorti*), and [the proposition] is not modal.[63] Or it can determinate the verb itself in respect of (*propter*) its inherence [in] or composition [with the subject], in which case the sense is "the composition 'Socrates is running' is contingent." In this case [the proposition] *is* modal, since [the adverb] determinates the action of the predicate in the subject.[64]

Here is a similar case: 'the soul of Antichrist will necessarily be'; for if the [adverbial] mode determinates the action of the verb in respect of its composition, then [the proposition] is modal and the sense is "the composition 'the soul of Antichrist will be' is necessary," which is false (*et falsa*).[65] If, however, [the adverbial mode] determinates the verb's action as such, then the sense is 'necessary being goes together with the soul of Antichrist,' in which case it is not modal, and in which case it is true.[66] And so also with respect to the other modes.[67][41]

---

[63] The suggestion seems to be that the Latin adverb '*contingenter*' was sometimes used in the way we use 'aimlessly' or 'erratically,' so that in this first use of '*contingenter*' we should understand the example as 'Socrates is running erratically,' the "sense" of which is the ascription of an erratic course to Socrates. The adverb's determinating "the action as such" is simply its modifying the verb in the way adverbs usually modify verbs.

[64] The adverb's determinating "the action of the predicate *in* the subject" is its modifying the relation between the subject and the predicate, a kind of modification possible only with *modal* adverbs (or "adverbial modes"), although, as the previous example shows, modal adverbs can *sometimes* modify verbs in the way other adverbs *usually* modify verbs.

[65] At the end of the twelfth century the eschatological writings of Joachim of Floris (ca. 1145–1202) inaugurated a period "in which eschatology, and above all the expectation of the coming of Antichrist, exercised a great influence on the world's history" (*Encyclopaedia Britannica*, 11th ed., 2.123, "Antichrist"). The logicians of the period began employing examples dealing with Antichrist, often revolving around the open question whether Antichrist would be a man (and thus have a soul) or a supernatural being. Thus in the late twelfth-century *Fallacie parvipontane* (edited by De Rijk in *Logica modernorum*, Vol. I, pp. 551–609) there are several Antichrist sophismata and examples, including (on p. 569) '*anima Antichristi erit*' — 'the soul of Antichrist will be.'

[66] It seems that the "senses" of the contrasting examples might be accurately rewritten as follows: (1) 'Antichrist will have a soul' is necessary. (2) Necessary being is a condition of the soul of Antichrist. Then, since it is an open question whether Antichrist will be human, (1) is false. But (I take it) every soul insofar as it is a soul at all has necessary being, even the soul of Antichrist, should he have one; so (2) is true. Notice that in expressing the second sense Sherwood ignores the future tense of the original example; the distinction between the two senses would certainly be blurred and perhaps obliterated if he had written "necessary being *will* go together with . . ."

[67] I.e., similar examples making similar points might be provided for the other two adverbial modes — 'possibly' and 'impossibly.'

25. THE EFFECTS OF NOMINAL MODES

Nominal modes[68] enter into discourse in the following way, as if I were to say 'that Socrates is running is contingent.' And Aristotle said that just as things are the subjects in assertoric statements, while being or not being[69] is predicated, so in modal statements being or not being is the subject, while modes are the appositions — i.e., the predicates.[70] And so it appears that the dictum[71] 'that Socrates is running' is the subject, and the mode is the predicate.[72]

On that view, however, it appears that [the statement] is not modal, because just as a statement in which the predicate is a word signifying exception is not an exceptive statement or a statement in which the predicate is a word signifying [exclusion] is not an exclusive statement, so a statement in which the predicate is a word signifying a mode is not a modal statement.[73] Again, the predicate is naturally prior to the composition [of subject and predicate], while the disposition of the composition is naturally posterior to the composition itself; but one and the same thing cannot be both prior and posterior to anything. Therefore the predicate cannot be the disposition of the composition, and therefore it cannot produce a modal proposition.

It may be said that in discourse of this kind there are two compositions — one between the verb in indirect discourse and its suppositum (inter infinitum et suum suppositum),[74] and the other between the

---

[68] Just as Sherwood's 'adverbial modes' seems to be an awkward designation for modal adverbs, so here 'modal nouns or adjectives' would seem less awkward than 'nominal modes.' There is a marginal note in the manuscript at this point: "How nominal modes produce modal propositions."

[69] G has 'inesse'; 'non esse' in manuscript.

[70] Cf. De int., Ch. 12 (21b27ff). Grabmann's reference at this point to An. pr., Bk. I, Ch. 8 (29b29), is mistaken.

[71] 'Dictum' is a technical term for the clause in indirect discourse and will be retained in the translation.

[72] G has 'modus predicati'; 'modus predicatum' in manuscript.

[73] 'Alone' is a word signifying exclusion, but when it occurs as a predicate — as in 'Socrates is alone'— the result is not an exclusive statement — i.e., a statement in which some or most individuals or kinds are excluded from a predication that can be affirmed (or denied) of the others. Thus 'Socrates alone is running' is an exceptive statement but 'Socrates is running alone' is not. Cf. Abelard, Logica "ingredientibus" in Peter Abaelards Philosophische Schriften, ed. Geyer, p. 483. (Exception and exclusion were usually distinct notions; see, for example, Sherwood's contrasting treatments of 'praeter,' an exceptive, and 'solus,' an exclusive, in the Syncategoremata.) Similarly, 'squaring the circle is impossible' is not modal but assertoric, while 'the hypotenuse is necessarily greater than either of the other two sides' is a modal statement.

[74] The Latin phrase 'inter infinitum et suum suppositum' (here translated as

entire dictum and the mode. The mode can make the first composition modal (*potest modus modificare primam*), since it is predicated of it, but not the second, for the reasons given above.[75]

On the other hand, a statement is modal not because just any composition [in it] is made modal, but because its principal composition is so; for if I say 'that God necessarily is is known to me' no one says that *this* is modal, although the composition within the dictum is made modal. In modal statements, therefore, if the principal composition is made modal, the composition of the dictum is also made modal, as has been agreed (*sicut responsum est*). Therefore that composition will be the principal composition, and therefore its extremes — viz., the verb in indirect discourse and its suppositum — will be the subject and predicate. Therefore the mode is not the predicate.[76]

In response to this we must point out that expressions of this kind have, with respect to both the form of discourse and the construction,

---

'between the verb in indirect discourse and its suppositum') presents two problems, the second of which is more interesting than the first. (1) The Latin construction for a declarative sentence in indirect discourse is "the infinitive with subject accusative"; however, the *verbum infinitum* is not the infinitive but the infinite verb (see p. 24). In the thirteenth century the usual designations for the infinitive seem to have been '*infinitivum*' and '*verbum infiniti modi*,' so Sherwood's '*infinitum*' here may be a scribe's error for '*infinitivum*' (which is unlikely since the whole phrase is repeated exactly on p. 44) or an unusual and misleadingly abridged version of '*verbum infiniti modi*.' (2) The phrase 'its suppositum' may, and in Chapter Five certainly does, represent an important technical notion. But there are a number of reasons for thinking that in this case it is just a fancy word for the subject, perhaps especially appropriate to the subject accusative in indirect discourse. That Sherwood was not overly conscious of the special technical senses of '*suppositum*' and related words may also be seen on p. 28, where he suggests '*suppositiva*' as a Latinization of 'hypothetical.'

[75] (1) Every mathematical truth is necessary; (2) that 7 is prime is necessary. In both cases the nominal mode is used to ascribe necessity to the subject, and neither (1) nor (2) is, strictly speaking, modal. But in (2) the subject is itself a composition of subject and predicate, and the ascription of a mode to such a composition produces a modal statement; so although (2) is, strictly speaking, assertoric, its effect is the transformation of '7 is prime' into the modal '7 is necessarily prime.'

[76] This paragraph contains an attempt to argue that, despite what has been said so far, statements having an assertoric statement in indirect discourse as subject and a nominal mode as predicate are genuinely modal. The first sentence of the paragraph is quite correct. The second sentence, however, seems to be a fundamental distortion of what "has been agreed," for it does not refer to the kind of statement that has been under discussion. Instead, the claim here seems to be that although (1) 'that God necessarily is is known to me' is not modal, (2) 'that God is is necessarily known to me' would be modal (which is correct); and that in (2) "the composition of the expression in indirect discourse is also made modal," which has *not* been agreed and which is, moreover, not correct, as can be seen in (3) 'that I am is necessarily known to me.' But if we ignore the confusion introduced in the second sentence and try to apply the conclusion in

the dictum as subject and the mode as predicate; therefore they ought not to be called modal. Nor does Aristotle call them modal, but rather *de modo*.[77]

In another respect, if we consider what is signified (*rem significatum*) we shall say that the subject of the dictum *is* the principal subject and that its predicate *is* the principal predicate and that the mode *is* a disposition of that composition, and that therefore they *are* modal statements. For if I say 'that Socrates is running is contingent,' it is just the same, with respect to what is signified (*secundum rem*), as if I were to say 'Socrates is contingently running.'[78]

It is clear, then, how these [nominal] modes produce a modal proposition, [42] for since the modes occur as predicates with respect to both the form of speaking and the construction, [the propositions] are not modal. [But] with respect to what is signified, these modes make the composition of the dictum modal, while its subject is the principal subject and its predicate the principal predicate.[79] Propositions of this

---

the last two sentences to the kind of statement that has been under discussion, we come up with something like this: A statement such as (4) 'that Socrates is an ass is impossible' has the character of a modal statement, and yet we are prevented from calling it modal because the mode is the predicate. But, as has been agreed, the mode as predicate has the effect in (4) of making a modal statement of 'Socrates is an ass.' Now a statement whose principal composition is made modal is genuinely modal, and since our instincts are to consider (4) as genuinely modal, why not recognize the composition 'Socrates is an ass' as the principal composition? If we do so, then 'an ass,' not 'impossible,' is the predicate and 'Socrates,' not 'that Socrates is an ass,' is the subject, and the principal composition is made modal by the occurrence of the nominal mode 'impossible' in the secondary composition. Sherwood's rejoinder (in the next paragraph) to this elaborate move is, in essence, that so gross a distortion of the plain structure of the statement is too high a price to pay for calling such statements "modal"; let them instead be called statements "*de modo*," statements involving a mode. However, as can be seen from the second paragraph following this one (p. 45), Sherwood's real objection is only to the argument developed here, not to the point of view that motivates it.

[77] This distinction evidently does not occur in Aristotle's discussions of modal propositions (in *De int.*, Chs. 12 and 13, and *An. pr.* I, Chs. 3 and 8–22). Since Aristotle does not use a term strictly corresponding with 'modal,' it is unlikely that the distinction originates with him.

[78] The Latin here is '*Sortes contingenter currit*,' while in the similar example discussed on p. 41, where there is said to be an ambiguity in the force of the adverb, the Latin is '*Sortes currit contingenter*.'

[79] The passage at the beginning of p. 43 in *G* reads as follows: "quia cum predicentur modi secundum formam loquendi et secundum constructionem, non sunt modales secundum rem, modificant compositionem dicti, cuius subiectum est principale subiectum et predicatum principale predicatum." This reading is faithful to the manuscript, but it cannot be read correctly without such emendations as the translation reflects.

sort are modal in one way — viz., with respect to what is signified — but not in another way — viz., with respect to the construction. For this reason, Aristotle [80] draws a distinction between these propositions and those that are assertoric simply and in every respect — e.g., 'every man is running' — especially because when these *de modo* propositions enter into a syllogism, they are accepted as modal. For the character (*virtus*) of a syllogism depends more on the condition of the things signified (*rerum conditio*) than on the way the propositions are constructed, as we shall see.[81] Therefore, since [these *de modo* propositions] are modal with respect to what is signified, they will occur as modal propositions in a syllogism.

26. NEGATION IN MODAL STATEMENTS

The foregoing remarks enable us to understand modals on the basis of their substance; [82] we have yet to look into their dispositions — i.e., how they are negated and of what quantity they are.

Aristotle says that in such propositions negation is not to be referred (*non referenda est*) to the predicate of the dictum but to the mode.[83] Thus, [the contradictory of 'that Socrates is running is contingent' is not 'that Socrates is not running is contingent' but] 'that Socrates is running is not contingent.'

But on the other hand the predicate of the dictum is in a way the principal predicate,[84] and so the negation must accordingly be referred to [that predicate] itself, as if one were to say 'that Socrates is not running is contingent.'

What we have to say here is that if the subject is considered with respect to the form of speaking, the negation must be referred to the mode. If, however, it is considered with respect to what is signified, then it must be referred to the predicate of the dictum, but with the mode included under it (*sed includendo sub se modum*), as if one were to say 'that Socrates is not running is contingent.'[85] But Aristotle understands it in the first way.

---

[80] See n. 77, this chapter. Grabmann cites *De int.*, Ch. 12, but no such distinction is provided there by Aristotle.

[81] P. 62.

[82] See p. 40.

[83] *De int.*, Ch. 12 (21b23ff).

[84] See p. 45.

[85] Here as elsewhere Sherwood makes his point so concisely that it is likely to be misunderstood. From what has gone before it seems clear that he wants to

27. THE QUANTITY OF MODAL STATEMENTS

The next thing is to see of what quantity such propositions are, and it appears, according to Aristotle, that they are singular.[86] For the dictum is the subject, and it is singular and predicable of one thing only.[87]

But on the other hand, a syllogism results from 'that every man is running is contingent' together with a singular proposition.[88] But there is no syllogism without a universal proposition; therefore 'that every man is running is contingent' is universal.

The rejoinder to this is obvious; for since quantity depends on the subject (*attenditur penes subiectum*), and since in all such propositions there are two subjects, there can be two quantities in all of them. If the dictum is considered as the subject, they are all singular. But if the subject of the dictum — i.e., the subject with respect to what is signified — is considered as the subject, [43] then some are universal, some particular, some indefinite, some singular.[89]

28. THE INTERRELATIONS OF THE MODES

We have yet to consider the relation of the modes to one another in inference (*secundum consequentiam*). In this connection it is important to realize that the two modes "possible" and "contingent" are interchangeable (*convertuntur*); they contradict "impossible," and they follow from "necessary" (but not vice versa). Therefore they are as if

---

claim the following: since with respect to what is signified we may treat 'that Socrates is running is contingent' as if it were 'Socrates is contingently running,' so we may treat 'that Socrates is not running is contingent' as if it were 'Socrates is not contingently running,' for in this case the negation is referred to the predicate of the expression in indirect discourse but "with the mode included under" that predicate.

[86] It seems Sherwood infers this from what Aristotle has to say in *De int.*, Ch. 12 (21b29ff), rather than finding it explicitly in Aristotle.

[87] Evidently he says it is singular simply *because* it is predicable of one thing only. But what is that one thing of which the expression in indirect discourse is predicable? The thing — i.e., state of affairs — signified? There is no other obvious possibility, but a rather elaborate semantic theory is presupposed by the notion that statements are predicated of states of affairs, and I know of no such theory on which Sherwood could be relying here.

[88] E.g., 'Socrates is a man; therefore that Socrates is running is contingent.' This seems to be what Sherwood has in mind. However, it is an invalid syllogism, for 'that every man is running is contingent' and 'that Socrates is running is not contingent (but necessary)' are compatible.

[89] I.e., 'that every man is running is contingent' is singular in the one respect, universal in the other; 'that some man is running is contingent' is singular in the one respect, particular in the other; and so on.

subalternated [to "necessary"], and they are interchangeable. The modes "impossible" and "necessary," on the other hand, are contraries.

But since each one of these modes can be taken in four different ways — viz., either [A] without negation; or with negation in two different ways: either [B] with more than one negation, or with one negation in two different ways: either [C] before [the mode], or [D] after it — each one of these modes can be altered in four respects to be made equipollent and opposite.[90] For every mode [A] is equipollent to its contradictory with [C] a preceding negation and to its subaltern with [B] two negations. Again, a mode with [D] a following negation is equipollent to its contrary with [B] two negations and to its subaltern with [C] one preceding. Again, a mode with [C] a preceding negation is equipollent to its contradictory [A] and to its subaltern with [D] a following negation. Again, a mode with [B] two negations is equipollent to its contradictory with [D] one following and to its subaltern [A] directly.

Thus there are four series (*ordines*). [Example of the first:] 'it is possible to be,' 'it is contingent to be,' 'it is not impossible to be,' 'it is not necessary not to be.' Example of the second series (*secunde linee*):

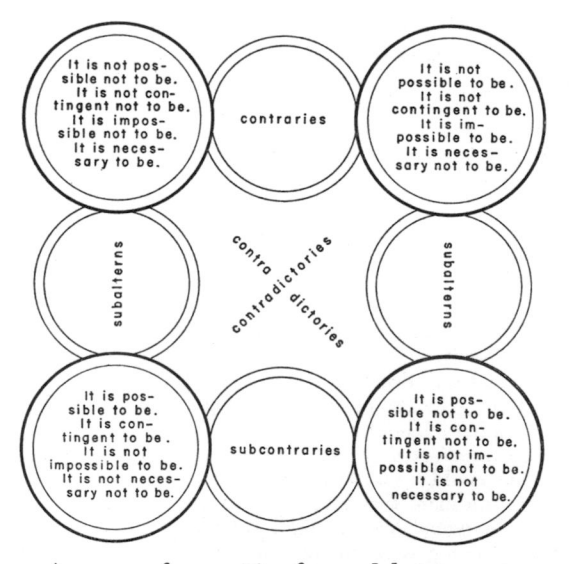

A square of opposition for modal statements

---

[90] See n. 33, this chapter.

'it is possible not to be,' 'it is contingent not to be,' 'it is not impossible not to be,' 'it is not necessary to be.' Example of the third: 'it is not possible to be,' 'it is not contingent to be,' 'it is impossible to be,' 'it is necessary not to be.' Example of the fourth: 'it is not possible not to be,' 'it is not contingent not to be,' 'it is impossible not to be,' 'it is necessary to be.'

Thus the first series is related to the second through subcontrariety, the third to the fourth through contrariety, the first and the third are contradictory, the second and the fourth are contradictory, the first is related to the fourth as subalternate to subalternant, and the second to the third likewise.

These relations can be retained by means of the following verses:

> Let the first series be for you the subcontrary of the second;
> The third series is always contrary to the fourth;
> The third series is contradictory to the first;
> The second conflicts with the fourth by contradicting;
> The first is under the fourth, in the role of a particular;
> And by this same law the second is related to the succeeding series.[91] [44]

All these relations also appear in the accompanying figure. The figure could be arranged differently, however, so that the contrary series could be put in the first, or upper, line, and the subcontraries in the lower. But [the arrangement as given] coincides more closely with Aristotle's.[92]

If 'possible' is attributed to anything, 'contingent' is attributed to it

---

[91] These mnemonic verses read as follows in Latin:

> Sit tibi linea subcontraria prima secunde.
> Tertius est quarto semper contrarius ordo.
> Tertius est primo contradictorius ordo.
> Pugnat cum quarto contradicendo secundus.
> Prima subest quarte vice particularis habens se.
> Hac habet ad seriem se lege secunda sequentem.

Several lines of the corresponding verses in Peter of Spain's *Summulae logicales* are identical with these, but as usual, he has more mnemonic verses and he has improved on Sherwood's. For example, although he retains the fifth line verbatim, he replaces the difficult last line with *"Ordo subalternus sit tertius atque secundus."* (Bocheński's edition has *'primus'* instead of *'tertius'* (p. 14), but this must be an error.)

[92] The arrangement Sherwood describes as an *alternative* to the one given is in fact the *given arrangement* in the only surviving manuscript and in this present translation of it. The arrangement Aristotle gives in *De int.*, Ch. 13 (22a23ff) (and corrects in 22b22ff), is as follows:

whether the proposition is affirmative or not; 'impossible' is separated from it; and 'necessary' is separated from its opposite. This rule governs (*continet*) the first and second series. There is another rule that governs the third and fourth series — viz., if 'possible' is separated from anything, 'contingent' is separated from it; 'impossible' is attributed to it; and 'necessary' is added to its opposite.[93]

A. It may be. It is contingent. It is not impossible that it should be. It is not necessary that it should not be.	B. It cannot be. It is not contingent. It is impossible that it should be. It is necessary that it should not be.
C. It may not be. It is contingent that it should not be. It is not impossible that it should not be. It is not necessary that it should be.	D. It cannot not be. It is not contingent that it should not be. It is impossible that it should not be. It is necessary that it should be.

Apparently some scribe or student revised Sherwood's original square of modal opposition in accordance with his suggestion, which of course brings it into line with the square of categorical opposition (on p. 32). Peter of Spain adopts this clearer, less Aristotelian, alternative (*Sum. log.*, ed. Bocheński, p. 14). He also makes his square more attractive to students by introducing letters of the alphabet corresponding to Sherwood's four ways in which to take the modes (p. 48) as follows: [1] — A; [2] — U; [3] — I; [4] — E. This enables him to name the four corners of the square as follows: upper left — "*Purpurea*"; upper right — "*Iliace*"; lower left — "*Amabimus*"; lower right — "*Edentuli*" (Bocheński ed., *loc. cit.*).

[93] For a brief, accurate summary of Sherwood's contributions to the discussion of modal statements see Kneale, *Development*, p. 232.

CHAPTER TWO

The Predicables

1. THE NATURE OF A PREDICABLE[1]

Turning our attention to the predicable, let us see first what a predicable is, and then how it is divided.

Just as a predicate is what *is* predicated of something else, so a predicable is what *can be* said (*est . . . dicibile*) of something else. However, the word 'predicable' is used both broadly and strictly. Broadly speaking, everything that can be joined to (*adjungere*) something else through the medium of (*mediante*) the verb 'is' is called a predicable, [45] whether it is common or individual. Strictly speaking, only what is common is predicable.

What is individual is what is predicable [broadly speaking] of one thing only — e.g., a proper name, a pronoun, and a common word together with a pronoun;[2] for it is called "individual" because it is not divided into parts belonging to the subject[3] (*partes subiectivas*).

On the other hand, what is common is the same as what is universal; for it is called "common" because it unites (*unire*) many things together (*simul*) — i.e., into a single nature; "universal" because it turns (*vertere*) several things into one — e.g., the noun 'man.'[4] What is universal is defined as follows: a universal is what can be said of several

---

[1] The chapter heading inserted in G is *"De Predicabili."* The manuscript contains no heading, but the beginning of a new treatise, or chapter, is clearly indicated by capitalization and indentation. This chapter should be compared generally with Aristotle's *Categories* and Porphyry's *Isagoge.*

[2] Although some personal pronouns might occasionally serve in this capacity — e.g., 'he,' 'his father' — they fail to do so on at least as many occasions — e.g., 'they,' 'his foot.' It is probable that Sherwood has only singular demonstrative pronouns in mind and that his examples here are intended as various forms in which "discrete terms" might occur. See p. 108.

[3] See p. 29.

[4] Sherwood is offering what he takes to be the etymological basis of the distinction — viz., *'commune'* from *'con'* and *'unire'* [actually *'con'* and the root *'mu-'* (to bind)], and *'universale'* from *'unus'* and *'verto.'*

things, up to the differentia of an individual[5] (*ad differentiam individui*). The universal is divided into genus, species, differentia, property, and accident.

2. GENUS [6]

A genus is what is predicated of several things differing in species, in respect of what they are (*in eo quod quid est*).[7]

The phrase (*Et hoc, quid dico*) "what is predicated of several things" occupies the place of the genus in this definition[8] (and [what is predicated of several things] is the same as a universal). The phrase "differing in species" is added because genus differs from species and property, which are not predicated of several things differing in species — i.e., of several species. The phrase "in respect of what they are" is added because genus differs from differentia and accident, which are not predicated in respect of *what*, but in respect of *how* things are;[9] for what is given in answer to a question asked by means of 'what?' is predicated in respect of what a thing is. For example, 'animal' is predicated of several species — since it is predicated of man and of the ass — and is predicated in respect of what they are; for if someone says 'what is man?' it is correct to answer 'animal.'

3. SPECIES

A species is what is predicated of several things differing numerically, in respect of what they are.

The phrase "what is predicated . . ." occupies the place of the genus in this definition. The phrase "differing numerically" is added because species differs from genus, which is predicated of several species and not of several things differing numerically — i.e., [not] of individuals

---

[5] Since the Taj Mahal is the only world-famous Indian tomb, world-famous-Indian-tomb is the differentia of an individual (as world-famous-tomb or Indian-tomb is not). From the first part of Sherwood's definition it seems clear that this 'up to' is *inclusive*, for there *could* be more than one world-famous Indian tomb. So the differentia of an individual is apparently a genuine universal, although a limiting case.

[6] Compare this section especially with *Topics*, Bk. I, Ch. 5 (102a30–102b3).

[7] This technical phrase is the Latin equivalent of Aristotle's "ἐν τῷ τί ἐστι" (*Topics*, 102a32) and is often translated simply as 'essentially,' or 'in essence.'

[8] Sherwood is alluding to the standard form of definition in terms of the genus and differentia of what is being defined — as in "man is a rational [differentia] animal [genus]." Thus what-is-predicated-of-several-things is the genus of *genus*.

[9] I.e., in respect of their *quality*.

in the primary sense (*individuis primo dico*). Through the medium of a species, however, a property likewise [is predicated of several things differing numerically]. For example, 'man' is predicated of several things differing numerically — i.e., of primary individuals — but not 'animal' (which is a genus) or 'risible' (which is a property); for each of these is predicated of a man through the species [10] (*utrumque enim per posterius predicatur de homine*). The phrase "in respect of what they are" is added because of the difference from differentia and accident, as above. Moreover, the species is predicated in respect of what [46] things are, since to the question 'what is Socrates?' it is correct to answer 'a man.'

Species is also defined as follows: a species is what is placed under a genus — e.g., the species *man* is directly under the genus *animal* [11] — and also: a species is that of which a genus is predicated in respect of what it is.

4. INTERRELATIONS OF GENERA AND SPECIES

Species is divided into most specific species and subaltern species, in which division the division of genus into most general and subaltern is also apparent.

A most specific species is a species that is not a genus, such as *man*. (The first definition fits this case.) A subaltern species is one that is a species in one respect and a genus in another, as we shall see. (The second two definitions cover this case.) [12]

A most general genus is one that is only a genus. A subaltern genus

---

[10] This sentence and the one immediately following are in the reverse order in the text. It seems apparent that '*per posterius*' here must be doing the same job as '*mediante specie*' in the preceding sentence; perhaps species is called '*posterius*' here because it is the latter of the two predicables so far discussed. When Sherwood denies that a genus or a property is predicated of an individual he is denying only something describable as *direct* predication, since of course he goes on to qualify these denials immediately by allowing such predication "through the medium of the species." Cf. *Categories* (hereafter cited as *Cat.*), Ch. 5 (2b6ff).

[11] In the text this example immediately follows the second rather than the first of these two definitions. The phrase '*directly* under' need not and evidently does not mean *immediately* under — i.e., with no intervening species — but may mean merely *perpendicularly* under, as in Sherwood's Tree of Porphyry on p. 54.

[12] In virtue of what was said in the paragraph immediately preceding the one containing the second and third definitions of species, the first definition does not apply strictly to subaltern species but only to most specific species. The second and third definitions, on the other hand, apply to most specific as well as to subaltern species.

is one that is both a genus and a species, but in different respects (*respectu tamen diversorum*). [In the accompanying figure,] for example, the arrangement (*ordo*) in the category of substance is such that *substance* is located in the top position with *body* under it; under

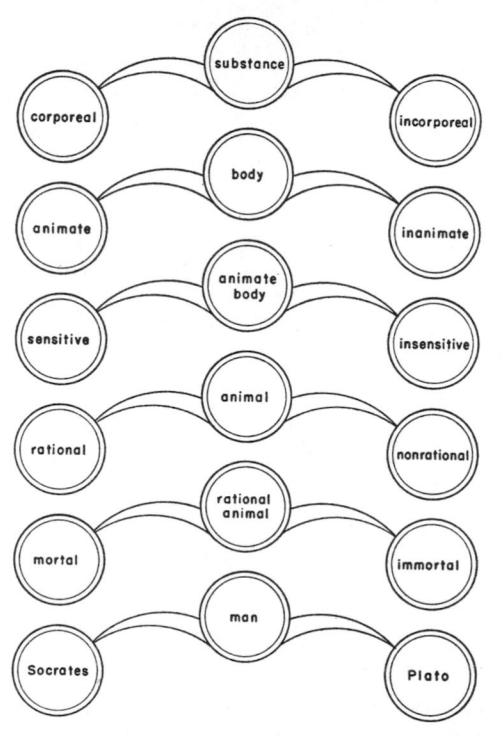

Interrelations of genera and species (Tree of Porphyry)

body, animate body; under *animate body, animal*; under *animal, rational animal*; under *rational animal, man*; under *man*, Socrates. *Substance* is the most general, because there is no higher genus; on the other hand, *man* is the most specific, because there is no lower species. Those in between are subalterns, and are genera with respect to those below, species with respect to those above.[13]

---

[13] The figure immediately following is usually called Porphyry's Tree because it is suggested by a passage in the *Isagoge* (in Bocheński, *History*, p. 135). Peter of Spain calls it *"arbor Porphyrii"* and *"arbor porphyriana"* and introduces it with the following "verse": "The Porphyrian Tree makes these matters plain to you" (*Sum. log.*, ed. Bocheński, pp. 17–18). On the Tree in Sherwood see Kneale, *Development*, p. 232.

5. DIFFERENTIA

The word 'differentia' is used in three ways: broadly, strictly, and especially strictly.

Broadly speaking, every form in which things differ is called a differentia, whether it is substantial or accidental. According to this, one may say that whiteness is a differentia of a white man with respect to what is black (*respectu nigri*).

Strictly speaking, a differentia is what makes a thing different [from other things] through a substantial form or an inseparable accident. According to this, one may say that whiteness is a differentia of a swan with respect to what is black.[14]

Speaking especially strictly, a differentia is only what makes [a thing] different [from other things] in a substantial form. According to this, it is said that *rational* is the differentia of a man with respect to an ass. A differentia in this last sense is a species of universal.

Differentia is defined as follows: a differentia is what is predicated of several things differing in species, in respect of *how* they are (*in eo quod quale*). The phrase "what is predicated . . ." occupies the place of the genus. By means of the phrase "differing in species" differentia is distinguished from property and species; and by means of the final phrase, from genus and accident. For since there are two kinds of quality — essential and accidental [47] — "how" is taken for essential quality. Genus, on the other hand, is predicated in respect of *what* [things are], and accident in respect of how [things are] *accidentally*.

It is also defined as follows: a differentia is that by means of which a species flows from the genus (*qua habundat species a genere*); for the form of a species is made up of the genus and a differentia. And it is also defined as follows: a differentia is what is naturally suited to divide the things that are under one and the same genus. For example, in the species *man* the genus is *animal* and the differentiae are *rational* and *mortal*, and so by means of these *man* flows from *animal*. On the other hand, they divide *man* from *ass* and from *immortal animal*, all of which are under the same genus, *animal*.

Differentia is divided into divisive and constitutive. Note that one

---

[14] Whiteness in man is a mere accident, but whiteness in swans (until black swans were discovered in Australia) was held to be an inseparable accident — a contingent but unvarying characteristic.

and the same differentia can be both divisive and constitutive, for *rational* constitutes *man* and divides *animal*.

6. PROPERTY [15]

A property is what is always and only associated with every [individual] belonging to a [given] species, as *risible* is associated always and only with every man. For although a man is not always laughing, he is always risible.

7. ACCIDENT [16]

An accident is what is present or absent without the corruption of the subject [17] — i.e., what happens to (*advenit*) a subject (supposing the subject to be already in existence) (*et intellige subiecto preexistenti*) or is absent [from the subject] without the corruption of it.

Accident is divided into separable and inseparable. A separable accident is one that the subject can be without, as *white* (*album*) is an accident of a man (*accidit homini*). An inseparable accident is one that the subject cannot be without, as *whiteness* (*albedo*) is an accident of a swan.

It must be understood that although a swan cannot be without whiteness, nevertheless whiteness is an accident of it, because if we suppose that a swan were to become black, the swan would nevertheless remain a swan. That would not be the result if whiteness were of the essence of the swan and not an accident of it. If, for example, we supposed a swan to be inanimate, the swan would not remain a swan. This is because *animate* is substantial rather than accidental.[18]

Let these remarks on the predicables suffice.

---

[15] Compare this section with *Topics*, Bk. I, Ch. 5 (102a17–102a30).

[16] Compare this section with *Topics*, Bk. I, Ch. 5 (102b4–102b26).

[17] The corruption of the subject is either its annihilation or its ceasing to be a certain *kind* of thing. The second sort of corruption is obviously somewhat vague, as the next paragraphs show.

[18] On this distinction between substantial and accidental cf. p. 55.

1. DEFINITION OF SYLLOGISM

Now that we are about to speak of the syllogism, which is the main purpose of logic, let us speak first of its definition and then of how many ways it can occur.

A syllogism, then, is discourse[1] in which, certain things having been propounded, [48] something else necessarily results from them and as a result of their having been propounded[2] (*Est igitur sillogismus oratio, in qua quibusdam positis necesse est aliud evenire ab hiis et propter hoc*).

Note that the discourse spoken of here is not an indicative, imperative, optative, conjunctive,[3] or interrogative [sentence], but a group of sentences[4] (*congeries orationum*) — e.g., 'every man is an animal, everything risible is a man; therefore everything risible is an animal.'

The phrase "certain things having been propounded" is added so that we may exclude ambiguous sentences (*orationes multiplices*) of the sort that constitute verbal fallacies[5] (*fallacie in dictione*); they produce not a *single* (*una*) but an *ambiguous* proposition.[6] And this phrase

---

[1] The Latin word here is *'oratio,'* "the derivation [of which] is frequently given from *oris ratio,* reason of mouth; [it] signifies therefore the expression of any act of reason by any effect of speech. Since it is the property of reason to compound and divide and to proceed discursively from one thing to another taking note of their causes, [*oratio*] expresses these processes in words; the syllogism is [*oratio*] which results from the latter property of reason" (McKeon, *Selections* (Glossary), 2.476). Cf. Sherwood's definition of *oratio,* p. 25 above.

[2] This is Aristotle's definition in *An. pr.,* Bk. I, Ch. 1 (24b18ff).

[3] I.e., subjunctive.

[4] Sherwood's point here is that *'oratio'* in the definition is not to be taken in that one of its ordinary senses in which it is used as is the English word 'sentence,' but in that other, equally ordinary sense in which it means extended discourse composed of sentences.

[5] See, e.g., pp. 134–135.

[6] Although Sherwood, toward the end of Chapter One, tended to ignore his original distinction between statements and propositions (p. 22), he is making use of it here — i.e., 'proposition' is being used as a synonym for 'premiss.'

ought to have the following gloss[7] on it: "certain (i.e., single [unambiguous]) things having been propounded (i.e., arranged in mood and figure)" (*positis id est dispositis in modo et figura*). As we shall see, useless groupings of sentences are thus ruled out as well.

By means of the phrase "necessarily results" all extra-verbal fallacies [49] except Begging the Original Issue and Mistaking the Cause[8] are ruled out, for they entail (*inferunt*) nothing by necessity. Begging the Original Issue, in which something *else* does *not* follow from the premisses (*premissis*), is ruled out by means of the phrase "something else . . . from them"; and Mistaking the Cause, in which the conclusion does not occur on account of all the premisses, is ruled out by means of the phrase "as a result of their having been propounded." (All these things can be explained by means of examples.)[9]

2. PERFECT AND IMPERFECT SYLLOGISMS

The syllogism is divided into perfect and imperfect.[10] A perfect syllogism is one in which the cause of its necessity is evident. An imperfect syllogism is one the cause of whose necessity is not evident. (This distinction will become clear further on.) Therefore an imperfect syllogism must be reduced to perfection in order for its necessity to appear. This reduction, however, is accomplished by means of the conversion of propositions, and so one must study conversion.

3. CONVERSION[11]

Conversion, then, is making a predicate out of a subject, and vice versa. But there are three kinds of conversion: simple, by limitation, and by contraposition (*per se, per accidens, per contrapositionem*).

Conversion is simple when the proposition is converted while the quality and quantity remain unchanged. The universal negative and the particular affirmative are converted in this way, for this follows:

---

[7] In the middle ages a gloss was a note or comment inserted into the margin or into the text itself (as here), especially as an explanation of words that were foreign or obsolete. Sherwood could take it for granted that his readers would recognize the above definition of a syllogism as Aristotle's, and he is here offering his glosses on a familiar text.

[8] See pp. 157–159 and 162–165.

[9] This may be a reference to Chapter Six, where examples of the fallacies can be found, or perhaps a suggestion to the reader — something like an exercise in a modern textbook.

[10] Cf. *An. pr.*, Bk. I, Ch. 1 (24b23–26).

[11] Compare this section with *An. pr.*, Bk. I, Ch. 2.

'no man is an ass; therefore no ass is a man'; similarly, 'some man is an animal; therefore some animal is a man.' And in both of them the quality and quantity remain unchanged.

Conversion is by limitation when the conversion is performed while the quality but not the quantity remains unchanged. The universal affirmative is converted in this way — e.g., 'every man is an animal; therefore some animal is a man.' The quality remains unchanged, but not the quantity.

Conversion is by contraposition when the conversion is performed with the quality and quantity remaining unchanged but with definite terms changed into infinite terms. A definite term is one presented in the form of an affirmation (*profertur sub affirmatione*), while an infinite term is one presented in the form of a negation, such as 'non-man,' 'non-animal.' The universal affirmative is converted by contraposition as follows: 'every man is an animal; therefore every non-animal is a non-man'; and the particular negative as follows: 'some man is not an ass; therefore some non-ass is not a non-man' (viz., that non-ass who is a man). But the universal negative is not converted in this way, for this does not follow: 'no man is an ass; therefore no non-ass is a non-man' — for some non-ass *is* a non-man, e.g., a lion. Likewise, according to some, the particular affirmative is not converted by contraposition [50] in case the subject is predicable of every being and of every non-being. For example, if the word 'intelligible' is of this sort, this does not follow: 'something intelligible is a man; therefore some non-man is unintelligible' — for every non-man is intelligible. But in every other case the particular affirmative *is* converted in this way — e.g., 'some animal is a man; therefore some non-man is a non-animal.'[12]

Let these remarks on conversion suffice.

4. THE STRUCTURE OF THE SYLLOGISM [13]

Let us return to the main topic and see in how many ways the syllogism can occur.

---

[12] Since conversion by contraposition admits of exceptions in the case of the particular affirmative, it is invalid in that case — i.e., an inference of the form 'some S is P; therefore some non-P is non-S' can have a true premiss and a false conclusion. But Sherwood (like most medieval logicians) is not principally concerned with strictly formal logic, and so, after pointing out the kind of circumstances in which inferences of this form will fail, he goes on to remark that they will hold in other (in this case, *most*) kinds of circumstances.

[13] This section and the remainder of this chapter should be compared with *An. pr.*, Bk. I, Chs. 4–7.

There are, then, at least two propositions[14] in every syllogism, because nothing follows syllogistically (*sillogistice*) from one. Moreover, those two propositions must share a term; otherwise nothing follows from them, as nothing follows from these: 'every man is running, Socrates is arguing.' But something does follow from these: 'every man is running, Socrates is a man,' because there is one term common to (*communicatus in*) the two propositions. There will be no more and no fewer than three terms, since propositions cannot share two terms, for then they would be one and the same proposition.[15] This is because there are exactly two terms in one proposition — viz., the subject and the predicate — for the proposition is analyzed (*resolvitur*) into the term. So there will be three terms in every syllogism.

5. THE FIGURES OF THE SYLLOGISM

A figure, in contexts other than this, is produced as a result of the arrangement of boundaries (*termini*), since a figure is a closure of boundaries; and so it is in the case of the syllogism [and its terms (*termini*)].[16] However, [the arrangement of syllogistic terms] cannot vary in more than three ways — viz., [1] the middle term is the subject in one proposition and the predicate in the other, or [2] the predicate in both, or [3] the subject in both — and so there are only three figures.[17] The first, when the middle term is the subject in one and the predicate in the other; the second, when it is the predicate in both; the third, when it is the subject in both. And the middle term in every figure is the one that is used twice before the conclusion. Whatever is predicated of the middle term in the first figure is the major term or extremity;[18]

---

[14] I.e., premises. The 'at least' suggests that Sherwood included syllogistic inferences of more than two premises (the kind that during the renaissance became known as "sorites") among syllogisms. However, he does not discuss such inferences.

[15] Even if we understand sharing two terms to be sharing the subject-term and the predicate-term as such (thus ruling out conversion), this is overstated; for of course 'every man is running' and 'no man is running' share both terms even in this strong sense. See p. 30.

[16] I.e., just as a geometrical figure is determined by (or identified as) an arrangement of geometrical *termini*, so a syllogistic figure is determined by (or identified as) an arrangement of syllogistic *termini*, the terms of the two premises.

[17] ". . . we have no trace of anyone who defended the doctrine of four figures before the end of the Middle Ages" (Kneale, *Development*, p. 183, *q.v.*; see also p. 101). But cf. Bocheński, *History*, pp. 216–219.

[18] The extremities of the syllogism are the terms of the conclusion, the minor and major terms. The middle term is the *means* whereby these *extremes* are connected.

and whatever is the subject with respect to the middle term is the minor term. The proposition in which the major term occurs is called the major proposition, and the one in which the minor term occurs is called the minor proposition.

It is known that in every figure there are certain combinations (*coniugationes*) of terms and propositions from which [51] a conclusion follows; such a combination is called a mood. The mood depends on the arrangement of the propositions with respect to quality and quantity. There are other combinations as well, from which nothing follows; they are called useless combinations.

6. THE MOODS OF THE FIRST FIGURE

In the first figure, then, there are four moods that lead directly to a conclusion (*directe concludentes*) and five indirectly. A conclusion is direct when the major is concluded of the minor, but indirect when it is the other way around.[19]

Thus the first mood of the first figure [*Barbara*][20] consists of two [universal] affirmatives leading to a universal affirmative conclusion — e.g., 'every *b* is *a*, every *c* is *b*; therefore every *c* is *a*.'[21] The necessity of this mood is revealed through its definition — i.e., the *dici de omni*; for whenever nothing is subsumed (*sumere*) under the subject of which the predicate is not asserted (*dicere*), that is *dici de omni*.[22] So, since

---

[19] Concluding the major of the minor means having the major term as predicate of the conclusion. The five indirect moods (see Kneale, *Development*, p. 100) are those in which the major term is subject and the minor term predicate of the conclusion. Note that this is *not* a violation of the definition of major term, which is given for the first figure as "whatever is predicated of the middle term" (p. 60). The five indirect moods of the first figure are those grouped together after the middle ages as the fourth figure.

[20] For Sherwood's introduction of these nicknames for the moods and a discussion of their significance, see n. 37, this chapter.

[21] Sherwood uses these term-variables (after the manner of Aristotle) only in his discussion of the first mood of the first figure. As has already been pointed out (n. 12, this chapter), such a strictly formal approach is not the principal aim of most medieval logicians. (Peter of Spain, for example, does not use variables at all in his discussion of syllogisms.) If there is any special point to Sherwood's use of the form instead of examples in this case, it may be the fact that this mood is not only one of two *perfect* moods but also the *primary* perfect mood. If infinite terms are used in the reduction of other moods of syllogism, they may all be reduced to this mood, which may therefore be considered the fundamental syllogistic form.

[22] The *dici de omni*, or *dictum de omni* (*et nullo*), was the most widely accepted formula for the essence of syllogistic reasoning. It is sometimes stated as "what is predicated of any whole is predicated of any part of that whole," which is traced to *An. pr.*, Bk. I, Ch. 1 (24b26): "That one term should be included in

'every *b* is *a*' is [an instance of] *dici de omni* and every *c* can be subsumed (*contingit sumere*) under *b* (since 'every *c* is *b*' is asserted), *a* is predicated of every *c*, and it follows that [every] *c* is *a*.

The second mood [*Celarent*] consists of a universal negative major and a universal affirmative minor leading to a universal negative conclusion — e.g., 'no animal is a stone, every man is an animal; therefore no man is a stone.'[23] And this conclusion follows by reason of the principle of operation (*virtus*) of the mood — i.e., the *dici de nullo*; for whenever nothing is subsumed under the subject of which the predicate is asserted, that is *dici de nullo*.[24] So, since the *dici de nullo* occurs in 'no animal is a stone' and every man can be subsumed under the subject of that proposition (since 'every man is an animal' is asserted), 'stone' is asserted of no man, and 'no man is a stone' follows.

Now these two moods are the most evident (*manifestissimi*), and syllogisms in them are perfect.[25] They therefore take precedence over all the others, and the first of them is prior to (*ante*) the second in the same respect as affirmation is prior to negation.

The third mood [*Darii*] consists of a universal affirmative major and a particular affirmative minor leading to a particular affirmative conclusion — e.g., 'every man is a substance, some animal is a man; therefore some animal is a substance.'

The fourth mood [*Ferio*] consists of a universal negative major and a particular affirmative minor leading to a particular negative conclusion — e.g., 'no man is an ass, some animal is a man; therefore some animal is not an ass.'

---

another as in a whole is the same as for the other to be predicated of all of the first. And we say that one term is predicated of all of another, whenever no instance of the subject can be found of which the other term cannot be asserted: 'to be predicated of none' must be understood in the same way." (Cf. Kneale, *Development,* pp. 79 and 272–273; Bocheński, *History,* pp. 79–80.) The *dici de omni* is called the "definition" of this mood because a definition is a presentation of a thing's essence. Cf. p. 62 below, where the *dici de nullo* is said to be the second mood's "principle of operation."

[23] All Sherwood's syllogistic examples are traditional, dating at least from the twelfth century. Many of them — such as this one — are not particularly apt, but there was a strong and perfectly understandable tendency among medieval logicians to develop their discussions around a single set of examples.

[24] See n. 22, this chapter.

[25] Cf. *An. pr.,* Bk. I, Ch. 4 (25b30ff): "Whenever three terms are so related to one another that the last is contained in the middle as in a whole, and the middle is either contained in, or excluded from, the first as in or from a whole, the extremes must be related by a perfect syllogism."

The necessity of the moods so far discussed is revealed in the figure.[26]

The fifth mood [*Baralipton*] consists of two universal affirmatives leading indirectly to a particular affirmative conclusion — e.g., 'every [52] animal is a substance, every man is an animal; therefore some substance is a man.' The minor is concluded of the major.[27] This syllogism is imperfect and reduces to the first mood [*Barbara*], in which it follows from its two premises that every man is a substance. And since this converts by limitation, it follows that [some] substance is a man.[28]

The sixth mood [*Celantes*] consists of a universal negative major and a universal affirmative minor leading indirectly to a universal negative conclusion — e.g., 'no animal is a stone, every man is an animal; therefore no stone is a man.' And since the universal negative converts simply, it follows that no man is a stone.[29]

The seventh mood [*Dabitis*] consists of a universal affirmative [major] and a particular affirmative [minor] leading indirectly to a particular affirmative conclusion — e.g., 'every man is an animal, some substance is a man; therefore some animal is a substance.' This reduces to the third [*Darii*] when the conclusion is converted simply.

The eighth mood [*Fapesmo*] consists of a universal affirmative major and a universal negative minor leading indirectly to a particular negative conclusion — e.g., 'every man is an animal, no stone is a man; therefore some animal is not a stone.' This reduces to the fourth [*Ferio*] by the conversion of the major by limitation, the simple conversion of the

---

[26] This remark is evidently intended to cover all four moods so far discussed, despite the special support for the first two moods in the *dici de omni et nullo*. What is meant by the remark? "Aristotle thinks that only syllogisms of the first figure are perfect or complete (τέλειος). His reason is presumably that only in the first figure, when the terms are arranged in his usual order, is the transitivity of the connexions between the terms obvious at a glance" (Kneale, *Development*, p. 73). For Aristotle's proof that the third and fourth moods are also perfect, see *An. pr.*, Bk. I, Ch. 4 (26a16–29).

[27] See n. 19, this chapter.

[28] "In origin the doctrine of reduction is connected with the view that only syllogisms of the first figure are perfect in themselves, that is to say, evidently conclusive without supplementary argument [*An. pr.*, Bk. I, Ch. 1 (24b22), Ch. 4 (26b28), Ch. 5 (28a4), Ch. 6 (29a14)]. For most of the moods in the imperfect figures such supplementary argument takes the form of conversion" (Kneale, *Development*, p. 76). Thus this reduction of *Baralipton* consists in showing that its premises lead, in *Barbara*, to a conclusion which, when converted by limitation, yields the stated conclusion in *Baralipton*.

[29] *Celantes* is reduced to *Celarent* by showing that a conclusion in *Celantes* yields, by simple conversion, a conclusion in *Celarent*, the premises remaining the same.

minor, and the transposition of the premisses.[30] For the converted major reads (*habetur*) 'some animal is a man,' and the converted minor reads 'no man is a stone.' The conclusion given above follows from these in the fourth mood [*Ferio*] when they are transposed.

The ninth mood [*Frisesomorum*] consists of a particular affirmative major and a universal negative minor leading indirectly to a particular negative conclusion — e.g., 'some lion is an animal, no man is a lion; therefore some animal is not a man.' This reduces to the fourth [*Ferio*]; for when the particular major and the minor are converted simply (*per se id est simpliciter*) and transposed, the fourth mood [*Ferio*] recurs.

7. THE MOODS OF THE SECOND FIGURE

In the second figure the middle term is the one that occurs as a predicate twice in the premisses, the major is the one that is the subject in the first premiss, and the minor is the one that is the subject in the second.[31]

There are four moods in the second figure. The first [*Cesare*] consists of a universal negative major and a universal affirmative minor leading directly to a universal negative conclusion — e.g., 'no man is a stone, every pearl is a stone; therefore no pearl is a man.' And this reduces to the second mood of the first figure [*Celarent*] by [53] the conversion of the major proposition.

The second mood [*Camestres*] consists of a universal affirmative major and a universal negative minor leading directly to a universal negative conclusion — e.g., 'every pearl is a stone, no man is a stone; therefore no man is a pearl.' And this reduces to the second mood of the first figure [*Celarent*] by the conversion of the conclusion and of the minor proposition and the transposition of the premisses.

The third mood [*Festino*] consists of a universal negative major and a particular affirmative minor leading to a particular negative conclu-

---

[20] The use of conversion by limitation here (as in the attempts to reduce *Darapti* to *Darii* and *Felapton* to *Ferio* on p. 65) does not produce a genuine reduction because this kind of conversion (unlike the other two kinds) is not a reversible operation. Thus, instead of showing that *Fapesmo* may be derived from *Ferio*, this "reduction" might be taken to show that *Ferio* may be derived from *Fapesmo*, which is of no use in this justification-procedure and certainly not what was intended. The mistake, however, is Aristotle's; Sherwood (and, e.g., Peter of Spain) can be blamed only for repeating it. See *An. pr.*, Bk. I, Ch. 6 (28a17–29).

[31] In the text this sentence occurs immediately after the discussion of the first mood of the second figure.

sion in this way: 'no man is a stone, some pearl is a stone; therefore some pearl is not a man.' It reduces to the fourth mood [of the first figure] [*Ferio*] by the conversion of the major.

The fourth mood [*Baroco*] consists of a universal affirmative major and a particular negative minor leading to a particular negative conclusion — e.g., 'every pearl is a stone, some man is not a stone; therefore some man is not a pearl.' It reduces to the first mood of the first figure [*Barbara*] *per impossibile*. To reduce *per impossibile* is to take one of the premises with the opposite of the conclusion and conclude the opposite of the other premiss.[32] In this case the major is taken together with the opposite of the conclusion — viz., 'every man is a pearl' — and the following syllogism is produced: 'every pearl is a stone, every man is a pearl; therefore every man is a stone.' This conclusion is the opposite of the minor proposition, and thus it [*Baroco*] becomes the first mood of the first figure [*Barbara*].

8. THE MOODS OF THE THIRD FIGURE

In the third figure there are six moods. The first mood [*Darapti*] consists of two universal affirmatives leading directly to a particular affirmative conclusion — e.g., 'every man is an animal, every man is a substance; therefore some substance is an animal.' It reduces to the third mood of the first figure [*Darii*] by the conversion of the minor.[33]

The second mood [*Felapton*] consists of a universal negative major and a universal affirmative minor leading to a particular negative conclusion — e.g., 'no man is an ass, every man is an animal; therefore some animal is not an ass.' And that reduces to the fourth mood of the first figure [*Ferio*] by the conversion of the minor.[34] [54]

The third mood [*Disamis*] consists of a particular affirmative major and a universal affirmative minor leading to a particular affirmative conclusion — e.g., 'some man is an animal, every man is a substance; therefore some substance is an animal.' It reduces to the third [mood of the first figure] [*Darii*] by the conversion of the major, the conversion of the conclusion, and the transposition of the premisses.

---

[32] Reduction *per impossibile*, or indirect reduction, is required for only two moods — *Baroco* and *Bocardo* (see pp. 65 and 66) — and is introduced by Aristotle in *An. pr.*, Bk. I, Ch. 23 (40b16ff). For a discussion of this procedure see Kneale, *Development*, pp. 76–77.

[33] See n. 30, this chapter.

[34] See n. 30, this chapter.

The fourth mood [*Datisi*] consists of a universal affirmative [major] and a particular affirmative [minor] leading to a particular affirmative conclusion — e.g., 'every man is an animal, some man is a substance; therefore some substance is an animal.' It reduces to the third mood of the first figure [*Darii*] by the conversion of the minor.

The fifth mood [*Bocardo*] consists of a particular negative major and a universal affirmative minor leading to a particular negative conclusion — e.g., 'some animal is not a man, every animal is a substance; therefore some substance is not a man.' It reduces to the first mood of the first figure [*Barbara*] *per impossibile* — viz., by taking the contradictory opposite of the conclusion together with the minor and concluding the contradictory opposite of the major, where the opposite of the conclusion is taken in place of the major.[35] So in this case the opposite of the conclusion — viz., 'every substance is a man' — [is taken together with] the minor — viz., 'every animal is a substance' — and the contradictory opposite of the major follows — viz., 'every animal is a man.'

The sixth mood [*Ferison*] consists of a universal negative [major] and a particular affirmative [minor] leading to a particular negative conclusion — e.g., 'no man is an ass, some man is an animal; therefore some animal is not an ass.' And it reduces to the fourth mood of the first figure [*Ferio*] by the conversion of the minor.

9. SUMMARY OF MOODS AND FIGURES

The difference of the figures is retained in this verse: *Sub pre prima bis pre secunda tertia bis sub.*[36]

The moods and their reductions, on the other hand, are retained in these verses:

> Barbara celarent darii ferio baralipton
> Celantes dabitis fapesmo frisesomorum
> Cesare camestres festino baroco
> Darapti felapton disamis datisi bocardo ferison.[37]

---

[35] See n. 32, this chapter.

[36] I.e., "[The middle is a] sub[ject and a] pre[dicate in the] first [figure], twice a pre[dicate in the] second, [and in the] third twice a sub[ject]." Peter of Spain spells it out: "*Prima prius medium subicit post praedicat ipsum; altera bis dicit; tertia bis subicit*" (*Sum. log.*, ed. Bocheński, p. 37).

[37] This is the oldest known surviving version of these famous mnemonic verses, and Sherwood may have been the inventor of them (cf. Grabmann, "Einleitung," p. 27; Kneale, *Development*, pp. 232–233). However, there were earlier attempts

In these lines 'a' signifies a universal affirmative proposition, 'e' a universal negative, 'i' a particular affirmative, 'o' [55] a particular negative, 's' simple conversion, 'p' conversion by limitation, 'm' transposition of the premisses, and 'b' and 'r' when they are in the same word signify reduction *per impossibile*.[38] The first two lines are devoted to the first figure, the four words of the third line to the second figure, and all the other words to the third figure.

From what has been said so far it is clear that all the other moods reduce to the four [direct] moods of the first figure. However, the third mood of the first figure [*Darii*] can be reduced *per impossibile* to the second mood of the second figure [*Camestres*], and likewise the fourth mood of the first figure [*Ferio*] to the first mood of the second figure [*Cesare*]. Furthermore, these two moods [*Camestres* and *Cesare*] (and through them all the moods that reduce to the third and fourth moods of the first figure [*Darii* and *Ferio*]) reduce by conversion to the second mood of the first figure [*Celarent*]. Thus all other moods reduce to the first two moods of the first figure [*Barbara* and *Celarent*].[39]

---

at the same sort of device in the thirteenth century, and the word *'Festino'* appears "in a MS dating at the latest from 1200" (Bocheński, *History*, p. 211; and see pp. 210–216). The word *'camestres'* appears as *'campestres'* in G and in the manuscript, and Kneale (*loc. cit.*) reproduces that spelling. But this must be an error, for as the next paragraph of the text explains, the presence of 'p' indicates the use of conversion by limitation in the reduction of the mood, and this plays no part in the reduction of *Camestres*. Peter of Spain has it without the 'p' (*Sum. log.*, ed. Bocheński, p. 41).

[38] Peter of Spain gives a fuller, and in some respects a different, account of these verses. He points out, as Sherwood does not, that each indirect mood of the first figure and each mood of the second and third figures has a nickname beginning with the same consonant as the nickname of the direct mood of the first figure to which the mood in question is reduced. Moreover, he says that it is the occurrence within a word of the letter 'c' rather than the combination of 'b' and 'r' that indicates reduction *per impossibile* (*Sum. log.*, ed. Bocheński, pp. 42–43; translated in Bocheński, *History*, pp. 213–214). As for Sherwood's claim that the combination of 'b' and 'r' signifies reduction *per impossibile*, it includes *Baralipton* and *Barbara* along with *Baroco* and *Bocardo*. *Barbara*, I suppose, might be explained on the ground that it is the mood to which reduction *per impossibile* is directed, but that still leaves *Baralipton* unaccounted for. (Incidentally, it seems that *'Baralip'* and *'Frisesmo'* would be improvements over *'Baralipton'* and *'Frisesomorum,'* at least as far as the code is concerned.) The treatment of these verses in both Sherwood and Peter of Spain strongly suggests at least one earlier version on which both men are drawing. In fact, if Sherwood is, as he certainly seems to be, simply mistaken about the code for reduction *per impossibile* and Peter of Spain's book is later than Sherwood's, there *must* have been such a source.

[39] This paragraph has been more nearly reconstructed than translated. There are several attempted corrections in the manuscript which Grabmann incorporates in his edition, where this paragraph reads as follows: "Ex predictis patet, quod in

Note that nothing follows from two negatives or from two particulars. In the first figure nothing follows directly if the major is particular or the minor negative. In the second, nothing follows from two affirmatives. In the third, nothing follows if the major is negative.

Let these remarks on the syllogism suffice.

---

quattuor modis prime figure reducuntur omnes alii, tertius autem prime figure potest reduci in secundum secunde. Et quartus prime in primum, primus et secundus secunde per conversionem per impossibile et alii ab hiis duobus modis scilicet tertio et quarto prime possunt reduci in secundum prime et sic in duos primos prime figure reducuntur omnes alii." This is undoubtedly a mangled copy of Sherwood's version of Aristotle's proof (in *An. pr.*, Bk. I, Ch. 7 (29b1–25)) that all the moods reduce to the two "most evident" moods, *Barbara* and *Celarent*. On this attempt at a systematic treatment of the syllogism see Jan Łukasiewicz, *Aristotle's Syllogistic*, Section 15, especially pp. 44–45.

CHAPTER FOUR

Dialectical Reasoning

1. DEMONSTRATIVE, DIALECTICAL, AND SOPHISTICAL SYLLOGISM[1]

For a thorough understanding of the syllogism we need to understand it not only with respect to its definition but also with respect to its division. Some of the divisions that must be presented apply to the syllogism in general — e.g., a syllogism is either perfect or imperfect, either affirmative or negative, and so on.[2] However, other divisions that must be presented apply to the syllogism in such a way as to separate it into distinct types. The following division is of this kind: a syllogism is either demonstrative, or dialectical, or sophistical.[3]

A demonstrative syllogism is one that produces scientific knowledge on the basis of necessary [premisses] and the most certain reasons for the conclusion. A dialectical syllogism, however, is one that produces opinion on the basis of probable [premisses]. Finally, a sophistical syllogism is one that either syllogizes on the basis of seemingly probable [premisses] or seemingly syllogizes on the basis of probable [premisses]; in either case it is strictly aimed at glory or victory.

It is our plan to disregard the other types [for now] and to consider the dialectical syllogism.[4] The dialectical syllogism, indeed, is based on

---

[1] Compare this chapter generally with Aristotle's *Topics* and Boethius's *De differentiis topicis* (hereafter cited as *De diff. top.*).

[2] Chapter Three above considers the syllogism with respect to its definition and such general divisions as these.

[3] For this division, see *Topics*, Bk. I, Ch. 1 (100a25ff). ". . . in the *Topics* the word 'syllogism' was used in accordance with its etymology for any conclusive argument of more than one premiss" (Kneale, *Development*, p. 44). Sherwood, however, has not even this etymological justification for his use of 'syllogism' in this chapter. Most of his examples are of one premiss only, and he does not always construct a categorical syllogism as a warrant for the dialectical argument under discussion. See n. 15 and n. 142, this chapter.

[4] Sherwood takes up sophistical arguments in Chapter Six, but he never discusses the demonstrative syllogism, the subject matter of Aristotle's *Posterior Analytics*. Konstantyn Michalski ("Le criticisme et la scepticisme dans la philoso-

probable [premisses], but it derives its probability from [dialectical] grounds[5] (*probabilitatem autem habet ex locis*). Therefore we have to determine the nature of dialectical grounds.

2. THE DEFINITION AND DIVISION OF DIALECTICAL GROUNDS

In the case of natural objects a ground (*locus*), properly so-called, is that which contains a thing and from which it is possible to extract the thing. A dialectical ground[6] (*locus dyalecticus*) [is so called] because of its similarity to [a ground in that sense]. [56] It is defined as follows: A dialectical ground is the basis of an argument (*sedes argumenti*) or that from which an argument is conveniently extracted. (This definition will become clear in what follows.)

A dialectical ground is divided into the maxim[7] and the differentia of the maxim. The ground considered as a maxim (*locus maxima*) is a

phie du XIVᵉ siècle," pp. 56–57) argues that dialectic and sophistic are the focal points of the works of the terminist logicians — e.g., Sherwood, Peter of Spain, Lambert of Auxerre — and of Sherwood in particular he says, "D'abord Guillaume de Shyreswood compose son manuel de façon que toutes les parties de celui-ci convergent comme vers leur terme, vers les deux chapitres [IV and VI] consacrés à la dialectique et à la sophistique" (p. 56).

[5] '*Locus*' is the Latin equivalent of Aristotle's 'τόπος.' It was introduced for this purpose by Cicero in his *Topica*, where '*locus*' is defined as '*sedes argumenti*' (see p. 70 below), and transmitted to the medieval logicians through Boethius. (See Kneale, *Development*, pp. 33–34 (Aristotle), 178–179 (Cicero), 193 (Boethius), 216–217 (Abelard), 233 (Sherwood).) Sherwood evidently sees this chapter as an attempt to supply justification for arguments which, unlike the syllogisms discussed in Chapter Three, are not justifiable simply in virtue of their structure or of their reducibility to arguments that are so justified.

[6] In the remainder of this chapter Sherwood usually uses simply '*locus*' rather than '*locus dyalecticus*.' The translation will often read 'dialectical ground' for '*locus*' alone, as on p. 70 above.

[7] The maxim (*propositio maxima*) was introduced into the discussion of *loci* or topics by Boethius in his *De differentiis topicis*. The *ground* of the dialectical argument is the necessary (or probable) connection supporting the inference, while the *maxim* is the formula expressing that connection in general terms. Cf. *De diff. top.*, Bk. II (*P.L.*, 64.1185D): "Thus both universal and maximal propositions are called *loci*, since they are the ones that contain other propositions and since the consequence and valid conclusion depend on them. And just as a *locus* contains the quantity of a body in itself, so these propositions that are maxims contain within themselves the inferential force (*vim consequentiam*) of the derivative propositions (*posteriorum*) and of the conclusion itself. And so in one sense the maximal, principal proposition supporting belief in another proposition is called a *locus* — i.e., a basis of argument" (quoted in Latin by Kneale, *Development*, p. 193).

known[8] general proposition containing and confirming many arguments — e.g., 'the genus is predicated of whatever a species is predicated of.'[9] The differentia of the maxim is the respect in which one maxim differs from another — in the example above, the words 'genus' and 'species'[10] (*quale est hoc, quod dico genus, et hoc, quod dico species*).

[Dialectical grounds] are also divided into intrinsic, extrinsic, and mediate grounds, [a division] which is to be understood in the following way. When there is some doubt about a proposition we first put it in the form of a question;[11] then we find a middle term; and then we syllogize it, either affirmatively or negatively. So when the argument is extracted from an internal property of one of the terms of the question, the ground is called intrinsic; when from an extrinsic property, the ground is called extrinsic; when from a mediate property, the ground is called mediate.[12]

3. *ARGUMENTS FROM INTRINSIC GROUNDS

One kind of argument from an intrinsic ground is from substance — i.e., from an accepted definition (*Locus intrinsecus alius a substantia et hec est a diffinitione sumpta*). (I use "accepted definition" generally for definition properly so called, for description, and for the interpretation of a noun.) The other kind of argument from an intrinsic ground is from the concomitants of substance.[13]

---

[8] I.e., self-evident, or accepted without a supporting argument of its own. Cf. Boethius, *De diff. top.*, Bk. I (*P.L.*, 64.1176C).

[9] See p. 77.

[10] The division here is not into two types of dialectical grounds but more nearly into two senses of 'dialectical ground.' The ground may be identified with the maxim or with the particular kind of connection expressed in that maxim (the differentia of the maxim). Thus the words 'genus' and 'species' distinguish Sherwood's example here from one containing, for example, the words 'what is defined' and 'the definition' in the corresponding positions in the formula '——— is predicated of whatever ——— is predicated of.' (See p. 72.)

[11] Cf. Aristotle's "dialectical proposition" and "dialectical problem," *Topics*, Bk. I, Ch. 10 (104a3ff).

[12] What Sherwood means by these distinctions will appear as he considers each of these divisions in detail. Cf. Boethius, *De diff. top.*, Bk. II (*P.L.*, 64.1186D). By "internal property of one of the terms" he evidently does not mean what he means by "a property of a term" in Chapter Five.

[13] I.e., concepts closely connected with but separable from the concept of substance itself, such as *genus* and *species*. For Boethius's treatment of the arguments from intrinsic grounds see *De diff. top.*, Bk. II (*P.L.*, 64.1186D–1190B).

3.1. Arguments from Substance

As is already clear, arguments from substance are divided into arguments from definition, from description, and from the interpretation of a noun.

3.1.1. *From Definition.*[14] A definition is an expression indicating what the essence of a thing is. We argue from definition (*iuxta quam argumentatur*) both constructively and destructively. Constructively, in case the middle is the definition of the subject or of the predicate [of the conclusion] — e.g., 'a mortal rational animal is running; therefore a man is running.'[15] Maxim: *Whatever is predicated of the definition is predicated also of what is defined*[16] (*quicquid predicatur de diffinitione, et de diffinito*).[17] Again, 'Socrates is a mortal rational animal; therefore Socrates is a man.' Maxim: *What is defined is predicated of whatever the definition is predicated of* (*de quocunque predicatur diffinitio, et diffinitum*).

"Destructively" [like "constructively"] is taken in two ways — e.g., 'a mortal rational animal is not an ass; therefore a man is not an ass.'

---

[14] Cf. Boethius, *De diff. top.*, Bk. II (*P.L.*, 64.1187A–B).

[15] His terminology suggests that Sherwood thought of the dialectical argument as a syllogism (see n. 3, this chapter). In this case the syllogism would be in *Disamis* and the suppressed minor premiss would read 'every mortal rational animal is a man.' That premiss, however, is only entailed by, not equivalent to, the definition in question: 'man is defined as mortal rational animal,' or, perhaps, 'every man is a mortal rational animal, and conversely.' Moreover, if it were possible in this case or generally to show that the dialectical argument was only a truncated syllogism, the maxims would have no point. In fact they are clearly propounded as warrants independent of (though not on a par with) the figures of the categorical syllogism. (For Sherwood's explicit use of syllogistic figures together with maxims see, e.g., p. 76.)

[16] Here, as elsewhere in this chapter, there is an apparent inconsistency stemming from the traditional vagueness about the status of subjects and predicates. The definition is said to be an *expression* (cf. *Topics*, Bk. I, Ch. 5 (101b37ff)), but nothing is predicated of the expression 'mortal rational animal' in this example. Sherwood seems to have been aware of this inconsistency. His discussion of the "objection" introduced on p. 73 looks like an attempt to avoid the difficulty by suggesting that these maxims are to be read as abbreviated versions of the principles that are actually supporting these arguments. (See also p. 75.)

[17] The Latin given here and immediately following the translations of the next three maxims represents a set of standard formulas for the maxims in this chapter. In English the standard formulas are Constructive: (a) Whatever is predicated of (or goes together with) ——— is predicated also of (or goes together also with) ———; and (b) ——— is predicated of (or goes together with) whatever ——— is predicated of (or goes together with); or Destructive: (a) Whatever is denied of (or is separated from) ——— is denied also of (or is separated also from) ———; and (b) ——— is denied of (or is separated from) whatever ——— is denied of (or is separated from).

Maxim: *Whatever is separated from the definition is separated also from what is defined* (*quicquid removetur a diffinitione, et a diffinito*). Again, 'Brownie[18] is not a mortal rational animal; therefore Brownie is not a man.' Maxim: *What is defined is separated from whatever the definition is separated from* (*a quocunque removetur diffinitio, et diffinitum*).

Each of these cases is an argument from definition, because the foregoing maxims proceed from definition (*Et est hic ubique locus a diffinitione, quia predicte maxime a diffinitione exeunt*). [57]

Suppose someone objects to the foregoing maxims as follows: "'mortal rational animal' is a definition, but a man is not a definition" (*animal rationale mortale est diffinitio, non tamen homo est diffinitio*). Then we must point out that the maxim is to be understood as follows: *Whatever goes together with the definition with respect to individuals (secundum singula) goes together also with what is defined, and vice versa.*[19]

Note that a simple revision of the maxims makes it possible to argue in the same number of ways from what is defined.[20]

3.1.2. **From Description.**[21] Next is the argument from description. Now a description is [a predicate] that does not indicate what the essence of a thing is but nevertheless belongs to that thing alone and is predicated convertibly of it.[22]

We argue constructively from description in two ways. For example, 'a risible animal is running; therefore a man is running.' Maxim: *Whatever is predicated of the description is predicated also of what is described.* Again, 'Socrates is a risible animal; therefore he is a man.' Maxim: *What is described is predicated of whatever the description is predicated of.*

---

[18] Just as Socrates is the medieval logicians' standard example of a man, Brownie (*Brunellus*) is their standard example of an ass.

[19] See n. 16, this chapter. Cf. p. 75. Sherwood's consideration of "objections" here and elsewhere in this book is one of the more important features distinguishing it from the immensely popular *Summulae logicales* of Peter of Spain. (See Introduction, pp. 4–5 above.)

[20] E.g., in the case of the first maxim, "*whatever is predicated of what is defined is predicated also of the definition.*"

[21] Cf. Boethius, *De diff. top.*, Bk. II (*P.L.*, 64.1187B–D).

[22] Cf. *Topics*, Bk. I, Ch. 5 (102a17ff). Sherwood here uses 'description' where Aristotle uses 'property,' but he sometimes reverts to 'property' in this same sense. See, e.g., p. 75 below.

"Destructively" is also used in two ways [in connection with this argument] — e.g., 'an animal capable of braying does not exist; therefore an ass does not exist.' Maxim: *Whatever is separated from the description is separated also from what is described.* Again, 'earth is not naturally borne upwards; therefore it is not fire.' Maxim: *What is described is separated from whatever the description is separated from.*

A simple revision of the maxims makes it possible to argue in the same number of ways also from what is described.

3.1.3. *From the Interpretation of a Noun.*[23] Next is the argument from the interpretation of a noun. Now the interpretation of a noun is the exposition of it either in the same language (*ydioma*) or in another.

We argue from the interpretation of a name in as many ways as from the preceding grounds. First, 'a foot-bruiser does harm; therefore a stone does harm.'[24] Maxim: *Whatever is predicated of the interpretation is predicated also of what is interpreted.* Second, 'this is a foot-bruiser; therefore this is a stone.' Maxim: *What is interpreted is predicated of whatever the interpretation is predicated of.*

Destructively, too, as follows: [First,] 'a lover of wisdom[25] is not envious; therefore a philosopher is not envious.' [Maxim: *Whatever is separated from the interpretation is separated also from what is interpreted.*] Second, 'an evil man is not a lover of wisdom; therefore an evil man is not a philosopher.' Maxim: *What is interpreted is separated from whatever the interpretation is separated from.*

A simple revision of the maxims makes it possible to argue in the same number of ways from what is interpreted.[26]

Suppose someone objects that an interpretation is not convertible with what is interpreted. Then we must point out that an expositive expression can be taken in two ways: either insofar as it is expositive,

---

[23] Cf. Boethius, *De diff. top.*, Bk. II (*P.L.*, 64.1187D–1188A).

[24] The argument depends on the mistaken medieval derivation of *'lapis'* ('stone') from *'laedens pedem'* ('foot-bruiser'). Peter of Spain makes this a little clearer when he says in a parallel passage " *'laedens pedem'* is the interpretation of *'lapis'* " (*Sum. log.*, ed. Bocheński, p. 48).

[25] G has *'philosophiam'*; *'sapientiam'* in manuscript. Evidently the *lapis/laedens-pedem* example is a case of exposition within the same language, whereas the *philosophus/amans-sapientiam* example rests on the exposition of a Greek name in Latin.

[26] In the text this sentence occurs between the two objections following.

in which case it *is* convertible [with what is expounded], or simply as it stands (*secundum se*), in which case it is not convertible.[27] [58]

Suppose, further, that someone objects to the maxims of interpretation and description in the same way as to the maxims of definition earlier.[28] This is to be resolved just as before, by pointing out that the maxims are to be understood as follows — e.g., *Whatever is predicated of a description in such a way as to be predicated of an individual contained under it is predicated of what is described.* The other maxims are to be similarly filled out.

3.2. *Arguments from the Concomitants of Substance

Next are the arguments from the concomitants of substance (*a concomitantibus substantiam*), which are so called because they are drawn from [states or circumstances] attendant on (*ab hiis, que concomitantur*) the substance of the subject or of the predicate of a [dialectical] problem[29] — e.g., the universal whole, generation, and the like.

*3.2.1. *From Genus.*[30] Now the first of these arguments is from genus, or from a universal whole, since genus is the formal part of definition, the part that indicates the essence of what is defined (for the material part of definition indicates the essential parts of what is defined)[31] (*Materialis enim pars indicat, ex quibus est diffinitum*). "Genus" here means (*Dicitur autem hic genus*) the superior substantial predicate.[32] Thus genus, species, definition, and property[33] with respect to an individual is called the differentia here.[34]

---

[27] This objection seems to apply especially well to the *lapis/laedens-pedem* example, for of course there are foot-bruisers that are not stones. We might indicate that the expression was occurring as an expositive expression by enclosing it in quotation marks: "this is a 'foot-bruiser'; therefore this is a stone."

[28] See p. 73 above; see also n. 16, this chapter.

[29] On the nature of the *problema*, or dialectical problem, see *Topics*, Bk. I, Ch. 11 (104b1–19). Cf. Kneale, *Development*, pp. 34–35.

[30] Cf. Boethius, *De diff. top.*, Bk. II (*P.L.*, 64.1188B–C).

[31] Sherwood seems to be designating the genus and the differentia as the "formal" and "material" parts, respectively, of a real definition. This terminology was evidently not widespread.

[32] I.e., if a definition is divided into two parts, the genus and the differentia, these two parts may be considered two substantial predicates, and the genus will, in that context, be the substantial predicate occurring "higher" than the differentia in the *linea predicamentali*, or in a Tree of Porphyry (see p. 54 above).

[33] See n. 22, this chapter.

[34] See Chapter Two, section 5, on differentia. Sherwood is evidently referring to the "differentia of the maxim" (see p. 71) and suggesting that genus as the differentia of the maxim in this dialectical ground must be interpreted very broadly.

We argue only destructively from genus, as follows: 'a man is not a quantity; therefore a man is not a line.' Maxim: *The species is separated from whatever the genus is separated from.* And this reduces to a syllogism in the fourth mood of the second figure [*Baroco*], as follows: 'every line is a quantity, an animal is not a quantity; therefore it is not a line.'[35]

We argue destructively in another way, too. 'It is not the case that an animal is running; therefore it is not the case that a man is running' (*Non animal currit. Ergo non homo currit.*). Maxim: *Whatever is separated from the genus is separated from the species.* Let this be reduced to the second mood of the first figure [*Celarent*], as follows: 'it is not the case that an animal is running, every man is an animal; therefore it is not the case that a man is running.'

The objection here is that the argument from genus does not hold if we argue as follows: 'an animal is not running; therefore a man is not running.' This is not valid (*Non valet*); and yet since it proceeds from the superior to the inferior by negating, it is an argument from genus. In this connection we must point out that whenever an argument is from genus the whole genus must be negated. Thus the negation must be put before the genus. But in 'an animal is not running' the genus *animal* is not negated universally, and so in that case it is not superior to *man*. For that reason this argument does *not* proceed from the superior to the inferior by negating, insofar as the rule is understood.

Again, suppose someone objects that 'it is not the case that an animal is running; therefore it is not the case that a man is running' is an argument from a quantitative whole[36] [rather than from genus]. Then we must point out that this is true, but as a consequence (*per consequens*) [of its being an argument from genus]. The name of the genus is ampliated[37] (*ampliatur*) in the way just mentioned [i.e., to that of a quantitative whole] because the force of arguing [59] from one superior to an inferior is the same as that of arguing from another superior, whether it is a genus or not. Therefore it is the same kind of argument;

---

[35] It seems the minor term should be 'man' rather than 'animal' and that the syllogism should be characterized as *Camestres* rather than as *Baroco*. However, see p. 114 on the status of indefinite propositions as syllogistic premisses. On the use of syllogistic figures in connection with dialectical arguments see n. 15, this chapter.

[36] See p. 79.

[37] 'Ampliated' has a technical sense in the doctrine of the property of terms (see, e.g., p. 129). The technical sense seems inappropriate here (as in the case of '*ampliatur*' and '*supponitur*' in the paragraph immediately following).

for the argument from genus is distinguished by a diversity of inferential force [38] (*Diversificatur enim locus presens diversitate virtutis inferendi*).

3.2.2. *From Species.*[39] Next is the argument from species. Now a species is what is placed under a genus (*supponitur generi*), but it is ampliated in the same way as a genus.

We argue from species constructively only, in such a way that the middle is a species of the subject of the conclusion. Thus 'a man is running; therefore an animal is running' is an argument from species. Maxim: *Whatever is predicated of a species is predicated of the genus.* Let this be reduced to the third mood of the third figure [*Disamis*], as follows: 'a man is running, every man is an animal; [40] therefore an animal is running.'

Alternatively, in such a way that the middle is a species of the predicate of the conclusion. Thus 'Socrates is a man; therefore Socrates is an animal' is an argument from species. Maxim: *The genus is predicated of whatever a species is predicated of.* And let this be reduced to the third mood of the first figure [*Darii*] as follows: 'every man is an animal, Socrates is a man; therefore Socrates is an animal.'

Suppose someone objects that we can argue only[41] destructively (*destructive solum*) from species, as follows: 'a man is not running; therefore an animal is not running'—for this does follow in case a man exists.[42] In response we must point out that in this case we are *not* argu-

---

[38] The objection seems to be that in this example we are basing an inference not on a *property* of the genus (as in the first example on p. 76) but on what is contingently denied of every member of the genus — i.e., of every part of a quantitative whole. The first part of Sherwood's reply seems to be that we can view it as a valid argument from a quantitative whole only *because* the genus-species relation between *animal* and *man* makes every man a part of that quantitative whole (as is brought out in the minor premiss of the reconstructed syllogism supporting this example on p. 76). The second part of the reply seems to be that the genuinely fundamental dialectical ground here (and elsewhere in this chapter) is the argument from some (predicamental) superior to some inferior, and that many of the arguments traditionally distinguished are thus really versions of the argument from genus. (He nevertheless goes on to discuss the traditional kinds of dialectical argument separately.)

[39] Cf. Boethius, *De diff. top.*, Bk. II (*P.L.*, 64.1188C–D).

[40] G has '*omne animal est homo*'; '*omnis homo est animal*' in manuscript.

[41] In view of what has gone before in the discussion of arguments from species and the proviso following this example it looks as if this 'only' should have been 'also.'

[42] I.e., the premiss might have been true simply because no such thing as a man existed, much less was running. In that case the conclusion could, of course, have been false although the premiss was true.

ing negatively [i.e., destructively] from species, since the genus is not negated insofar as it is a genus. Instead, [it is negated] only for that same thing for which 'man' [is negated].[43]

Moreover, it is proved that we argue [A] constructively from genus and [B] destructively from species in the following way: [A] 'an animal is running; therefore either a man is running, or an ox, etc.'; [44] [B] 'neither a man nor an ox, etc., is running; therefore it is not the case that an animal is running.' In response we must point out that in both these cases we are arguing from what is *equal* [to the conclusion], or from description.[45]

*ARGUMENTS FROM WHOLES [46]

3.2.3. *From an Integral Whole.*[47] Next is the argument from an integral whole, for the integral whole follows the universal whole and is posterior to it in logic. It is the kind of whole that consists of the parts that make it a whole[48] (*ex partibus integrantibus ipsum*).

We argue from an integral whole constructively only, in such a way that the middle is the whole of the subject of the conclusion. Thus, 'the house exists; therefore a wall exists' is an argument from an integral whole. Maxim: *What goes together with an [integral] whole in respect of proportional*[49] *and perceptible parts (secundum partes proportion-*

---

[43] In this argument the negations are for a single individual rather than for the species and the genus. If the argument were revised so as to contain negations for the species and the genus and thus to qualify as a genuine destructive argument from species it would be made invalid: 'it is not the case that a man is running; therefore it is not the case that an animal is running.'

[44] The 'etc.' here (as in [B] immediately following) is intended to indicate a disjunction of statements exhaustive of all the species of animal.

[45] Cf. definition of description, p. 73 above; also *Topics*, Bk. I, Ch. 7 (103a13ff).

[46] Although Sherwood speaks of genus and species here as "universal wholes," in his catalogue of arguments from intrinsic grounds (p. 92) he separates the arguments from genus and species from the arguments from wholes and parts.

[47] Cf. Boethius, *De diff. top.*, Bk. II (*P.L.*, 64.1188D–1189A). See also p. 26 above.

[48] An integral whole is distinguished from a universal whole — i.e., a genus or species (see p. 75) — by the fact that it is *really* and not just *conceptually* divisible into its parts; and it is distinguished from a quantitative whole (see pp. 79–81) by the fact that its parts are genuinely *components* — parts that play different roles in the whole and that make it the kind of whole it is, parts the absence of one of which not merely *diminishes* but *destroys* the whole. (See especially Aristotle's chapter on various notions of a whole — *Met.*, Bk. V, Ch. 26 (1023b26–1024a1).)

[49] The proportional parts seem to be those which on the next level of analysis would be considered the largest wholes. Thus the proportional parts of a paragraph are sentences, not words, and the proportional parts of a sentence are words, not syllables or letters.

ales et notabiles) goes together with a part. For this does not follow: 'a house encloses; therefore a wall encloses,' because enclosing does not go together with [the whole] in respect of the nature of a part but as a result of the interconnection of the parts. Nor [60] does this follow: 'the house is seen; therefore the wall is seen'; nor this: 'the house is tall; therefore the foundation is tall'; for predicates of this kind do not go together with the whole in respect of the individual parts. Moreover, something can go together with the whole in respect of the countable parts — e.g., a pebble as part of a house (*secundum partes numerales ut lapillus domus*) — which does not go together with a part such as a wall, or the roof, or the foundation, which make up its [proportional and] perceptible parts.

Arguments from an integral whole reduce to the third mood of the first figure [*Darii*], as follows: 'every part of the house exists (since the house exists), a wall is part of the house; therefore a wall exists.'[50]

But the argument does not follow if the middle is the whole of the *predicate* [of the conclusion] — e.g., 'this is a house; therefore this is a wall' — since an integral part and a whole are not one and the same, as are a definition and what is defined, [but their relation is like that between] a species and a genus (*non sunt idem, ut diffinitio et diffinitum est genus et species*).

We argue from an integral part destructively only, in such a way that the middle is a part of the subject of the conclusion. Thus, 'the wall does not exist; therefore the house does not exist' is an argument from an integral part. Maxim: *What fails to go together with (disconvenit) an [integral] part fails to go together with the whole.* Let this be reduced to the fourth mood of the first figure [*Ferio*], as follows: 'no [integral] whole, one of whose parts does not exist, exists; the house is an [integral] whole, one of whose parts does not exist (since the wall does not exist); therefore the house does not exist.'

3.2.4. **From a Quantitative Whole.*[51] Next is the argument from a quantitative whole, for the quantitative whole, since it consists in number, follows the integral whole.

We argue from a quantitative whole constructively as follows: 'every

---

[50] In this case, the reduction is to a syllogism whose major premiss is presented as a *conclusion from* the premiss of the original argument. The clause 'since the house exists' is attached also to the minor premiss, but this must be a scribe's error.

[51] On this and the three following subsections cf. Boethius, *De diff. top.*, Bk. II (*P.L.*, 64.1189A–C), where these grounds are discussed together.

man is running; therefore Socrates is running.' Similarly: 'no man is running; therefore Socrates is not running'; for the inferential force is the same [in both cases]. Maxim: *Whatever goes together with a [quantitative] whole either affirmatively or negatively goes together with a part.* Let this also be reduced to a syllogism [*Darii*] in similar fashion, as follows: 'every man is running, Socrates is a man; therefore Socrates is running.' Similarly [*Ferio*]: 'no man is running, [Socrates is a man]; therefore Socrates is not running.'[52]

However, we argue from a quantitative part destructively as follows: 'Socrates is not running; therefore not every man is running.' Maxim: *Whatever fails to go together with a [quantitative] part fails to go together with the whole.* Let this be reduced to the fifth mood of the third figure [*Bocardo*], as follows: "Socrates is not running, Socrates is included under 'every man' (*sub eo quod est omnis homo*) (make a universal proposition of the minor premiss as follows: 'whatever is Socrates is included under "every man"');[53] therefore not every man is running."

The word "quantitative" appears in the terminology of these arguments[54] because in them we argue especially on the basis of quantity

---

[52] This paragraph reads as if only constructive arguments from a quantitative whole were being considered. It seems very likely, however, that the paragraph is actually a compressed treatment of both constructive and destructive arguments. Cf. Peter of Spain, *Sum. log.*, ed. Bocheński, p. 49: "The ground of the argument from a quantitative whole is the relation of the whole to its part and is both constructive and destructive. E.g., 'every man is running; therefore Socrates is running.' Maxim for the argument from a quantitative whole: *Whatever is predicated of a quantitative whole is predicated also of any of its parts.* Destructively, as follows: 'no man is running; therefore Socrates is not running.' Maxim for the argument for a quantitative whole: *Whatever is denied of a quantitative whole is denied also of any of its parts.* Alternatively: *If a universal [proposition] is true, each of its singular propositions is true.*" Sherwood's single maxim here is analogous to the single maxim Peter offers as an alternative.

[53] Notice that a singular statement is taken to be particular for purposes of the major premiss and universal for purposes of the minor premiss, and that the minor term is mentioned rather than used in the minor premiss. Sherwood's difficulties with syllogistic reduction in cases such as this may partially account for the fact that Peter of Spain completely avoids attempting to justify dialectical arguments by reducing them to syllogisms. Peter's treatment of arguments from a quantitative part is quite different from Sherwood's. His constructive example is " 'Socrates is running, Plato is running, (and so on for the individuals [included under "every man"]); therefore every man is running.' Maxim: *Whatever is predicated of quantitative parts taken together at one time is predicated of their whole*" (*Sum. log.*, ed. Bocheński, p. 50). He also presents an analogous destructive example and maxim.

[54] The phrase translated as 'quantitative whole' is '*totum in quantitate,*' and so Sherwood speaks here not of the word 'quantitative' but of the '*nomen quantitatis.*'

and containment (*continentia*). For this kind of whole contains parts *under* itself, while an integral whole contains parts *within* itself.[55] [61]

3.2.5. *From a Temporal Whole.* Next is the argument from a temporal whole, which is indicated affirmatively by the adverb 'always,' negatively by the adverb 'never.'

We argue from a temporal whole affirmatively, as follows: 'Socrates is always running; therefore Socrates is running now.' Maxim: *What goes together with [something] with respect to a temporal whole goes together with [it] with respect to the parts.* And this reduces to the third mood of the first figure [*Darii*], as follows: "always Socrates is running, now is included under 'always'; therefore now Socrates is running," for we can syllogize using oblique [cases] and by means of convertible terms, as Aristotle teaches in the *Prior Analytics.*[56]

However, we argue from a temporal part destructively, as follows: 'Socrates is not now running; therefore Socrates is not always running.' Maxim for the argument from a temporal part: *What fails to go together with [something] with respect to a part fails to go together with [it] with respect to the whole.* Let this be reduced to the fifth mood of the third figure [*Bocardo*], as follows: "not now Socrates is running,

---

[55] Arguments from a quantitative whole or from a quantitative part are important in connection with certain types of supposition — e.g., distributive (see pp. 108–109 below) — although Sherwood does not introduce them under that designation in his treatment of supposition in Chapter Five. In his *Syncategoremata* Sherwood does refer to these arguments several times by name — e.g., on pp. 58, 73, 82 (O'Donnell ed.).

[56] Grabmann supplies a reference to *An. pr.*, Bk. II, Chs. 8–10 (59b1–61a16); however, those chapters deal with the conversion of syllogisms generally and seem not to contain any material particularly relevant here. Sherwood is more likely to have been thinking of *An. pr.*, Bk. I, Ch. 36 (48a40–49a5), which does deal with terms occurring in oblique cases and contains other remarks that might be thought of as dealing with convertible terms ('ϕ' and 'ψ' are convertible terms if and only if '$(x)(\phi(x) \equiv \psi(x))$' is true). *An. pr.*, Bk. II, Ch. 22 (67b26ff), deals with convertible terms in detail. However, none of this Aristotelian doctrine seems genuinely pertinent here. The "terms" of Sherwood's "syllogism" do not occur in oblique cases; in fact, it is easier to say that about the terms than to identify them. Moreover, nothing resembling convertible terms occurs here. Sherwood's appeal to Aristotle is perhaps an ellipsis for something like this: "The fact that this is not a standard categorical syllogism ought not to vitiate this attempted reduction, for Aristotle himself accepted deviations from the standard form — e.g., when he allowed syllogisms with terms in oblique cases or with two convertible terms where we should normally find two occurrences of one and the same term." And the "syllogism" might better be put as follows: 'at all times Socrates is running, this time is included under all times; therefore at this time Socrates is running.' Sherwood's use of adverbs as syllogistic terms is one source of the difficulties in this and the following section.

every now is included under 'always'; therefore not always Socrates is running."[57]

*3.2.6. *From a Locational Whole.* Next is the argument from a locational whole. A locational whole is indicated universally by the affirmative adverb 'everywhere,' or by the negative adverb 'nowhere.'

We argue from a locational whole constructively, as follows: 'Socrates is everywhere; therefore Socrates is here.'[58] Maxim for the [constructive] argument from a locational whole: *What goes together with* [*something*] *with respect to a locational whole goes together with* [*it*] *with respect to a part.* This reduces to the third mood of the first figure [*Darii*] as follows: "everywhere is Socrates, here is included under 'everywhere'; therefore here is Socrates."[59] We argue negatively in like fashion by means of the adverb 'nowhere,' [and a negative argument from a locational whole reduces] to the fourth mood of the first figure [*Ferio*].[60]

We argue from a locational part destructively, as follows: 'Socrates is not here; therefore Socrates is not everywhere.' Maxim: *What does not go together with* [*something*] *with respect to a locational part does not go together with* [*it*] *with respect to the whole.* This reduces to the fifth mood of the third figure [*Bocardo*], as follows: "here is not Socrates, every here is included under 'everywhere'; therefore everywhere is not Socrates."[61]

Suppose someone asks why Boethius assigns distinct arguments to

---

[57] Perhaps this would benefit from a less literal translation — e.g., 'it is not the case that Socrates is running at this time, every time is included under all times; therefore it is not the case that Socrates is running at all times.'

[58] Boethius's example, the one usually found in this context, is, as might be expected, 'God is everywhere . . .'

[59] Or, 'for every location, Socrates is in it, this place is a location; therefore Socrates is in this place.'

[60] The missing example, maxim, and reduction are easily supplied.

[61] As it stands, this conclusion is ambiguous and probably more readily interpretable as 'Socrates is nowhere' than as the required 'Socrates is not everywhere.' The Latin '*ubique non est Sortes*' may, however, be a scribe's error for '*non ubique est Sortes*,' in which case the conclusion would be the acceptable 'not everywhere is Socrates.' Even with this emendation this "syllogism" is an especially striking example of the difficulties involved in Sherwood's use of reduction in this chapter. Most of those difficulties stem from his attempt to preserve the natural wording of the original argument in the terms of the reductive syllogism. There is no special difficulty in providing a standard case of *Bocardo* as the reductive syllogism if one is willing to blur the connections between it and the original argument — e.g., "Some location is not a location of Socrates, every location is a location included under 'everywhere'; therefore some location included under 'everywhere' is not a location of Socrates."

location and time[62] since the [inferential] force is the same in arguing from that which is in every location, from that which is everywhere, from that which is always, and from that which is in every time. Then we must point out that this is the case because location and time are the first principle (*sunt principium primum*) of generation — not [62] in the sense in which they are measures, but in the sense in which they are natural conditions inseparable from the things that are in them[63] (*sed secundum quod nature concordes hiis, que insunt*). Furthermore, they are naturally signified by a single word since they are not divided except in relation to something; nor do they become many adverbially or because they have reference to the motion designated by a verb[64] (*Preterea dictione una naturaliter significantur, quia non dividuntur nisi secundum quid nec fiunt plura adverbialiter aut quia spectant ad motum designatum verbo*).

3.2.7. *From a Modificational Whole.* We argue from a modificational whole (*a toto in modo*) destructively only, and a modificational whole is a verb used without modification (*dictum simpliciter*) — e.g., 'Socrates is not running; therefore he is not running well.' Maxim: *What does not go together with [something] with respect to a modificational whole does not go together with [it] with respect to a part.* This reduces to the fourth mood of the first figure [*Ferio*], as follows: 'not running is Socrates, running well is running; therefore not running well is Socrates'[65] (*non currit Sortes. Bene currere est currere. Ergo non bene currit Sortes*).

---

[62] In *De diff. top.*, Bk. II (*P.L.*, 64.1189A–B).

[63] Cf. Aristotle, *De generatione et corruptione* (hereafter cited as *De gen. et cor.*), Bk. II, Ch. 10 (337a16–34).

[64] This is evidently at least in part a reference to Aristotle's introduction of the categories (including place and time) as "things said without combination"— i.e., without the requirement of combining words into a statement. (Cf. *Cat.*, Ch. 4 (1b25–2a10)). Aristotle also maintains that "time, past, present, and future, forms a continuous whole. Space, likewise, is a continuous quantity . . ." (*Cat.*, Ch. 6 (5a6ff)). Therefore neither location nor time is divisible as such (*simpliciter*) but only in relation to something (*secundum quid*). But when we do thus divide space and time ("adverbially," by the use of such words as 'sometime,' 'somewhere'; or with "reference to the motion designated by a verb," 'x has moved (is moving, will move) y from w to z'), we do not really make many spaces or many times. What Sherwood has to say in response to the question regarding Boethius's treatment of these arguments is obscure, but it is even more difficult to see how this is to constitute an answer to that question.

[65] Leaving aside the serious flaws that this reduction has in common with others, it seems it would have been slightly improved if the syllogism had been interpreted as an instance of *Celarent* rather than of *Ferio*.

From a modificational part — i.e., a modified (*determinatum*) verb — we argue constructively only, as follows: 'Socrates is running well; therefore Socrates is running.' Maxim: *What goes together with [something] with respect to a modificational part goes together with [it] with respect to the whole.* This reduces to the third mood of the first figure [*Darii*] as follows: 'every running well is running, Socrates is running well; therefore Socrates is running.'[66]

*ARGUMENTS FROM CAUSES [67]

Next are the arguments from causes, since from a logician's point of view the causes of a thing follow after the matters we have already discussed, although from the natural scientist's (*phisici*) point of view they precede those matters. A cause is whatever conduces to being (*quod conducit ad esse*).

3.2.8. *From a Material Cause.*[68] A material cause is the source (*principium*) from which something comes, which is also in that thing.[69] I say "which is also in that thing" because of the ambiguity (*multiplicatem*) of the preposition 'from' (*ex*). Notice that sometimes it indicates an order, as in 'from — i.e., after — morning comes the day' [or] 'from these come the Olympian games' (*ex hiis fiunt olimpia*);[70] sometimes the material, as in 'a knife is made from iron.' That same example also enables us to set aside transient matter (*materia transiens*) — e.g., grass is the transient matter of cattle (*filix est materia transiens vitri*)[71] and flour of bread; but iron is the permanent matter of a knife.

---

[66] Although Boethius's only example of this kind of argument involves the modification of a verb, as Sherwood's examples do, he describes the ground in terms that make it available also in connection with nouns: "if we set forth anything simply, it is a modificational whole; if with modification (*adjectione*), it becomes a modificational part" (*P.L.*, 64.1189B). Peter of Spain confines this ground to nouns as Sherwood confines it to verbs (see *Sum. log.*, ed. Bocheński, p. 50).

[67] Cf. Boethius, *De diff. top.*, Bk. II (*P.L.*, 64.1189C–1190A). At the end of his discussion of the arguments from causes Sherwood indicates that he considers them as grouped under arguments from the concomitants of substance (p. 88 below). His reasons for doing so are obscure (see n. 91, this chapter).

[68] Cf. Boethius, *De diff. top.* (*P.L.*, 64.1189C–D). In the manuscript and in G this subtitle occurs later, just before the first complete paragraph on p. 85.

[69] Cf. Boethius, *De diff. top.* (*P.L.*, 64.1188A–B): "*Materia vero ex qua fit aliquid, vel in qua fit.*" Sherwood's Latin here is "*Materialis autem est principium, ex quo fit aliquid cui insit.*"

[70] See Aristotle, *Met.*, Bk. II, Ch. 2 (994a23): "For one thing comes *from* another in two ways — not in the sense in which 'from' means 'after' (as we say 'from the Isthmian games come the Olympian') . . ."

[71] Reading '*vituli*' for '*vitri*.' Cf. Peter of Spain, *Sum. log.*, ed. Bocheński, p. 51: "*transiens, ut in pane farina, vel in vitulo foenum et filix.*"

We argue from a material cause destructively, but this is to be understood as having to do with permanent matter — e.g., 'the Moors do not have iron; therefore they do not have iron weapons.' Maxim: *If the matter is lacking, then what depends on that matter is lacking (deficiente materia deficit materiatum)*. Let this be reduced to the fourth mood of the first figure [*Ferio*], as follows: 'no people who do not have iron are people who have iron weapons, the Moors are people who do not have iron; therefore the Moors are not people who have iron weapons.' [63]

We argue constructively, however, from what depends on the matter, as follows: 'the Moors have weapons; therefore the Moors have iron.' Maxim: *If what depends on the matter exists, then that matter exists*. This reduces to the third mood of the first figure [*Darii*] as follows: 'all people who have weapons have iron, the Moors are people who have weapons; therefore the Moors are people who have iron.'

3.2.9. *From a Formal Cause*.[72] According to Boethius, we argue from a formal cause destructively;[73] and a form, as Aristotle says, is that which was to be[74] (*que quid erat esse*) — e.g., 'Daedalus did not have wings; therefore Daedalus could not fly.' Maxim: *Everything is capable of only as much as its natural form permits*. This reduces to the fourth mood of the second figure [*Baroco*] as follows: 'nothing not having wings could fly, Daedalus did not have wings; therefore Daedalus could not fly.'[75] (This is not an argument from an efficient cause,[76]

---

[72] Cf. Boethius, *De diff. top.* (*P.L.*, 64.1189D–1190A).

[73] Apparently Boethius does not say this explicitly, but in his presentation of the argument from a formal cause he gives only the Daedalus argument — "Daedalus could not fly, since in his natural form he had no wings" — (a variant of which is given here by Sherwood) and the accompanying maxim given by Sherwood with only slight grammatical differences. Boethius's (implicit) doctrine is cited at this point because Sherwood wants to introduce a different approach to arguments from a formal cause in the next paragraph. (A reference is supplied in *G* to *De diff. top.*, Bk. II "(Migne *P.L.* 64.1096)," which is actually a part of Boethius's commentary on Cicero's *Topica* and contains nothing relevant here.)

[74] In *De gen. et cor.*, Bk. II, Ch. 9, Aristotle discusses form (and matter) in connection with coming-to-be in ways that suggest this view — e.g., "So coming-to-be and passing-away must occur in the sphere of what can-be-and-not-be. This, then, is the cause, in the sense of material cause, of things which are of a nature to come-to-be, *whereas cause in the sense of their 'end in view,' is their shape and form*; and this is the definition of the essential nature of each of them" (335b4ff). Thus wingedness has no place in what Daedalus was to be — viz., a man.

[75] Another particularly unsatisfactory reduction, especially in the treatment of the major premiss as a universal affirmative.

[76] See pp. 86–87.

since a thing does not bring about its own capacity (*non efficiat suam potentiam*) — e.g., wings do not bring about the capacity to fly.)

[Boethius to the contrary] notwithstanding, we can argue both destructively and constructively from a formal as well as from a material cause. For example, [constructively]: 'the Moors have the form of weapons; therefore the Moors have weapons'; also destructively: 'the Moors do not have the form of weapons; therefore the Moors do not have weapons.'[77] Maxim: *What bears the form exists if [and only if] the form exists (existente forma existit formatum).*[78]

We argue constructively from what bears the form, as follows: 'the Moor has weapons; therefore the Moor has the form of weapons.' Maxim: *If what bears the form exists, then the form exists.* This reduces to the third mood of the first figure [*Darii*] as follows: 'everyone who has weapons has the form of weapons, the Moor has weapons; therefore the Moor has the form of weapons.' We also argue destructively [from what bears the form].[79]

3.2.10. **From an Efficient Cause.*[80] We argue from an efficient cause both constructively and destructively. I mean an immediate efficient cause, for we argue only destructively from a mediate efficient cause.[81]

---

[77] Of course 'have the form' here means 'possess the form,' not 'are in the form.' But what does it mean to possess the form of something? Medieval writers often follow Boethius in using 'form' ('*forma*') where 'formal cause' ('*causa formalis*') would be more exact, and some sense might be made of the statement that the Moors possess the formal cause — designs, technological skills, etc. — of weapons. On that interpretation, however, Sherwood's argument would not be valid, since the Moors could of course possess the formal cause but lack the material, efficient, or final cause, and so lack the weapons. In any case it is more likely (especially in view of the accompanying maxim) that Sherwood is relying here on an Aristotelian position that he states explicitly in the next chapter (p. 111 below) — viz., that a form exists only in existent bearers of that form. Thus if we can, however oddly, say of the Moors that they possess the form of weapons, it follows that they possess the weapons, the bearers of that form.

[78] The maxim as it stands covers only the constructive argument; as emended, it covers both arguments. Perhaps it would be more consistent with Sherwood's practices (see, e.g., the next paragraph) to leave this maxim as it stands and attach it to the constructive argument while introducing a new maxim — *If the form does not exist, then what bears the form does not exist* — for the destructive argument. The omitted reductions would, no doubt, closely resemble the reduction in the next paragraph. On arguments from a form see also p. 87.

[79] The omitted example, maxim, and reduction are easily supplied.

[80] Cf. Boethius, *De diff. top.* (*P.L.*, 64.1189C).

[81] E.g., it is justifiable to "argue destructively" that for want of a nail the battle was lost, but if the nail had stayed in the horseshoe and the battle had been won it would not do to argue that since the nail had held the battle was won.

Now an efficient cause is the principle whereby motion [is started], as Aristotle says,[82] as a building [is caused] by a builder. For example, 'human society (*congregatio hominum*) gives rise to justice and is natural; therefore justice is natural.' Maxim: *As the efficient cause is, so is its effect.* This reduces to the third mood of the first figure [*Darii*] [64] as follows: 'every human society that gives rise to justice is natural, justice derives from a human society that gives rise to justice; therefore justice is natural.'[83]

[We argue from an efficient cause] destructively as follows: 'there is no such thing as nature; therefore there is no such thing as natural motion.' Maxim: *If the efficient cause is not, then its effect is not.* This reduces to the third mood of the second figure [*Festino*], as follows: 'it is not the case that there is nature, natural motion derives from nature; therefore it is not the case that there is natural motion.'

From an immediate effect, I maintain, we argue both constructively and destructively, but from a mediate effect, [we argue only] destructively, as is obvious from a simple revision of the foregoing examples and their maxims.

*3.2.11. *From a Final Cause.*[84] An end is that for the sake of which other things are or come to be[85] (*cuius gratia fiunt alia vel aliqua et sunt*). Some ends are *per se*, others *per accidens*, but the arguments may be understood as arising from an end *per se*. Moreover, some ends are inherent (*intra*), others extraneous (*extra*). An inherent end is the form of a thing; an extraneous end is that for the sake of which a thing comes to be — e.g., it is for the sake of health that medicine comes to be. Thus we argue from an inherent end just as from a form, since they are the same.[86]

---

[82] Several times in the *Metaphysics* — e.g., 983a30, 984a27, 988a33, 994a5, 1064a12.

[83] Cf. Boethius's example of an argument from an efficient cause in *De diff. top.* (*P.L.*, 64.1189C): "human society is natural, but human society gave rise to justice; therefore justice is natural," and Boethius's more restricted version of the accompanying maxim: "Those things whose efficient causes are natural are themselves natural." In Sherwood's reduction the question-begging phrase 'that gives rise to justice' might better have been omitted.

[84] Cf. Boethius, *De diff. top.* (*P.L.*, 64.1189D).

[85] Cf. Aristotle, *Met.*, 994b9: "The wherefor is an end, and an end of the sort which is not for the sake of something else, but for the sake of which other things are." Also 996a20ff: "anything good in itself or by its own nature is an end and serves to explain things only in the sense that it is for its sake that other things are or come to be . . ."

[86] See p. 85.

We argue from an extraneous end constructively, as follows: 'all health is good; therefore medicine is good.' Maxim: *A thing whose end is good is good as a whole.* This reduces to the third mood of the first figure [*Darii*], as follows: 'all health is good, medicine is a condition of health (*Potio antecedit sanitati*); therefore medicine is good.' We argue similarly with the word 'evil'; for *a thing whose end is evil is itself evil.* Hence we argue destructively also, as follows: 'health is not evil; therefore medicine is not evil.' But this does not follow: 'there is medicine; therefore there is health,' nor does the reverse.

We argue from a fully realized thing to its end just as we argue from an end[87] (*A finito autem finis argumentatur sicut a fine*). (Notice, however, that we do not argue quite so properly from a fully realized thing, or from what depends on the matter,[88] or from what is defined,[89] as from an end, or from the matter, [or from the definition,] since [strictly speaking] we argue from things better known to what is less well known, and not vice versa. These grounds are to be understood on that basis.)[90] As for the remainder (*Iuxta reliquos*), the arguments from a fully realized thing are obvious on the basis of a simple revision of the examples and maxims for the arguments from an end.

The arguments from causes are called arguments from the concomitants of substance because they limit one another[91] (*Dicuntur autem loci a concomitantibus substantiam a causis, quia sese diffiniunt*).

---

[87] Sherwood seems to have in mind arguments such as this: 'a just man is an asset to the community; therefore justice is an asset to the community.'

[88] See p. 85.

[89] See p. 73.

[90] It is unlikely that Sherwood intends this remark to apply only to the grounds actually cited. But it is not clear whether it is intended to apply to the secondary arguments in the case of *every* ground considered so far, since this criterion — "from things better known to what is less well known" — is itself far from clear. Cf. Aristotle, *Analytica posteriora* (hereafter cited as *An. post.*), 71b20: "the premisses of demonstrated knowledge must be true, primary, immediate, *better known than* and prior to the conclusion . . ."

[91] I cannot make good sense of this explanation — "because they limit (or define) one another." Perhaps 'they' is a pronoun for 'the four causes' rather than for 'the arguments from causes,' and it may make sense to say that the four causes limit or define one another as principles of explanation — i.e., we may be said to discover one of the four causes on the basis of establishing another one of them, or to define one in terms of the others. But what has this to do with the notion of concomitants of substance? We may, I suppose, define a given substance by its concomitants, but that is hardly relevant here. Perhaps the passage '*quia sese diffiniunt*' should be emended as '*quia esse diffiniunt*' and the emended passage translated as follows: "because they [like other concomitants of substance] set a limit to being." This seems to make some sense as applied to the four causes and also to be relevant

3.2.12. *From Generation.[92] Generation is the coming into being of anything whatever, whether substantial or accidental, as healing is moving into health. [65] (Every motion gets its name from its goal, as Aristotle declares in the fifth book of the *Physics,*[93] since it is proper that everything be named after its end, as he declares in the second book of the *De anima.*)[94]

We argue from generation both constructively and destructively, as follows: 'healing is good; therefore health is good.' Maxim: *What goes together with the generation with respect to the nature of what is generated goes together with what is generated.* This reduces to the third mood of the first figure [*Darii*], as follows: 'all healing is good, health is the goal of healing; therefore health is good.' Alternatively, in such a way that the middle has to do with the goal and is more evident (*Vel aliter, ut sit medium termini et evidentius*): 'every goal of healing (since healing is good) is good, health is a goal of healing;[95] therefore health is good.'

What is added to the middle in this case[96] is used [also] destructively by virtue of [another] maxim as follows: 'healing is not evil; therefore health is not evil.' Maxim: *What is separated from the generation with respect to the nature of what is generated does not go together with what is generated.* This reduces to the fourth mood of the first figure [*Ferio*], as follows: 'no healing is evil, health is the goal [of healing]; therefore health is not evil' — or by means of an addition, as above.[97]

We argue this way from what is generated on the basis of a simple revision of the [foregoing] arguments and their maxims.

---

as an explanation of the inclusion of the arguments from causes under the arguments from the concomitants of substance. The troublesome phrase 'sese diffiniunt' (or one closely related) occurs in similar contexts on pp. 91 and 92, however.

[92] Cf. Boethius, *De diff. top.* (*P.L.,* 64.1190A).

[93] 224b7: "it is the goal rather than the starting-point of motion that gives its name to a particular process of change. Thus 'perishing' is change *to not-being,* though it is also true that that which perishes changes *from being;* and 'becoming' is change *to being,* though it is also change from not-being."

[94] 416b22: "it is right to call things after the ends they realize . . ."

[95] Here, and frequently in the remainder of this chapter, the text does not spell out portions of examples that are merely repetitions of other portions. The Latin for this minor premise is '*Sanitas est terminus etc.*' All instances of '*etc.*' used in this way are spelled out in the translation.

[96] I.e., the subordinate premiss 'since healing is good.'

[97] I.e., 'no goal of healing (since healing is good) is evil, health is a goal of healing; therefore health is not evil.'

*3.2.13. *From Corruption.* Corruption is the passing of anything out of being into nonbeing.

We argue from corruption constructively, as follows: 'the corruption of health is not good; therefore health is good.' Maxim: *What is separated from*[98] *the corruption with respect to the nature of what is corrupted goes together with what is corrupted.* This reduces to the third mood of the first figure [*Darii*], as follows: 'everything corrupted by the corruption of health ([since the corruption of health] is not good) is good (*omne corruptum cum corruptione sanitatis non bona est bonum*),[99] health is corrupted [by the corruption of health]; therefore health is good.'

Destructively, as follows: 'the corruption of health is evil; therefore health is not evil.' Maxim: *What goes together with the corruption with respect to the nature of what is corrupted is separated from what is corrupted.* This reduces to the fourth mood of the first figure [*Ferio*], as follows: 'nothing corrupted by the corruption of health (since the corruption of health is evil) is evil, health is corrupted [by the corruption of health]; therefore health is not evil.'

We argue from what is corrupted on the basis of a simple revision of the [foregoing] examples and maxims.

If someone objects that arguments from these grounds do not follow because generation and corruption are not simultaneous with their end results (*termini*), for while healing is, health is not ([and therefore is] neither good nor evil), then we must point out that [66] the end results are not taken simply to be supposita in a state of real being [100] (*non sumuntur termini i.e. supposita entitati rei simpliciter*).

Finally, [arguments from generation and from corruption] are called [arguments] from the concomitants of substance because motion of

---

[98] Reading '*non removetur*' as '*removetur.*'

[99] Reading '*omne corruptum corruptione sanitatis, cum corruptio sanitatis sit non bona, est bonum*' for the passage as given in parentheses.

[100] Sherwood's point seems to be that considerations of simultaneity of process and end result are not relevant to the foregoing arguments and maxims because they are concerned not with this particular (healing) process and its particular end result but with the (healing) process and its end result *generally*. Part of what makes Sherwood's explanation difficult is the Latin of this passage, which seems confused. Outside the context of supposition theory (as presented in Chapter Five) the word '*supposita*' is usually used to refer to individual primary substances underlying all modifications.

that kind and the end result of such motion limit each other [101] (*quia motus et motus terminus secundum quod huiusmodi sese diffiniunt*).

3.2.14. *From Uses.*[102] We can argue constructively from a use (a use being an operation by means of some instrument, such as riding a horse) — e.g., 'riding is good; therefore a horse is good.' Maxim: *What goes together with a use insofar as it is a use goes together with that of which it is the use.* This reduces to the third mood of the first figure [*Darii*] as follows: 'all riding is good, a horse is for riding; therefore a horse is good.' (The solution of the argument 'riding is [a kind of] moving; therefore a horse is [a kind of] moving' (*equitare est agere. Ergo equus est agere*) is clear: '[a kind of] moving' does not apply to riding insofar as it is a use, but to riding as such.)

Destructively, as follows: 'riding is not good; therefore a horse is not good.' Maxim: *What is separated from a use insofar as it is a use is separated from that of which it is the use.* The reduction of this to the fourth mood of the first figure [*Ferio*] is clear. (The solution of the objection 'riding is not good (supposing the horse is sleepy); nevertheless a horse is good' is also clear: terms are understood either simply or together with a reduplication, as follows: 'riding is not good insofar as it is a use (*equitare non est bonum, quando est*); therefore a horse is not good,' which follows correctly.[103])

We argue similarly from what is used — i.e., the instrument — on the basis of a simple revision of the maxims.

Suppose someone objects that an argument from a use is the same as an argument from an effect.[104] Then we must point out that in one sense that is true — viz., insofar as riding is associated with (*comparatur ad*) the principle of moving by means of a horse. On the other

---

[101] The difficulty here centers around the phrase '*sese diffiniunt*,' as in the explanation of the classification of the arguments from causes. See n. 91, this chapter.

[102] Cf. Boethius, *De diff. top.* (*P.L.*, 64.1190A–B).

[103] A reduplication is a phrase attached to the subject of a proposition and containing a "reduplicative expression" such as 'insofar as,' 'to the extent that' ('*inquantum*,' '*secundum quod*,' etc.). Sherwood makes use of this notion in a different connection in Chapter Five, p. 112. On reduplication generally see the *Tractatus de exponibilibus* attributed to Peter of Spain (in Joseph Patrick Mullally, *The Summulae Logicales of Peter of Spain*, especially pp. 110–115). The reduplication in Sherwood's example here seems incomplete at least, and possibly also mistaken — i.e., '*quando est*' for '*inquantum usus est.*' But even after such an emendation his reply to this objection seems too general; it differs in no essential way from his solution to the fallacious argument in the preceding paragraph.

[104] See p. 87.

hand, insofar as riding is associated merely with a horse and its use the objection is not true.

Use and instrument accompany each other in definition [105] (*Et concomitantur usus et instrumentum sese in diffinitione*).

*3.2.15. *From Associated Accidents.*[106] Those accidents are said to be associated (*communiter*) which [A] happen at the same time necessarily, or which [B] frequently accompany each other. From [A] we argue both constructively and destructively; from [B] likewise, but with probability (*probabiliter*).[107] For example, 'a wise man commits no crime; therefore a wise man will not repent.' Maxim: *If one associated accident is separated from anything, the remaining ones are separated [from it] also.* Let this be reduced to the fourth mood of the first figure [*Ferio*], as follows: 'no one who does no wrong will repent, a wise man is one who does no wrong; therefore [67] a wise man will not repent.'[108] Since the maxim is probable, the argument is probable also.

3.3. Catalogue of Arguments from Intrinsic Grounds

Now the number of intrinsic grounds is apparent. There are three arguments from substance (together with their correlatives),[109] besides the arguments from genus and from species, plus ten from part and from whole, plus four from causes (together with their correspondents), plus the two from generation and from corruption and a third from use (together with their correlatives), plus one from associated accidents, which is the twenty-third.

---

[105] See n. 91 and n. 101, this chapter. Evidently this sentence, like the similar sentences on pp. 88 and 91, is meant to explain the inclusion of arguments from use under arguments from the concomitants of substance. It seems possible also to read this sentence as 'use and instrument are defined in terms of each other,' but that less literal reading seems no better (or worse) as an explanation of the classification.

[106] Cf. Boethius, *De diff. top.* (*P.L.*, 64.1190B).

[107] For the sake of clarity, clauses have been rearranged and identifying letters introduced in these first two sentences.

[108] Notice the incompleteness of this discussion. Only the fourth of the four cases distinguished above is considered in detail. Moreover, Sherwood does not introduce as many cases initially as might be, and frequently were, distinguished in this connection. Cf. Abelard, *Dialectica* (ed. De Rijk, pp. 437–438); Peter of Spain, *Sum. log.* (ed. Bocheński, pp. 52–53).

[109] The correlatives (or, in the case of causes, the correspondents) are the subordinate arguments. E.g., the arguments "from what is defined," "from what bears the form," "from an instrument."

4. *ARGUMENTS FROM EXTRINSIC GROUNDS [110]

We have yet to consider arguments from extrinsic grounds. Now an argument is from an extrinsic ground when the middle lies outside the subject or the predicate of the [dialectical] problem [111] (*cum medium est extra extremum problematum*). Arguments of this type are divided into arguments from authority or from judicious opinion (*a rei iudicio*) (which is the same thing), from likeness, from the superior, from the inferior, from opposites, from proportion,[112] and from transposition.[113]

4.1. Miscellaneous Arguments from Extrinsic Grounds

*4.1.1. *From Authority.*[114] Since authority considered as a dialectical ground consists in something that is said, it comes first from the logician's point of view [115] (*Est autem locus ab auctoritate primus quoad logicum, cum consistat in dicere*); for authority, properly so called, is the confirmed opinion of some wise man or, alternatively, a saying worthy of imitation (*sententia ymitatione digna*). 'Authority' is being used broadly here, however, in the sense of a judgment, or something said by several wise men (*Sumitur tamen hic communiter ut et iudicium, ut dicatur dictum plurium sapientium*).

We argue from authority constructively, as follows: 'the astronomers say that the heavens are revolving (*celum esse volubile*); therefore the heavens are revolving.' Maxim: [*What is said*] *by many insofar as they are wise men* [116] *is not to be contradicted.* Let this be reduced to the third mood of the first figure [*Darii*], as follows: 'everything said by the astronomers to be revolving is revolving, the heavens are said by the astronomers to be revolving (since the astronomers say that the heavens are revolving); therefore the heavens are revolving.'

Destructively, as follows: 'Aristotle does not mention more than four

---

[110] Cf. Boethius, *De diff. top.* (*P.L.*, 64.1190B–1192B).

[111] See n. 11, this chapter.

[112] Reading '*proportione*' for '*propositione*'; see p. 96.

[113] What is called "transposition" here is called "transumption" when it is discussed on p. 99 and in n. 145.

[114] Cf. Boethius, *De diff. top.* (*P.L.*, 64.1190C); also Aristotle, *Topics*, Bk. I, Ch. 14 (105a35ff).

[115] Because logic is a sermocinal science (see p. 21), primarily concerned with what takes place in language.

[116] This proviso seems designed to prevent arguments from misplaced authority, appeals to the opinions of experts regarding matters outside their field. Thus Peter of Spain defines authority as "the judgment of a wise man in his own science" (*Sum. log.*, ed. Bocheński, p. 55).

causes; therefore there are no more than four causes.' The maxim is the same as above.[117] Let this be reduced to the fourth mood of the first figure [*Ferio*], as follows: 'no things said by Aristotle not to be are, more causes than four are said by Aristotle not to be (since Aristotle says that there are no more than four causes);[118] therefore there are no more causes than four.'

4.1.2. *From Likeness.*[119] Likeness (*Similitudo*) is oneness in quality.

We argue from likeness (*a simili*) [constructively] as follows: 'Socrates is white and Plato is like Socrates; therefore Plato is white.' Maxim: *Of things that are alike,*[120] *a like judgment* [*is to be made*]. This reduces [68] to the third mood of the first figure [*Darii*], as follows: 'everyone who is like Socrates (since he is white) is white, Plato is like Socrates (since Socrates is white);[121] therefore Plato is white.'

Likewise destructively, as follows: 'in like manner, quantity is neither in Socrates nor in Plato, but quantity is not in Socrates; therefore quantity is not in Plato'[122] (*Destructive similiter sic: similiter non inest quantitas Sorti nec etiam Platoni. Sed Sorti non inest quantitas. Ergo Platoni non inest quantitas*). The maxim is the one above. Let this be reduced to the fourth mood of the first figure [*Ferio*], as follows: 'no one in whom quantity is not, such as Socrates (since quantity is not in Socrates), is one in whom quantity is; Plato is one in whom in like

---

[117] Since the appeal is to the authority of Aristotle alone, the maxim cannot be quite the same.

[118] Note that this differs from the premiss in the original example, which makes the weaker claim that Aristotle does *not* say that there *are* more than four causes.

[119] Cf. Boethius, *De diff. top.* (*P.L.*, 64.1190C–D).

[120] If the example is to be accepted, the things in question must be alike in every respect, must share every quality. That requirement seems not only false in the case of the example but absurd generally. Perhaps Sherwood intended to treat this as a merely probable argument (see p. 92). In any case, his treatment of this ground differs from the tradition established by Boethius, which is well represented in the example given by Peter of Spain: "The ability to laugh belongs to a man in the same way as the ability to whinny belongs to a horse, but the ability to laugh is a property [as opposed, say, to an accident] of a man; therefore the ability to whinny is a property of a horse" (*Sum. log.*, ed. Bocheński, p. 54).

[121] The insertion of this subordinate premiss here must be a mistake.

[122] This example is confusing, and the accompanying reduction compounds the confusion. It seems just possible that something like the following is intended: 'if quantity is not in Socrates, then, since Socrates and Plato are alike, quantity is not in Plato.' This emended version retains at least part of the confusion of the original, however, since the premiss 'quantity is not in Socrates' seems obviously false unless Socrates (as well as Plato) is being used here (unexpectedly) as an example of a long-dead individual, one that *now* lacks quantity. (Cf. example on p. 82 – 'Socrates is everywhere'; also on p. 76 – 'a man is not a quantity.')

manner [quantity is not]; therefore quantity is not in Plato' (*nulli cui non inest quantitas ut Sorti, cum Sorti non insit quantitas, inest quantitas. Plato est illud, cui similiter etc. Ergo Platoni non inest quantitas*).

However, the noun 'likeness' is [also] used broadly so as to include unity in any disposition whatever.[123] Thus this is an argument from likeness: 'Socrates and Plato are equal, and Socrates is two cubits[124] (*est bicubitus*); therefore Plato is two cubits'; and so is this: 'Socrates is as much a man as Plato (*eque est Sortes homo ut Plato*), but Socrates is a man; therefore Plato is a man.'

4.1.3. *From the Superior.*[125] The superior (*maius*) is what exceeds something else in quantity or in power.

We argue from the superior destructively only, as follows: 'a king cannot take the castle by storm; therefore neither [can] a knight.' Maxim: *What does not go together with something with which it seems [to go together] the more does not go together with something with which [it seems to go together] the less.* Let this be reduced to the fourth mood of the first figure [*Ferio*], as follows: 'no one inferior to a king (since a king cannot take the castle by storm) can take the castle by storm, a knight is inferior [to a king]; therefore a knight cannot [take the castle by storm].'

Suppose someone offers the following in opposition to this kind of argument: 'an elephant cannot pass through the enemy lines; therefore a man cannot' — or 'a priest cannot take a wife; therefore neither can an acolyte.' Then it must be declared that all sophistical arguments of this type are to be solved on the basis of a correct understanding of the nature of the superior and the inferior; for it must be understood that the kind of superior from which we argue is one whose superiority is such as to aid the thing in relation to which it is superior to take on the predicate in question[126] (*Intelligendum enim argumentari a maiori,*

---

[123] Cf. Boethius, *De diff. top.*, *loc. cit.*: "likeness consists either in quality or in quantity, but in quantity it is named 'equality,' in quality, 'likeness.'"

[124] An unnecessarily confusing example in view of the facts that all quantity was denied to Socrates and Plato in the preceding paragraph and that two cubits ordinarily equal only about three feet.

[125] Cf. Boethius, *De diff. top.* (*P.L.*, 64.1190D–1191A).

[126] I.e., an elephant's superior size and strength are not qualities that enhance its chance of slipping through battle lines, whereas the superior military force under the command of a king is the sort of quality that does enhance his chances of taking a castle by storm.

cuius maioritas adiuvaret unus, cui comparatur ad predicatum recipiendum).

4.1.4. *From the Inferior.[127] The inferior is what is exceeded in some quantity or power.

We argue constructively from the inferior, as follows: 'a knight can take the castle by storm; therefore a king [can] too.' Maxim: *What goes together with something with which it seems [to go together] the less goes together with something with which [it seems to go together] the more.* This reduces to the third mood of the first figure [*Darii*], as follows: 'everyone superior to a knight (since a knight can take the castle by storm) can take the castle by storm, a king is superior [to a knight]; therefore a king can [take the castle by storm].'

There are objections to this argument like those to the one preceding, and the objections are similarly resolved.

4.1.5. *From Proportion.[128] [69] A proportion is a certain relation (*habitudo*) among things of the same genus. Proportionality, however, is likeness of proportions.[129] But a proportion is here taken [to hold] among things of different genera, such as man and whiteness. For the following is an argument from proportion: 'as man[130] is to substance, so whiteness is to quality; but man is a species of substance; therefore whiteness is a species of quality.' Maxim: *From proportions a proportional judgment is inferred* (*arguitur*).

We argue from proportion in the following way as well: 'as the master of a ship (*rector navis*) is to the ship, so the master of a school (*rector scole*) is to the school; but the master of a ship is not chosen by lot; therefore the master of a school is not [chosen by lot].' The maxim is the one above. This reduces to the fourth mood of the first figure [*Ferio*], as follows: 'no one proportionate to the master of a ship (since a ship's master is not chosen by lot but by skill) is chosen by lot, the master of a school is proportionate [to the master of a ship]; therefore the master of a school is not chosen by lot but by skill.'

---

[127] Cf. Boethius, *De diff. top.* (*P.L.*, 64.1191A).

[128] Cf. Boethius, *De diff. top.* (*P.L.*, 64.1191A–B).

[129] McKeon's "Glossary" in *Selections*, p. 484: "PROPORTIO, 'proportion' (in modern usage 'ratio'), a certain order between two terms, as a proportion between arithmetical quantities is called a relation (*habitudo*) or order between equal or unequal numbers. PROPORTIONALITAS, 'proportionality' (in modern usage 'proportion'), a certain order or likeness between two proportions, that is, proportionality is a proportion of proportions."

[130] Reading '*homo*' for '*corpus.*'

This kind of argument differs from the argument from likeness because this kind depends on what state a thing is in while the other depends on what a thing is [131] (*hic fit per habere, ille autem per esse*).

4.2. *Arguments from Opposites [132]

4.2.1. *From Contrary Opposites.[133] Next are the arguments from opposites, and first of all from contraries. Contraries are naturally suited to occur in connection with the same thing successively (*regressive*) but not simultaneously.

We argue from contraries destructively, as follows: 'Socrates is white; therefore Socrates is not black.' Maxim: *If one contrary is in a thing, the other is not.* This reduces to the fourth mood of the first figure [*Ferio*], as follows: 'no one who is white is black, Socrates is white; therefore Socrates is not black.'

We do not argue constructively from contraries except from exhaustive (*immediatis*) contraries and in case the subject continues to be (*cum constantia subiecti*). For example: 'Socrates is not healthy, and he exists (*Sortes non est sanus et est*); therefore he is ill.' Maxim: *If one exhaustive contrary is not in a thing, then the other is, provided that the subject exists.* Its reduction [to *Darii*] is clear: 'every existing man who is not healthy is ill, Socrates is [an existing] man [who is not healthy]; therefore Socrates is ill.'

4.2.2. *From Privative Opposites.[134] We argue from privative opposites [135] destructively, as follows: 'Socrates is blind; therefore Socrates is not sighted.' Maxim: *If one privative opposite is in a thing, the other is not.*

We do not argue constructively, however, unless the subject continues to be and is one of those existing things in which the other privative opposite ought to be [136] (*nisi cum constantia subiecti et ipsis*

---

[131] Cf. Boethius, *De diff. top.* (*P.L.*, 64.1191A–B): "This kind of argument differs from that drawn from things that are alike, since in that case one thing is compared to any other thing, while in the argument from proportion, it is not the likeness of things but a certain comparison of their condition."

[132] Cf. Boethius, *De diff. top.* (*P.L.*, 64.1191B–C).

[133] Cf. Boethius, *De diff. top.* (*P.L.*, 64.1191C).

[134] Cf. Boethius, *De diff. top.* (*P.L.*, 64.1191C).

[135] On the place of the notion of privation in the theory of opposites, see Aristotle, *Met.*, Bk. X, Ch. 4 (1055a33–b29); also Bk. V, Ch. 22 (1022b22ff).

[136] Cf. Aristotle's third sense of 'privation,' *Met.*, Bk. V, Ch. 22 (1022b27): "We speak of 'privation' . . . (3) If, though it would naturally have the attribute, and when it would naturally have it, it has it not; for blindness is a privation, but one is

existentibus, in quo alterum debeat inesse). For example: 'Socrates is not blind, and Socrates exists, and [70] this is a time at which he ought to be either blind or sighted; therefore Socrates is sighted.' Maxim: *If one privative opposite is not in a thing, the other is, provided that the subject exists and the time is determinate.*

4.2.3. *From Contradictory Opposites.*[137] We argue from contradictory opposites constructively, as follows: 'man is risible; therefore non-man is not risible.' Maxim: *If one contradictory is predicated of another contradictory, the opposite of the first is also predicated of the opposite of the second*[138] (*si contradictorium de contradictorio, et reliquum de reliquo*).[139] Let this be reduced to the third mood of the first figure [*Darii*], as follows: 'every contradictory opposite of man (since man is risible) is not risible, non-man is a contradictory opposite of man; therefore non-man is not risible.'

In the case of non-convertibles, however, we argue the other way around — e.g., since immobile (*non moveri*) is higher than inanimate (*non animare*) but animate is higher than mobile, [we argue] destructively on the basis of this ordering (*ordine destructive*), as follows: 'immobility (*non moveri*) is not a property[140] of what is inanimate; therefore mobility is not a property of what is animate.' Maxim: *If one contradictory is separated from another contradictory, the opposite of the first is also separated from the opposite of the second.* This reduces to the fourth mood of the first figure [*Ferio*], as follows: 'nothing contradictory to immobility (since immobility is [not] a property of what is inanimate) is a property of what is animate, mobility is contradictory [to immobility]; therefore mobility is not a property of what is animate.'

4.2.4. *From Mutually Related Opposites.*[141] We argue from mutually related opposites (*a relative oppositis*) constructively, as follows: 'a

---

not 'blind' at any and every age, but only if one has not sight at the age at which one would naturally have it . . .''

[137] Cf. Boethius, *De diff. top.* (*P.L.*, 64.1191D–1192A).

[138] Of course the maxim does not hold in the unrestricted form in which it is stated, but, as the beginning of the next paragraph shows, this first maxim is intended to cover only cases involving *convertible* terms, such as 'man' and 'risible.' (See n. 56, this chapter.)

[139] The maxims from this point onward are extremely elliptical in the Latin, and the English versions are generally much more fully spelled out.

[140] Not a "property," as risibility is of man, but merely an "accident" of some inanimate entities (as well as of some animate entities).

[141] Cf. Boethius, *De diff. top.* (*P.L.*, 64.1191D).

father is a begetter; therefore a son is begotten.' Maxim: *If one mutually related opposite is predicated of another mutually related opposite, the opposite of the first is also predicated of the opposite of the second.* This is syllogized [142] as follows: 'everything mutually related to a father (since a father is a begetter) is begotten, a son is mutually related [to a father]; therefore a son is begotten.'

We argue destructively as follows: 'a master is not a model; therefore a servant is not a copy.' Maxim: *If one mutually related opposite is separated from another mutually related opposite, the opposite of the first is also separated from the opposite of the second.* This is syllogized as follows: 'nothing mutually related to a master (since a master is not a model) is a copy, a servant is mutually related [to a master]; therefore a servant is not a copy.'

Although proportion plays a part in (*concomitatur*) these methods of arguing, they are not arguments from proportion,[143] but arguments by virtue of opposition.

4.3. *From Transumption [144]

Transumption is translation from the less known to the better known.[145] This occurs either in connection with terms — e.g., from the noun 'anthropos' to [71] the noun 'man' — or in connection with things — e.g., from justice in other things to justice in a republic.[146] For it may happen that a thing is better known in one [context] or under one property than in another [context] or under another [property].

We argue from transumption constructively, as follows: "justice in a republic is desirable; therefore justice in other things is desirable.' Maxim: *What goes together with something more evident as such*

---

[142] Note the shift from 'reduced' to 'syllogized' and the omission of mood and figure identification. Perhaps the awkwardness of the attempts at rigid reduction prompted the change, which is adhered to through the remainder of the chapter.

[143] See pp. 96–97.

[144] See Boethius, *De diff. top.* (*P.L.*, 64.1192A–B).

[145] See n. 113, this chapter. Cf. Quintilian, *Institutiones Oratoriae*, 3.6.46: "metalepsis, which we variously call 'translation,' 'transumption,' and 'transposition' . . ."; cf. *ibid.*, 8.6.37; also John of Salisbury, *Metalogicon*, Bk. I, Ch. 16 (tr. McGarry, p. 50). In Quintilian the notion is narrower than in its use here in a logical context. Cf. p. 135 below where Sherwood uses 'transumptively' in the narrower sense.

[146] This is, of course, the "transumption" carried out by Socrates in the *Republic*. Boethius uses this example, attributing it to Socrates (*De diff. top.* (*P.L.*, 64.1192A–B)).

(planiori secundum se) goes together with something less evident. This is syllogized as follows: 'all justice in a republic is desirable, justice in other things is either justice in a republic or of the same nature; therefore justice in other things is desirable.'

Again, [destructively, as follows:] 'no man is an ass; therefore an anthropos is not an ass.' Maxim: *What is separated from something more evident as such is separated from something less evident.* This is syllogized by the addition of 'an anthropos is a man.'

Transumption is called an extrinsic ground because the middle under one name (or under one property) is extrinsic to the middle under another name (or property).

5. *ARGUMENTS FROM MEDIATE GROUNDS [147]

We have yet to consider mediate grounds (*loci medii*), which are so called because the middle is taken to be partly in and partly outside one or the other of the extremes [of the conclusion].[148] Thus 'just' is partly in 'justice' (*quod ergo est iustum est partim in hoc, quod est iustitia*) (since they share in signification and also in utterance) and partly outside it (which is clear since neither is predicated of the other).

Now there are three mediate grounds — viz., from coordinates, from grammatically related forms, and from division.[149]

5.1. *From Coordinates [150]

[Those words] are called coordinates [151] (*coniugata*) that are under the same signification as under a yoke — i.e., [on the one hand] denominative, subsumed, or concrete, and [on the other hand] principal or abstract (*ut denominativum sive sumptum sive concretum et principale sive abstractum*) — e.g., 'white,' 'whiteness'; 'just,' 'justice.'[152]

---

[147] Cf. Boethius, *De diff. top.* (*P.L.*, 64.1192B–1194A).

[148] Cf. p. 104.

[149] The first two grounds are listed in the reverse order in the text.

[150] Cf. Boethius, *De diff. top.* (*P.L.*, 64.1192B–C).

[151] See Aristotle, *Topics*, Bk. II, Ch. 9 (114a26–114b5), where coordinates and grammatically related forms are considered together.

[152] This division between denominative and principal forms has its source in Aristotle's discussion of paronyms in *Cat.*, Ch. 8 (10a27ff): "These, then, that we have mentioned are *qualities*, while things called paronymously because of these or called in some other way from them are *qualified*. Now in most cases, indeed in practically all, things are called paronymously, as the pale man from paleness, the grammatical from grammar, the just from justice and so on." The semantics of denominatives, or paronyms, was a favorite topic among dialecticians of the

We argue from coordinates constructively, as follows: 'a just man (*iustus*) is good (*bonus*); therefore justice is good' (*bona*). Maxim: *If one coordinate is predicated of another coordinate, then a coordinate of the first is also predicated of a coordinate of the second.*[153] This is syllogized as follows: 'everything denominative from justice (since justice is good) is good, what is just is denominative [from justice]; therefore what is just is good.'

Destructively, as follows: 'justice is not a vice; therefore what is just is not vicious.' Maxim: *If one coordinate is separated from another coordinate, then a coordinate of the first is also separated from a coordinate of the second.* This is syllogized as follows: 'nothing denominative from justice (since justice is not a vice) is vicious, what is just is denominative [from justice]; therefore what is just is not vicious.'

Suppose someone offers the following in opposition to this method of arguing: 'seated is a white man (*sedens est albus*); therefore sitting (*sessio*) is whiteness.' Then we must point out that we argue only from coordinates that are [72] of the same genus and are related to each other *per se* (*et per se ad invicem se habentibus*), as in the examples above.

5.2. *From Grammatically Related Forms[154]

A grammatically related form [in this context] is the inflection of a noun or adjective into an adverb (*casus ex inflexio nominis in adverbium*)[155] – e.g., 'just,' 'justly.'[156]

Suppose the problem is whether what is done justly is done well. We argue constructively, as follows: 'what is just is good; therefore what is done justly is done well.' Maxim: *If one grammatically related form is predicated of another grammatically related form, the form related to the first is also predicated of the form related to the second.* This is syl-

---

eleventh century according to St. Anselm (1033–1109) at the end of his dialogue on denominatives, *De grammatico.*

[153] Thus not only '*iustus*' and '*iustitia*' are coordinates, but also '*bonus*' and '*bona.*' Part of what is meant by calling the latter a pair of coordinates is, of course, absent in English, where there is no grammatical distinction between the first occurrence of 'good' and the second, but it may be said that these two occurrences of 'good' are "yoked under the same signification" rather than *identical* in meaning, since the word 'good' is used in two different but closely related senses in these two predications.

[154] Cf. Boethius, *De diff. top.* (*P.L.*, 64.1192B–C).

[155] Reading '*est*' for '*ex.*'

[156] See n. 151, this chapter. On '*casus*,' see n. 11, Chapter One.

logized as follows: "everything done in accordance with a grammatical form related to 'just' (since what is just is good) is done well, what is done justly is done in accordance with a grammatical form related to 'just'; therefore what is done justly is done well."

A further problem: is what is done justly done viciously? This may be answered negatively (*destruatur*) as follows: 'what is just is not vicious; therefore what is done justly is not done viciously.' Maxim: *If one grammatically related form is absent from (absit) another grammatically related form, the form related to the first is absent from the form related to the second.* This is syllogized as follows: "nothing done in accordance with a grammatical form related to 'just' (since what is just is not vicious) is done viciously, what is done justly is done in accordance with a grammatical form related to 'just'; therefore what is done justly is not done viciously."

If someone objects here as above [in connection with the argument from coordinates], let it be resolved in like fashion.

5.3. *From Division [157]

Division, as Boethius says, is the distribution of a genus into its proximate species;[158] and it is also taken in the sense of a distribution of something general into what is less general — e.g., of an utterance into its significations.[159] Sometimes this is done by means of negation, sometimes without it. Again, it is sometimes done in connection with the subject, sometimes in connection with the predicate.

[It is done] without negation [in connection with the predicate] as follows: 'Socrates is either healthy or ill, and he is not healthy; therefore he is ill.' Maxim: *If one member of a division is separated from some-*

---

[157] Cf. Boethius, *De diff. top.* (*P.L.*, 64.1192C–1194A).

[158] See his *Liber de divisione* (*P.L.*, 64.877): "The word 'division' is used in several ways; for there is the division of a genus into species; and it is division as well when a whole is divided into its proper parts; and there is another division when an utterance signifying many things is separated into its proper significations. . . ."

[159] See pp. 103–104, where Sherwood's example makes it clear that he has in mind here the kind of utterance that, like 'dog,' does have several distinct significations. (The Latin word '*canis*' was used not only in the ordinary sense of the English word 'dog,' but also for a constellation — *Canis maior* — and for a kind of shark, the "dog-fish.") Still, there is something peculiar about the notion that the word '*canis*' is related to these distinct significations as a genus is to its species. Notice that this sense of 'division' is present in Boethius (n. 158 above), and may have little or nothing to do with the notion of signification Sherwood presents at the beginning of the next chapter, where he is far less indebted to well-established traditions.

thing, the other goes together with it. This is syllogized in the following way: 'everything that is either healthy or ill and is not healthy is ill, Socrates is either healthy or ill and is not healthy; therefore Socrates is ill.'

[The same is done] by means of negation as follows: 'Socrates is either running or not running, and he is not running; therefore he is not running.' The maxim is the one above.

If someone objects that this is Begging the Original Issue,[160] then let the following be said: In one sense [of 'not running'] the conclusion is taken to be asserting not-running of Socrates, and in another sense [the last] part of the premiss is taken to be denying running of Socrates, so that (since running has been denied and the division thus completed) we may infer not-running [of Socrates][161] (*alia intentione sumit conclusionem, quia intentione asserere non currere Sorti et alia partem premisse, quia intentione removendi currere a Sorte, ut hoc remoto et divisione perfecta inferatur non currere*).

[We argue] from division in connection with the subject as follows: 'animal is on the one hand rational, on the other, nonrational; *simpliciter*, both rational and nonrational run; therefore, [73] *simpliciter*, animal runs.'[162] Maxim: *What goes together simpliciter with the members of a division goes together simpliciter with what is divided.* This is syllogized as follows: 'everything [the division] of which is into rational and nonrational (since, *simpliciter*, both rational and nonrational run) runs *simpliciter*; animal is something the division of which is into rational and nonrational; therefore, *simpliciter*, animal runs.'

[We argue] similarly from the division of an utterance into its significations,[163] as follows: 'a dog [is either] an animal capable of barking [or something that is not an animal capable of barking] (*Canis animal latrabile, etc.*); *simpliciter*, both what is capable of barking and what is not capable of barking is a substance; therefore, *simpliciter*, a dog is

---

[160] See pp. 157–159.

[161] The Latin is not so clear as it might be, but the sense is plain enough. Sherwood is pointing out that this is *not* an instance of *petitio principii* if it is read as follows: 'Socrates is either running, or not-running, but he is not running; therefore he is not-running.'

[162] The point of the '*simpliciter*' seems to be to prevent anyone's reading this example as having to do with particular rational and nonrational animals and their actual running here and now. Cf. the doctrine of simple supposition in the next chapter.

[163] See n. 159, this chapter.

a substance.' The maxim is the one above, and this is syllogized as above.

Finally, it is apparent that the middle is partly within and partly outside [one extreme or the other] in the two [i.e., constructive and destructive] kinds of the first [argument from mediate grounds], while in the remaining [arguments] the middle is within[164] (*Patet etiam partim medium esse intra et partim extra in duobus modis prime, in secundis autem est medium intra*).

---

[164] Cf. p. 100. This is an obscure passage. If the translation with its emendations is accurate, Sherwood seems to be claiming that only the arguments from coordinates satisfy his original definition of arguments from mediate grounds and that the arguments from grammatically related forms and from division are more suitably classified as arguments from intrinsic grounds. There may be some reason for including the arguments from division among those from intrinsic grounds, but there seems to be no such reason for distinguishing the first and second kinds of arguments in this group. Moreover, there seems to be no reason for Sherwood's treating the latter two kinds as arguments from mediate grounds only to classify them otherwise without explanation at the end of the chapter. Perhaps the principal difficulty in this passage (and in much of the chapter) is the notion of the middle as something inside, outside, or partly inside and partly outside the extremes. Evidently the notion is related, though not very closely, to Aristotle's discussion in, e.g., *An. pr.*, Bk. I, Ch. 4 (25b31ff): "When three terms are so related to one another that the last is wholly contained in the middle and the middle is wholly contained in or excluded from the first, the extremes must admit of perfect syllogism. By 'middle term' I mean that which both is contained in another and contains another in itself, and which is the middle by its position also; and by 'extremes' (a) that which is contained in another, and (b) that in which another is contained."

CHAPTER FIVE

Properties of Terms

1. SIGNIFICATION, SUPPOSITION, COPULATION, AND APPELLATION[1]

There are four properties of terms that we intend to distinguish now, since an understanding of them will contribute to the understanding of the term and thus to the understanding of the statement and the proposition. These properties are signification, supposition, copulation, and appellation.

Signification, then, is a presentation of the form of something to the understanding[2] (*presentatio alicuius forme ad intellectum*). Supposition, however, is an ordering of the understanding of something under something else (*ordinatio alicuius intellectus sub alio*); and copulation is an ordering of the understanding of something over something else (*ordinatio alicuius intellectus supra alium*).[3]

Note that 'supposition' and 'copulation,' like many names of this sort, are used in two ways: either with respect to an actual occurrence (*secundum actum*) or with respect to the capacity for such an occurrence (*secundum habitum*). The above definitions of supposition and copulation are with respect to what they are in actual occurrence. With respect to what they are in capacity, however, supposition is called a signification of something as subsisting (*significatio alicuius ut subsistentis*) (for what is of that sort is naturally suited to be ordered under something else), and copulation is called a signification of something as adjoining (*adiacentis*) (for what is of that sort is naturally suited to be ordered over something else).

---

[1] On this chapter generally, see Kneale, *Development*, pp. 246–265.

[2] Cf. John of Salisbury, *Metalogicon* (tr. McGarry), pp. 125–128 and 134, for passages illustrating the twelfth-century background of this doctrine of signification and of the (then implicit) distinction between signification and other properties of terms.

[3] These initial definitions seem unnecessarily vague and play no important part in the remainder of the chapter. Supposition is discussed in detail in the sections immediately following. On copulation see pp. 120–122. Cf. also the somewhat different definitions of supposition, copulation, and appellation on p. 122.

Appellation, finally, is the present correct application (*presens con-venientia*)[4] of a term — i.e., the property with respect to which what the term signifies can be [truly] said of something through the use of the verb 'is.'[5]

From these [definitions] it is clear that there is signification[6] in every word or part of speech, whereas there is supposition only in a substantive name, or a pronoun, or a substantive word[7] (for these signify a thing as subsisting and capable of being ordered under something else). There is copulation, however, in all adjectives, participles, and verbs. Finally, there is appellation in all substantives, adjectives, and participles, but not in pronouns (since they do not signify a form, but only a substance)[8] and not in verbs (since a verb does not signify something that [74] is attached [to something else] by means of the substantive verb,[9] because if it did so [the verb] would be beyond itself)[10] (*aliquid quod apponitur per verbum substantivum, quia sic esset extra ipsum*). Moreover, none of these three — supposition, copulation, appellation — is in the indeclinable parts of speech (since no indeclinable part signifies a substance or anything in a substance).[11]

Let us set signification aside and consider the other three properties.

---

[4] I.e., everything with which the term "goes together" (*convenit*) at the present time. See n. 73 and 74, this chapter.

[5] On appellation see p. 122.

[6] *G* has '*significatio non est*' (with no indication that the '*non*' is an emendation); '*significatio est*' in manuscript.

[7] By 'substantive word' (*dictio*) as distinct from 'substantive name' Sherwood probably means substantive expressions, such as definite descriptions — 'the father of the bride,' 'this man over here.'

[8] Note the discrepancy between this claim about pronouns and the claims on pp. 105 and 106 that signification is the presentation of a form and that every part of speech has signification. Cf. n. 11, this chapter.

[9] Viz., the verb 'to be.'

[10] The basis for this restriction is the traditional classification of the verb and the participle as distinct parts of speech, the participle "participating" in the characters of both the verb and the name (substantive or adjective). Evidently in 'Socrates is white' the adjective 'white' signifies something — whiteness — attached to something else and does so by means of the substantive verb, while in 'Socrates runs' the verb 'runs' does not by means of the substantive verb signify running as something attached to something else. As Aristotle and the medievals (including Sherwood) recognized, however, 'Socrates runs' may be analyzed into 'Socrates is running,' which does employ a participle and the substantive verb (see Chapter One, n. 25). Sherwood evidently would allow that in such a case the participle does signify by means of the substantive verb something attached to something else.

[11] On indeclinable parts and their signification see Chapter One, Section 7. As this sentence suggests, the supposition, copulation, and appellation of a term are functions of its signification. It is evidently for this reason that Sherwood believes

2. THE DIVISION OF SUPPOSITION

To begin with, [let us consider] supposition: first, as such; afterwards,[12] [with respect to] the rules given for it. And since we already have the definition, let us look at the division of it.[13]

Supposition, then, is on the one hand material, on the other hand formal. It is called material[14] when a word itself supposits either [A] for the very utterance itself or [B] for the word itself, composed of the utterance and the signification — as if we were to say [A] 'man is a monosyllable' or [B] 'man is a name.' It is formal when a word supposits what it signifies.

Formal supposition is divided into simple and personal supposition. It is simple[15] when a word supposits what it signifies *for* what it signifies[16] (*supponit significatum pro significato*), as in 'man is a species.' It is personal, however, when a word supposits what it signifies, but for a thing that is subordinate [to what it signifies], as in 'a man is running' (*homo currit*); for running is in man because of some individual[17] (*Cursus enim inest homini gratia alicuius singularis*).

---

that he can treat the four properties of terms without providing a specific treatment of signification.

[12] See pp. 117ff.

[13] Among several twelfth-century sources for the doctrine of supposition, the doctrine of univocation has many instructive parallels, in its "divisions" as well as in the central notion. See, e.g., the anonymous twelfth-century *Fallacie parvipontane* (ed. De Rijk, *Logica modernorum*, Vol. I), p. 562: "Univocation is the varied supposition of a name, the signification remaining the same; for although supposition varies, signification remains the same." The treatise goes on to discuss three kinds of univocation. The first includes *both* 'master' in 'master is a noun' and 'man' in 'man is a species.' The second includes *both* 'man' in 'man is the noblest of creatures' and 'pepper' in 'pepper is sold here and in Rome.' The third introduces the notions of ampliation and restriction. (See De Rijk, *Logica modernorum*, Vol. I, pp. 561–571 and 51–56.) Sherwood discusses these (or very similar) examples and introduces the notions of ampliation and restriction later in this chapter.

[14] Some insight into the origin of this division and its terminology may be found in John of Salisbury's *Metalogicon* (tr. McGarry), p. 175.

[15] Cf. John of Salisbury's *Metalogicon* (tr. McGarry), p. 119: "Our understanding at times looks directly at the simple essence of things, simply, as when it conceives of *man* as such, or *stone* as such, in which operation it is simple."

[16] It seems that the first occurrence of 'what it signifies' is intended to distinguish simple supposition (as a division of formal supposition) from the kind just discussed (material), in which a word supposited something other than what it signified. The second occurrence of 'what it signifies' indicates that in simple supposition the suppositum is *a form* which, on p. 105, was said to be the significatum of every word.

[17] The force of this observation might be made plainer by adopting the ordinarily unnatural translation 'man runs' (rather than 'a man is running') for the example '*homo currit.*'

There is also another division of formal supposition — viz., into common and discrete. Common supposition is that which occurs through a common term, as in 'a man is running'; discrete, that which occurs through a discrete term, as in 'Socrates is running' or 'that man is running'[18] (*ut Sortes currit vel iste*).

Note that both these divisions are completely exhaustive of what I call formal supposition; for every suppositing word is either common or discrete, and [every formally suppositing word] is taken either for the signified form (in which case it is simple supposition) or for a thing bearing the form (in which case, personal).

Personal supposition is divided as follows: on the one hand determinate, on the other hand confused. Confused supposition is divided into merely confused and distributive confused supposition, the latter being divided into mobile and immobile distributive confused supposition.

Personal supposition is determinate when the locution can be expounded by means of some single thing[19] (*exponi . . . per aliquod unum*), which is the case when the word supposits for some single thing, as when I say 'a man is running.' Therefore it can be true for anyone running.

[Personal supposition is] confused, on the other hand, when the word supposits for many, and distributive when it supposits for many in such a way as to supposit for any — e.g., the word 'man' when I say 'every man is an animal.' It is merely confused, [however, when it supposits as does] the word 'animal' [in that statement]. [Distributive confused supposition is] mobile when a descent can be made, as in the term 'man' in the example above.[20] It is immobile when a descent cannot

---

[18] Cf. p. 51.

[19] Expounding the locution seems tantamount to answering the question 'which one?' or attaching a namely-rider to a case of determinate supposition — 'a man, namely Socrates, is running.' Cf. Geach, *Reference*, p. 64.

[20] Sherwood's notion of a logical descent is quite stringent as compared, say, with Ockham's (see *Philosophical Writings*, tr. Boehner, pp. 71–74). It seems clear from this and other passages — e.g., pp. 109 and 119 — that Sherwood means by 'descent' a valid inference from an original proposition whose subject is a common term to a single singular proposition whose subject is a discrete term under the original common term in the "predicamental line." Thus where Ockham will descend from 'every man is running' to the exhaustive conjunction 'man$_1$ is running and man$_2$ is running and . . . and man$_n$ is running,' which Ockham seems to have considered equivalent to the original proposition, Sherwood's descent is unquestionably irreversible — 'therefore this man is running.' (Cf., however, his descent in the case of "distributive copulation," on p. 121.)

be made, [75] as here: 'only every man is running' (for one cannot infer 'therefore only Socrates is running').[21]

3. A DOUBT REGARDING THE DIVISION MOBILE/IMMOBILE

But it seems a descent can be made in every case of distributive supposition, for a word supposits distributively that supposits for many in such a way as to supposit for any; therefore a descent can be made to any. And it must be said that a descent *can* be made in every case of distributive supposition considered in itself [22] (*quantum est de se*); nevertheless, the descent can be impeded by means of an adjunct, as by means of the word 'only' in the example above.

4. *A DOUBT [REGARDING THE DIVISION MATERIAL/FORMAL]

There is some doubt (*Dubitatur*) regarding the first division of supposition, for it seems that [material and formal supposition] are not different ways of suppositing but rather of signifying, since signification is a presentation of the form of something to the understanding. Therefore, [where there is] a different presentation [there is] a different signification. Now when a word supposits materially it presents either itself or its utterance; but when it supposits formally it presents what it signifies. Therefore it presents something different; therefore it signifies something different.

This is not true, however, because words considered in themselves (*quantum de se est*) always present what they signify; and if they present their utterance they do so not in themselves but as a result of adjunction to a [certain] predicate. For one predicate is disposed to have reference to (*vult respicere*) only the utterance or the word but another to what is signified.[23] But this does not produce a different

---

[21] For a further discussion of "immobility," see p. 119 below. Cf. also Sherwood's *Syncategoremata*, where such examples are frequently discussed. Of course one cannot infer the exhaustive conjunction of singular propositions here, but in accordance with Ockham's notion of descent it seems correct to infer a proposition the subject of which is an exhaustive conjunction of discrete terms under the original common term. 'Only every man is running; therefore only man$_1$ and man$_2$ and . . . and man$_n$ are running.' As far as I know, Ockham does not, however, produce this result. Cf. Geach's discussion of "conjunctive supposition," *Reference*, p. 72.

[22] I.e., a case of distributive supposition that is not embedded in another syntactic context. Cf. Sherwood's remarks about supposition *de se*, or *secundum se*, pp. 130–131 below.

[23] E.g., the predicates '*est nomen*' and '*est species*' respectively, when attached to '*homo*.'

signification, for just as a word is a word before it is arranged [with other words] in an expression, so it has [its] signification beforehand, not as a result of being arranged together with something else.[24]

5. *A DOUBT [REGARDING THE RELATION BETWEEN THE DIVISIONS SIMPLE/PERSONAL AND COMMON/DISCRETE]

There is some doubt regarding [the relation between] the second and third divisions, for some maintain that the division into simple and personal is a division [only] of common supposition, since that difference does not occur within discrete supposition.[25] This is because it is never anything but personal, since in discrete supposition an individual is always supposited.

We must point out, however, that it is not the fact that an individual is supposited that produces personal supposition, but the fact that a thing bearing the form signified by the name is supposited, and this can occur in a proper name when it signifies a substance together with a quality.[26] Thus when I say 'Socrates is running' it is with respect to his real being (*respicitur pro sua re*); when I say 'Socrates is predicable of one only'[27] it is with respect to the form signified by the name.

6. *A DOUBT [REGARDING THE DIVISION SIMPLE/PERSONAL] [76]

There is likewise some doubt regarding the division into simple and personal supposition, for this division seems to produce equivocation,

---

[24] This sentence seems to contain a clue to the motivation behind supposition theory. The *definition* is supposed to provide the fixed signification — e.g., 'man' considered in itself always does or should present the form *mortal rational animal*. But there are countless legitimate uses of the word 'man' that cannot be explained if we are provided with no other account of its meaning than the simple, rigid signification presented in the definition. That supplementary account of the meaning of a term as a function of its various uses is provided in supposition theory.

[25] Peter of Spain divides supposition first into discrete and common, common supposition into natural and accidental, and accidental (common) supposition into simple and personal (*Sum. log.*, ed. Bocheński, p. 58), thus taking the position opposed here by Sherwood. Ockham, on the other hand, considers the division common/discrete to be a division only of *personal* supposition (*Summa logicae*, tr. Boehner in *Philosophical Writings*, p. 70).

[26] Priscian (*Inst. gram.*, 1.55) says that *every* name signifies a substance together with a quality. Cf. Abelard, *Dialectica* (ed. De Rijk), p. 93, lines 5–6. Sherwood's use of this doctrine to support the division of discrete (as well as common) supposition into simple and personal seems quite unusual, as does his arrangement of those divisions.

[27] See p. 114, on singular propositions "taken indefinitely." See also n. 69, this chapter.

since when a name supposits simply it presents to the understanding the form signified by the name, but when it supposits personally it presents a thing bearing the form.

We can respond to this just as to [the doubt regarding the division material/formal], or we can say that [in formal supposition a word] always supposits the same thing — viz., what it signifies — but in two ways: either *for* what it signifies (in which case it supposits simply) or for a thing signified [28] (in which case, personally).

7. *A NOTE ON THE THREE MODES OF SIMPLE SUPPOSITION

It should also be noted that simple supposition can occur in three ways, because there are three ways in which a word can be posited (*potest poni*) for its significatum [29] — [A] without any connection with things, or [B] for the significatum connected with things insofar as it is actually preserved in every single thing and is predicable of it, or [C] for the significatum connected with things insofar as it is related to anything generally, in an unfixed way, and is not identified with anything in a determinate way.

7.1. 'Man Is a Species'

The first mode occurs as follows: 'man is a species.' It is often said that this is manerial supposition, because ['man' here] supposits for the specific character in itself [30] (*suppositio manerialis, quia supponit pro ipsa manerie speciei*).

7.2. 'Man Is the Noblest of Creatures'

The second mode occurs as follows: 'man is the noblest of creatures.' This is unlike the preceding supposition since the predicate is not ascribed to the abstract species itself but to the species insofar as it is in things. Thus such a predicate can be ascribed to any of the things belonging to the species insofar as it shares the nature of the species; and so one can say 'this man, insofar as he is a man, is the noblest of creatures.' This [mode of simple] supposition occurs wherever the things belonging to a species acquire some predicate only with [that kind of] redupli-

---

[28] This must be elliptical for 'or for a thing bearing the form signified.'

[29] The translation 'what it signifies' for '*significatum*' seems clumsy in the context of this note and is therefore temporarily abandoned.

[30] G has '*suppositio materialis*'; '*suppositio manerialis*' in manuscript. Cf. Kneale, *Development*, p. 255. On the notion of *maneries*, apparently a twelfth-century innovation, see John of Salisbury, *Metalogicon* (tr. McGarry), p. 116; also De Rijk, *Logica modernorum*, Vol. I, p. 139.

cation of the species and in no other way. Thus if I say 'man is an animal,' ['man' has] *personal* supposition, since the individuals acquire this predication without reduplication of the species.[31]

7.3. 'Pepper Is Sold Here and in Rome'

The third mode occurs as follows: 'pepper is sold here and in Rome.' This supposition is unlike the first, since the species itself is not sold, and unlike the second, since 'pepper' is not used here [for everything belonging to the species] insofar as it is pepper. Instead, 'pepper' here supposits for its significatum [as] related in a general, unfixed way to the things belonging to it. Thus it is often said that this is unfixed (*vaga*) supposition. [A term having this third mode of simple supposition] supposits for a species insofar as [it does so] through individuals belonging to the species, but undesignated (*non signata*). It is as if someone asked 'what animal is useful for plowing?' and one answered 'the ox'; in answering one does not intend to speak of a particular ox, but simply of *ox*. Likewise, whoever says 'pepper [77] is sold here and in Rome' does not intend to speak of some pepper in particular, but simply of *pepper*.[32]

8. *QUESTION: [WHETHER SIMPLE SUPPOSITION IS A PROPERTY OF PREDICATES]

Suppose someone asks whether or not a word that occurs as a predicate predicates a form only and thus stands simply.[33] It seems it does

---

[31] If 'man is the noblest of creatures' were a case of personal supposition, the following descent would be valid: 'therefore this man is the noblest of creatures, or that man . . .' The reduplication of the species is the insertion of the phrase 'insofar as he is a man,' which validates the descent to 'therefore this man, insofar as he is a man, is the noblest of creatures, and that man . . .' But the need for reduplication in the descent marks this as simple rather than personal. Ockham attacks this kind of treatment of this example and claims that 'man' here has *personal* supposition but that the proposition is false "taken literally as it stands" (*de virtute sermonis*) (*Summa logicae*, 1.66).

[33] Ockham likewise opposes the treatment of this example as an instance of simple supposition. Again he thinks the statement is false "taken literally as it stands" and that it must be analyzed into 'pepper is sold here and pepper is sold in Rome,' as a result of which analysis it becomes interpretable as two distinct instances of *personal* supposition (*Summa logicae*, 1.66). (For another treatment of this example see n. 13, this chapter.) Sherwood's point in the ox example might be described (anachronistically) as an observation that not only mass nouns such as 'pepper' but also count nouns such as 'ox' admit of "unfixed supposition" — e.g., 'The ox has been domesticated for centuries in Europe and Asia.'

[33] Reading '*et sic stet simpliciter*' for '*et si stet simpliciter*.' Sherwood sometimes, as here, uses 'stands' where he ordinarily uses 'supposits'; cf. pp. 116 and 117.

not, for if that were the case one would truly say 'some species is a man' just as one says 'man is a species.'

We must point out, however, that this does not follow; for *every* name signifies a form only — not separately (*absolute*), but insofar as it informs a substance bearing it and thus in some way makes the substance intelligible. I maintain, therefore, that a name *in the predicate* makes a form intelligible to the extent to which it is the form of the substance of the subject;[34] and so, since that substance is understood in the subject, it is not understood a second time in the predicate. So the predicate does predicate (*dicit*) a form only.

Nevertheless, it is not true to say 'a species is a man,' since the word 'man' signifies humanity to the extent to which it is the form of [certain] individuals.[35] Therefore it is not predicated of the species, since it is not the form of the substance of the species. Note, moreover, that because a predicate is said to be in a subject, a form is always predicated to the extent to which it inheres in and informs [the substance of the subject].

A subject, on the other hand, sometimes supposits a form separately and sometimes does not, depending on what the predicate demands, in accordance with the following [principle]: *Subjects are of such sorts as the predicates may have allowed (talia sunt subiecta, qualia permiserint predicata).*

(It should be pointed out, however, that the authoritative opinion of Boethius is as follows: *Predicates are of such sorts as the subjects may have allowed, and not vice versa*; and his example in the same passage is 'a man is just; God is just,' the word 'just' being taken differently in the two cases, depending on what the subject demands.[36])

9. SIMPLE SUPPOSITION AND SINGULAR, INDEFINITE, OR PARTICULAR PROPOSITIONS

It seems that propositions such as 'man is a species' are singular since the subject is the proper name of a species.

---

[34] Making a form intelligible by supplying an instantiation of it.

[35] Cf. p. 131.

[36] At this point Grabmann supplies a reference to Boethius's *Introductio ad syllogismos categoricos* (Migne, *P.L.*, 64.768). Neither the principle as Sherwood cites it nor the examples he quotes appear there. In 768B Boethius does indicate that a singular subject has a certain effect over its predicate, and he introduces the verb '*suppono*' in an interesting way: "in singular propositions an individual is always supposited by the predicate term, as in 'Socrates is wise,' for Socrates is singular and individual . . ." The nearest approach to the principle in column 768 appears

We must point out, however, that this is not the case, for a common name is common just because it is a proper [name] of one form, and so to be proper in that respect is to be common. But if such propositions are indefinite, then it seems [A] they can be made definite through the application of a sign[37] — for example, one might say "some man is a species." And this seems right also because [B] particular and indefinite propositions are interchangeable.[38]

With respect to [A] we must point out that that procedure is to be understood [as applying only] to an indefinite proposition in which the supposition is particular;[39] in this case, however, it is applied to an indefinite proposition taken indefinitely (*indefinite sumpta*). Singular propositions taken indefinitely[40] are also of this sort, [78] as are certain singulars taken universally — e.g., 'all (*totus*) Socrates is white.'[41]

With respect to [B] we must point out that particular and indefinite propositions are interchangeable not as regards the truth but as regards syllogistic procedure. This is because anything that follows [syllogistically] from some proposition together with an indefinite proposition follows from that same proposition together with a particular proposition, and vice versa.

10. °QUESTION: [WHETHER EXPRESSIONS SUCH AS 'THIS PLANT GROWS HERE AND IN MY GARDEN' CAN BE TRUE]

It is also asked whether these expressions can be true: [A] 'this plant grows here and in my garden';[42] [B] 'woman, who has damned us, has also saved us'[43] (*mulier que damnavit salvavit*). And it seems they can-

---

at 768C: "A subject is that which supports the expression (*dictionem*) of the predicate . . ." There is at least a suggestion of the example Sherwood cites in 780C–781A, but the passage is badly confused, and it is difficult to know exactly what Boethius intended to illustrate by means of it.

[37] I.e., a word such as 'every,' 'some,' or 'no.' See pp. 28–29.

[38] See p. 30.

[39] I.e., *determinate* supposition, as in the indefinite proposition 'a man is running' (*homo currit*).

[40] See p. 110 — 'Socrates is predicable of one thing only.'

[41] Cf. Sherwood's *Syncategoremata* (ed. O'Donnell), p. 54.

[42] Cf. Ockham's discussion of this example (*Philosophical Writings*, tr. Boehner, pp. 70–71).

[43] An allusion to Eve, on the one hand, and Mary on the other. Cf. John of Salisbury, *Metalogicon* (tr. McGarry), pp. 124–125: "However, there are also relations that are general, which, if they are to remain true and are to be properly understood, cannot be tied down to some particular subject. Examples of such

not. This is because a demonstrative pronoun [as in [A]] indicates (*demonstrat*) something under such conditions as can be seen with one's own eyes; therefore it points out an individual. But [A] is false regarding an individual plant; therefore it is absolutely (*simpliciter*) false. Likewise, the purpose of a relative pronoun [as in [B]] is to bind the succeeding part of the sentence to the same suppositum with which the sentence began (*Item relativum ad hoc est, ut continet sequentem sermonem ad idem suppositum, de quo processit sermo*). But [if 'woman' is replaced] by the name of one and the same suppositum,[44] [B] is false (*Sed de nomine eiusdem suppositi est secundus sermo falsus*); therefore it is absolutely false.

In response to this we must point out that the term occurring with the demonstrative pronoun in [A] and the term occurring with the relative pronoun in [B] are suppositing simply in the third mode[45] (*in hiis sermonibus est demonstratio simpliciter et similiter relatio tertio modo*); for [the demonstrative pronoun] in [A] indicates *plant* insofar as it is related to more than one individual, which is also the way the relative pronoun functions in [B].

11. *A DOUBT [REGARDING THE DIVISION DETERMINATE/CONFUSED]

There is some doubt regarding the division of personal into determinate and confused supposition, for it seems that when I say 'a man is running' the term 'man' does not supposit determinately, since [A] the

---

are provided by the sayings: 'A woman both saved us and damned us'; 'A tree both bore the cause of our death, and that of our life'; 'The green leaves, which the freezing north wind bears off, the mild west wind restores.' In the instances which I have just mentioned, I believe that these relative expressions should not be conceived as descending to the specific and pointing out some particular person or thing, but rather that they should be understood as remaining general . . ." Cf. also *Secundum Magistrum Petrum Sententie*, XXIV (*Abaelardiana inedita*, ed. Minio-Paluello, p. 118): "When we say 'woman, who has damned us, has also saved us,' [we are speaking] not of one and the same person but of the nature of the female sex . . . for Eve damned us and Mary saved us. Neither does Priscian treat a construction of this kind as related to a person — viz., where he discusses the word '*sui.*'" (Cf. Priscian, *Inst. gram.*, 12.1–3.)

[44] I.e., both 'Eve, who has damned us, has saved us' and 'Mary, who has damned us, has saved us' are false, and, *a fortiori*, so are all other such instances.

[45] Although '*suppositio*' is not used in this passage, the reference is obviously to the third mode of simple supposition (see p. 112). The phrase '*demonstratio simpliciter*' is usually used to designate a logical demonstration which simply confirms a truth as distinguished from argumentative demonstrations such as *ad hominem* or *ad contradicendum*. Here, however, it must be a variant of '*demonstratio simplex*,' which might be read 'simple supposition in connection with a demonstrative

proposition is indefinite, and [B] it is uncertain for whom the term 'man' supposits. Therefore it supposits [A] indefinitely and [B] uncertainly; therefore indeterminately.

In response we must point out that there is a respect in which determinateness is opposed to uncertainty, and in that respect we can say that 'man' supposits indeterminately, as the objection has it. There is, however, another respect in which determinateness is opposed to plurality (*multitudini*) and whatever is single is determinate; and in this respect 'man' does stand determinately. For the sentence 'a man is running' means that the predicate is in some one individual, not in many, even though the predicate *is* in many — for [a sentence] sometimes *permits* this but does not *signify* it[46] (*Vis enim huius sermonis vult predicatum inesse alicui uni et non multis, licet predicatum insit multis. Hoc enim patitur aliquando, sed non significat*). And therefore 'man' supposits determinately, not confusedly, since by virtue of the expression (*de virtute locutionis*)[47] [in which it occurs] it supposits for one and not for many.

12. *A NOTE ON CONFUSED SUPPOSITION

Note that a word has confused supposition whenever it supposits either for many things or for one thing taken repeatedly with the capacity [79] of keeping one and the same thing [constant] for many things (*pro uno multotiens sumpto cum potentia ibidem tenendi pro multis*) — e.g., 'if everyone sees only Socrates, then every man sees a man.' Here [the second occurrence of] 'man' does not supposit for many things, but for one thing taken repeatedly with the capacity of keeping one and the same thing [constant] for many things. Understand, more-

---

pronoun.' Aquinas distinguishes *demonstratio simplex* and *demonstratio personalis* on the same grounds as are used to distinguish simple and personal supposition (see Deferrari, *Lexicon*, "*demonstratio*").

[46] Cf. Peter of Spain, *Sum. log.* (ed. Bocheński), p. 59: "Determinate supposition is the acceptance of a common term taken indefinitely or together with a particular sign — e.g., 'a man is running,' or 'some man is running.' Each of these is called determinate since the term 'man' in each of them may legitimately supposit for every man, not running as well as running. Nevertheless these propositions are true for any single running man; for it is one thing to supposit and another to render an expression true for something in predicates (*reddere locutionem veram pro aliquo in praedicatis*). In fact, as has been said, the term 'man' supposits for all [men], not running as well as running, but it renders the expression true only for one that is running."

[47] Cf. Ockham's frequent use of '*de virtute sermonis*' in *Summa logicae* (ed. Boehner), 1.66ff. Cf. n. 31, this chapter.

over, that [that occurrence of] the word 'man' supposits virtually as many times as [there are individuals] that can be descended to in the subject (*ly hominem totiens supponit virtualiter, quotiens potest descendi in subiecto*).[48] It is therefore important to know that every case of confused supposition is the result of (*omnis confusio est ab*) some distribution or something having the force of distribution.[49]

But suppose someone says 'every man sees Socrates.' Here 'Socrates,' although it supposits repeatedly, cannot be picked out separately (*cerni*) for many things. Therefore it does not stand confusedly.[50]

13. RULES REGARDING CONFUSED AND DETERMINATE SUPPOSITION [51]

13.1. *Rule I

It is, then, considered to be a rule that [A] *every distributive sign confuses the term immediately adjoining it confusedly and distributively*. But [B] *an affirmative [distributive] sign confuses the remote term merely confusedly*. Finally, [C] *a negative [distributive]*[52] *sign confuses the remote term confusedly and distributively*.

---

[48] The example under discussion is '*si quilibet videat Sortem tantum, tunc omnis homo videt hominem*,' and Sherwood's first remark on this example begins "*Hic homo non supponit pro multis . . .*" This wording might suggest that he intends this remark to apply to the *subject* of the consequent rather than the inflected form '*hominem*,' but the kind of confused supposition he describes can scarcely be considered a property of the subject. In his second remark on this example he does talk explicitly about the occurrence of '*hominem*,' but notice that when he does so he introduces it with '*ly.*' This medieval particle (frequently written '*li*') seems simply to indicate that one is referring to a particular *occurrence* of the word in question, so that '*ly*' (or '*li*') might be viewed as a precursor of quotation marks employed to distinguish between "mentioning" a word and "using" it. Thus in discussing the example in the paragraph just below Sherwood says "*hic Sortes licet supponit multotiens . . .*" although the proper name occurs in the example in the inflected form '*Sortem.*'

The second remark on the example seems to mean that we may infer from 'if everyone sees only Socrates, then every man sees a man' that if everyone sees only Socrates, then Plato sees a man, and Aristotle sees a man, and so on, and that in each conjunct in this descent 'man' supposits once for Socrates, now as the object of Plato's sight, now as the object of Aristotle's, and so on.

[49] The word 'not,' for example, although it is not a distributive sign, may count as "something having the force of distribution." See n. 52, this chapter.

[50] I.e., it does not supposit confusedly (see n. 33, this chapter) but determinately (and discretely). (This paragraph occurs in the original between the second and third sentences of the preceding paragraph.)

[51] On these rules, see Kneale, *Development*, pp. 258–259.

[52] Part A of Rule I and the two examples following part C support the interpolation of the word 'distributive' in part C. Sherwood may, however, intend part C to

Thus this follows: 'no man is an ass; therefore no man is this ass.' But this does not follow: 'every man is an animal; therefore every man is this animal.'

13.2. *Rule II

An argument from merely confused supposition to distributive confused supposition does not follow.

Thus when every man sees only himself this does not follow: 'every man a man does not see; therefore every man does not see a man.'[53]

13.3. *Rule III

An argument from many cases of determinate supposition to one of determinate supposition does not follow, but [only] to one of confused supposition.

Thus when every man sees only himself this does not follow: 'a man is seen by Socrates, and by Plato (and so on with respect to [all] individual [men]); therefore a man is seen by every man.'[54] But this does follow: '. . . therefore by every man a man is seen,' for a distribution has force in a succeeding phrase but not in a preceding phrase (*in consequens et non in antecedens*).

13.4. *Rule IV

An argument from determinate supposition to distributive confused supposition does follow, but not from merely confused supposition.

Thus this does not follow: 'a man is not seen by Socrates (*hominem*

---

apply also to such negative signs as 'not' (*non*), since the predicate term of the particular negative — 'some man is not *a philosopher*' — would probably also be said to have distributive confused supposition. See also the conclusion of the inference illustrating Rule II, where an occurrence of 'not' is evidently taken to produce distributive confused supposition in the predicate term of a universal affirmative proposition.

[53] The premiss of this example — '*omnis homo hominem non videt*' —seems correctly analyzable as 'for every man there is at least one man whom he does not see,' and on that analysis the premiss is true under the stated assumption that every man sees only himself. The conclusion — '*omnis homo non videt hominem*' — is intended to be equivalent to 'no man sees a man,' as is clear from Sherwood's discussion of equipollent signs in Chapter One (p. 35). Thus the second occurrence of 'man' in the premiss has merely confused supposition while the second occurrence of 'man' in the conclusion has distributive confused supposition as the predicate of a universal negative proposition. (See Rule I, part C.)

[54] The premiss as it stands is a single proposition with what might be described as a conjunction of discrete terms in the predicate, but taken as it stands the premiss is false under the stated condition and the inference is valid. Evidently Sherwood intended a conjunction of propositions as the premiss — viz., 'a man is seen

non videt Sortes);[55] therefore Socrates does not see a man' — as if there is only one he might see (*ut si videat unum solum*). But this follows correctly: 'a man is seen by every man; therefore every man sees a man.'

13.5. *Rule V [80]

An argument from distributive confused supposition to determinate supposition does follow, but not from merely confused supposition.

Thus this follows: 'Socrates does not see a man; therefore a man is not seen by Socrates.'[56] But this does not: 'every man sees a man (e.g., every man sees only himself); therefore a man is seen by every man.'[57]

Sometimes, however, distribution remains immobile, as in 'not every man is running,' 'only every man is running,' and other cases of that sort. It is called immobile, however, not because we cannot *ascend* in the subject but because we cannot *descend*.[58] This is due to the fact that distribution is of the supposita themselves,[59] and therefore when we cannot descend to one of them[60] (*ad hoc*) it is a case of what is properly called immobile distribution.[61]

---

by Socrates, and a man is seen by Plato, and . . . ' — otherwise he would not even have his "many cases of determinate supposition" in the premiss.

[55] Here as elsewhere Latin active constructions must be translated into English passive constructions in order to avoid ambiguity.

[56] *G* has '*hominem videt Sortes*'; '*hominem non videt Sortes*' in manuscript.

[57] "In effect the fourth of the rules . . . provides that a doubly general proposition with an existential quantifier in front of a universal quantifier implies the corresponding doubly general proposition with quantifiers transposed, while the fifth rightly rejects the converse implication" (Kneale, *Development*, p. 259).

[58] On immobile distributive supposition and logical descent see p. 109. Sherwood's notion of a logical ascent is probably that of a valid inference from a single singular proposition whose subject is a discrete term to a proposition whose subject is a common term over that discrete term in the predicamental line. His remark and examples here are evidently intended to show that since logical ascent is possible in *some* of these cases — e.g., his first example here — it is the general impossibility of logical descent despite the occurrence of a universal sign that is the criterion of immobility. (In the first of these examples Ockham's notion of logical descent would produce 'it is not the case that every man is running; therefore either it is not the case that man_1 is running, or it is not the case that man_2 is running, or . . . or it is not the case that man_n is running,' where the alternation is exhaustive. But for Ockham this descent would indicate that 'man' in 'not every man is running' had *determinate* supposition. See *Philosophical Writings*, tr. Boehner, p. 71.)

[59] Since the discussion here is only of varieties of *personal* supposition, the supposita are the individuals of which a given common term may be truly predicated.

[60] I.e., despite the occurrence of a universal sign.

[61] Note that Sherwood is speaking of distribution, not of distributive supposition, and that he goes on to make similar remarks about (distributive) supposition in the next paragraph. Distribution does not seem to be a thoroughly distinct or care-

Supposition is called immobile for a similar reason, viz., that we cannot descend to the supposita; for supposition is for a suppositum.[62]

14. *COPULATION [63]

As to copulation, it should be known that none of the following divisions applies to it: [A] material/formal, [B] common/discrete, [C] simple/personal. The reasons are as follows: [64] [A] if a copulating word [65] is posited (*ponitur*) *materially* it is said to supposit and not to

---

fully developed notion in Sherwood's book, but Peter of Spain devotes an entire chapter (Tractatus XII) to "Distributions," beginning with the following definition: "Distribution is the multiplication of a common term accomplished by means of a universal sign — e.g., when one says 'every man is running,' the term 'man' is distributed or confused for any of its inferiors by means of the sign 'every,' and so there is multiplication there" (*Sum. log.*, ed. Bocheński, p. 112). (Incidentally, passages such as this contradict Geach's claim, on p. 63 of *Reference*, that "the expression 'distributed term' is in fact a muddled memory of the medieval '(*suppositio confusa et) distributiva.*'" The distinction between distribution and distributive supposition as well as the expression 'distributed term' are themselves medieval, though they do seem muddled.) I can see no clear difference between the notions of distribution and distributive supposition in Sherwood unless it is that distribution emphasizes considerations of syntax and distributive supposition has more to do with semantical considerations. But even that is not an especially clear difference.

[62] There may be some clue to Sherwood's basis for distinguishing distribution from distributive supposition in the fact that he says that distribution is *of* the supposita themselves (*ipsorum suppositorum*) whereas supposition is *for* a suppositum (*pro supposito*).

[63] On the nature of copulation cf. pp. 105–106 and 122. Sherwood's notion of copulation as a property of terms is obscure and apparently different from the notions of copulation discussed by other medieval logicians. Peter of Spain, for example, has nothing on copulation in his *Summulae logicales* except the following remark in the chapter on supposition: "Copulation is the acceptance of an adjectival term for something" (ed. Bocheński, p. 58), having said a few lines earlier that "substantival names are said to supposit, while adjectival names as well as verbs are said to copulate" (p. 57). Lambert of Auxerre defines copulation as "the acceptance of a term [as] representing a dependent thing" — i.e., not a substance — and says that adjectives never supposit but only copulate (in Prantl, *Geschichte*, 3.31.127). By the time Walter Burleigh wrote his *De puritate artis logicae tractatus longior* (hereafter cited as *De puritate artis logicae*) (between 1325 and 1328) copulation apparently had lost its connection with supposition theory and was defined simply as "the union or composition of a predicate with a subject" (Boehner ed., p. 54). Cf. Mullally on this notion and its probable source in Boethius and Abelard in his partial edition and translation of the *Summulae logicales* of Peter of Spain, pp. xliv–xlv.

[64] The order of explanations here is revised from the original order so as to conform to the order of the divisions in the preceding sentence.

[65] Evidently a copulating word is (a) the name of an accident, (b) a word joined to a subject term somehow, especially by means of an occurrence of 'is' or 'are,' the copula. But not every such word has copulation. E.g., "the last word in the sentence is 'white,'" where 'white' is a copulating word that has material supposition rather than copulation.

copulate; [B] every copulating word is the name of an accident, but every name of an accident is common; therefore no copulation is *discrete*; [C] every copulating word signifies in adjunction to a substantive (*in adiacentia ad substantivam*)[66] and thus is copulated *personally* [if at all].

We do, however, find the following divisions in copulation: determinate/confused (determinate as in 'a man is white,' confused as in 'every man is white'); merely confused/distributive confused (merely confused as in the last example, distributive confused as in 'no man is white'). Distributive confused copulation occurs in connection with signs distributive of the copulata, such as 'of every sort' (*qualislibet*), 'of every amount'[67] (*quantuslibet*), and the like. Note that signs of that kind distribute the copulata in respect of their substantives; it is for this reason that the kind of copulation they give rise to (*unde sua copulatio*) is distributive. On the other hand, their substantives have merely confused supposition.[68] For example, when I say 'a man of every sort is running' the copulation is distributed; I can therefore descend to the specific copulata (*copulata specialia*) as follows: 'a man of every sort is running; therefore a white man is running, and a black [man is running], (and so on).' But the word 'man' [in the premiss] supposits merely confusedly, since we cannot descend as follows: 'a man of every sort . . . therefore Socrates . . .'[69] A sign such as 'of every sort' signifies some accident and distributes it in respect of its substantive.[70]

---

[66] See p. 105. Reading *"substantivam"* for *"substantiam."*

[67] Just as '*quilibet*,' ordinarily translated 'anyone,' must frequently be translated 'everyone' when found in medieval texts, so here the ordinary translations 'of any sort whatever' and 'of any amount whatever' must be altered. See Sherwood's example of distributive copulation in this paragraph. Cf. his treatment of '*qualelibet*,' introduced as a sign distributive of copulata, in his *Syncategoremata* (ed. O'Donnell), pp. 55–56.

[68] "The copulata" are instances of the accident(s) signified by the copulating word(s); "their substantives" are the common terms occurring as subjects in connection with the copulating words. The individuals, or substances, are the supposita of the substantives, and the accidents said to inhere in them are the copulata of the copulating words. Since "distribution is of the supposita themselves" (p. 119), and since accidents do not occur except as inhering in individuals, distributive copulation must distribute the copulata as inhering in the supposita for which the substantive in the proposition is suppositing. Nevertheless, the substantive itself will have merely confused (rather than distributive confused) supposition in cases where the copulating word has distributive copulation. (This seems to be the gist of Sherwood's doctrine here.)

[69] On logical descent, see n. 20, this chapter. Here Sherwood refuses to take the discrete term 'Socrates' as naming a *sort* of man, but cf. p. 110.

[70] 'Of every sort' ('*qualislibet*') thus combines the roles of copulating word and

We also find immobile distributive copulation, [81] as in 'not every sort of . . .'

Note also that where the inference does not hold (*ubi non tenet processus*) from the supposition to a suppositum it does not hold from the copulation to a copulatum.[71]

15. *APPELLATION

We have yet to examine appellation, which has already been defined.[72]

The difference between it and supposition is clear from its definition — i.e., supposition is in a term insofar as it is under another, but appellation is in a term insofar as it is [truly] predicable of the things subordinate to it (*predicabilis de suis rebus*) through the use of the verb 'is.' [The difference between appellation] and copulation [is likewise clear from the definition of appellation], because copulation is never lacking in a term when it is as such capable of being ordered over something else (*et ad copulationem, quia ipsa nunquam, cum est secundum se ordinabilis supra aliud, [non] inest termino*).[73]

Accordingly some say[74] that a term serving as a subject (*ex parte*

---

distributive sign into one word in Latin although the roles are played by separate words in the English translation.

[71] A medieval note in the margin of the manuscript at this point reads: "He says this because the rules given for supposition on the preceding page [pp. 117–120] hold likewise for copulation." Whether or not those rules do hold for copulation, the passage does not seem to have the purpose assigned it in this note, since those rules govern inferences from one kind of supposition to another kind of supposition, not "from the supposition to a suppositum." That phrase is certainly ambiguous, but it does suggest the sort of inference involved in Sherwood's notion of descent. He may, then, be pointing out that descent is blocked in copulation just as in supposition, an interpretation rendered more plausible by the fact that this passage immediately follows his remarks on *immobile* distributive copulation.

[72] On p. 106.

[73] I have inserted the word '*non*' before '*inest termino*' because the sense of the passage seems to demand it. Without this interpolation the English would read "because copulation is never in a term when . . ." With this interpolation the passage presents the distinction between copulation and appellation as based on the fact that copulation is a permanent property of such terms as it belongs to at all whereas the question of whether or not a term has appellation depends on the present existence of individuals bearing the form signified by the term. On p. 106 copulation is said to occur in adjectives, participles, and *verbs* while appellation is a property only of adjectives, participles, and *substantives*. Evidently this distinction is intended to apply only to adjectives and participles.

[74] I do not know which of Sherwood's contemporaries or predecessors maintained this distinction. Walter Burleigh, whose book was written about eighty years *after* Sherwood's, says "just as supposition strictly speaking is a property of

subiecti) supposits and that it appellates when it serves as a predicate. And it is true that a term serving as a subject supposits in accordance with both definitions of supposition,[75] while a term serving as a predicate supposits [only] in accordance with the [second] definition of supposition [as a signification of something as subsisting] (*secundum habitualem suam diffinitionem*).

It is also true, however, that a term serving as a subject appellates the things subordinate to it, but not as a result of its being a subject. A term serving as a predicate, on the other hand, does appellate as a result of its being a predicate, [because a predicate] is related to its subject through some of the things subordinate to it, and in that capacity it appellates.

16. A RULE REGARDING SUPPOSITION AND APPELLATION

Notice that sometimes a suppositum of a term is something that exists and at other times something that does not exist. An appellatum, on the other hand, is simply something that exists. Thus a suppositum and an appellatum are sometimes the same and at other times not; and the following rule is given for the purpose of determining when they are and when they are not the same: *An unrestricted common term, having sufficient appellata and suppositing in connection with a present-tense verb that has no ampliating force, supposits only for those [things subordinate to it] that do exist.*[76]

16.1. "Unrestricted"

The reason for adding the word "unrestricted" is that if a common term is restricted it can supposit for something that does not exist — e.g., a man who has been [but is not now] is something that does not exist. Understand that to restrict something is, strictly speaking, to force it to exist in a smaller space than it is naturally suited for (*quam sue nature competit*). Because of its resemblance [to restriction in the strict

---

the subject in so far as it is related to the predicate, so appellation is a property of the predicate related to the subject or to what is subordinate" (*De puritate artis logicae*, ed. Boehner, p. 47).

[75] A medieval note in the margin of the manuscript at this point reads: "Given above at the beginning of the third folio before this one" — i.e., on p. 105.

[76] G has '*suppositiones*'; '*supponens*' in manuscript. Pp. 123–131 contain a detailed explanation and discussion of the various conditions laid down in this rule, as the inserted subsection headings will indicate. On this rule and Sherwood's explication of it, see Kneale, *Development*, pp. 260–262.

sense], a relative clause (*implicatio*)[77] is also called [restriction]. [Finally,] an adjectival word is likewise said to restrict a common term.[78]

Thus the word "unrestricted" here is to be understood [as ruling out those] three kinds of restriction and not [the kind that occurs] in connection with a verb. [A verb,] however, may sometimes restrict, as in 'a man runs.'[79] The term 'man' as such can supposit [82] for past, present, and future men, but here it is confined to present men by the verb in the present tense.[80]

16.2. "Having Sufficient Appellata"

The reason for adding the phrase "having sufficient appellata" is that if [a common term] does not have sufficient appellata it can supposit for something that does not exist. And notice that sufficient appellata amount to at least three; therefore if there are not that many appellata a term can supposit for something that does not exist — e.g., if there are only two men 'every man exists' is false.

---

[77] Reading '*implicatio*' for '*inplicatio*.' On this technical sense of the word see Sherwood's *Syncategoremata* (ed. O'Donnell), pp. 50–51.

[78] The text is unusually compressed here and quite possibly corrupt. At the beginning of the next paragraph Sherwood refers to three kinds of restriction, which are evidently supposed to have been introduced in this paragraph, and distinguishes them from a fourth. It seems highly plausible that the intended distinctions are analogous to those developed in Tractatus XI, "On Restrictions," in the *Summulae logicales* of Peter of Spain (ed. Bocheński, p. 104): "Restriction is the contraction of a common term from a greater to a lesser supposition . . . One kind of restriction occurs as a result of an [*adjectival*] *name*, as when someone says 'white man,' the term 'man' does not supposit for black men nor for those colored with any color in between [black and white], but is restricted to white men. A [second] kind occurs as a result of a *verb*, as when someone says 'a man runs,' the term 'man' supposits for, or is restricted [to], presently existing men. A [third] kind occurs as a result of a *participle*, as in 'a running man argues'; the term 'man' is restricted to running men. A [fourth] kind occurs as a result of a relative clause (*implicationem*), as when someone says 'a man who is white is running,' the relative clause 'who is white' restricts the term 'man' to white men (*restringit homines ad albos*)." Peter's second kind is explicitly treated by Sherwood in the next paragraph, and the fourth and first kinds seem to have been mentioned by name in this paragraph. If there *is* a third kind of restriction mentioned in this paragraph, I suppose it could be Peter's third kind, although the description of restriction "strictly speaking" more nearly resembles the kind of general description with which Peter begins his account.

[79] '*Homo currit*' is not translated as 'a man is running' here only in order to retain the distinction between restriction by a verb and restriction by a participle.

[80] Sherwood seems thus to have explained that "unrestricted" in the rule is intended only to rule out such restrictions as may occur within the subject term itself — 'a white man,' 'a running man,' 'a man who is white'; a *further* condition laid down in the rule is intended to cover the effect of *verbs* on supposition and appellation. (See Section 16.3 below.)

Proof: The sign 'every' is imposed for the purpose of distributing for the greatest plurality and the sign 'both' for the least. Therefore since the least plurality is in a pair, the sign 'both' distributes only for two. But the greater plurality is in a group of three or more; therefore the sign 'every' distributes for at least three.[81] Therefore, since in the example above there are two supposita existing and the sentence means (*et vult iste sermo*) that the predicate is in [at least] three, it means that it is in something that does not exist. And so 'every man exists' is false and its contradictory, 'some man does not exist,' is true. Therefore a man does not exist. But nonexistence is not predicated of something that exists; therefore 'man' supposits for something that does not exist.

But [suppose someone says that] on the contrary 'every animal exists' is true and therefore 'every man exists' is true, for the term 'animal' has enough appellata.

[In that case] we must point out that in the case [in which there are only two men] this does not follow: 'every animal exists; therefore every man exists,' because the term 'animal' does have sufficient appellata, and so supposits only for what exists, while 'man' does not, and so supposits for something that does not exist. And by the same reasoning this does not hold: 'a man does not exist; therefore an animal does not exist.'

But again, consider this counterargument: 'every animal is, every man is an animal; therefore every man is.'[82] The first premiss is true, and the second is necessary, since the genus is predicated of a species.

[In response to this] we must point out that the argument is not valid (*non valet*), for when one says 'every animal is' one predicates *actual* being (*esse actuale*) — i.e., existence. But when I say 'every man is an animal' *relational* being (*esse habituale*) is predicated, and insofar as it is necessary it has the force of this conditional: 'if it is a man it is an animal' (*Si homo est, animal est*). For when 'is' is placed as a kind of means between the extremes 'a man' and 'an animal' it declares an interrelation between the two (*dicit habitudinem mediam inter hec duo*).

---

[81] Cf. Sherwood's *Syncategoremata* (ed. O'Donnell), pp. 49–50, where he develops this point and cites Aristotle (*De caelo*, 268a16: "Of two things, or men, we say 'both,' but not 'all': three is the first number to which the term 'all' has been appropriated"). In the discussion in the *Syncategoremata* Sherwood drops the unfortunate example 'every man exists' in favor of 'every man is colored.'

[82] '*Omne animal est*' and '*omnis homo est*,' which have been translated above as 'every animal exists' and 'every man exists,' are translated otherwise here to suit the argument.

Thus it is clear that the signification of 'is' in the first proposition differs from that in the second. Therefore the conclusion 'every man is' does not follow.

Nevertheless it may seem that 'every man is' is true because Aristotle says that the principle of *dici de omni* applies whenever there is nothing . . . etc.[83] But [83] nothing is to be found under this subject . . . etc., since there exist only two men of whom the predicate is asserted. Therefore this is an instance of *dici de omni*.

But we must point out that the term 'man' [in our example] does supposit for a nonexistent man, and that therefore there is something nonexistent under the term, to which the predicate does not apply. Therefore this is not an instance of *dici de omni*.

16.3. "Suppositing in Connection with a Present-Tense Verb"

The reason for adding the phrase "suppositing in connection with a present-tense verb" is that if the common term were to supposit in connection with a past-tense or future-tense verb it could supposit for something that does not exist. 'A man has run,'[84] for example, is true for Caesar.

[In this connection] it is customary to call attention to the following rule: *A common term suppositing in connection with a past-tense verb supposits for present things as well as for past things; likewise a common term suppositing in connection with a future-tense verb supposits for present things as well as for future things.*[85]

But [suppose someone says that] on the contrary the verb through its consignification of time *restricts* what the term supposits, and therefore a past-tense verb restricts it to past things and a future-tense verb to future things.[86]

Then we must point out that sentences such as 'a man has run,'[87] in which a past-tense (or future-tense) verb is predicated, have two senses

---

[83] See Chapter One, n. 22.

[84] G has '*currit*'; '*cucurrit*' in manuscript. Cf. Kneale, *Development*, p. 261, n. 2.

[85] The immediate purpose of this rule and the accompanying explication of it is evidently to justify the use of 'could' rather than 'would' in the preceding paragraph — "it *could* supposit for something that does not exist. . . ."

[86] This objection acquires special force from Sherwood's admission (at the end of Section 16.1 above) that verbs do sometimes restrict supposition, and thus it also provides the opportunity for stipulating conditions under which such restriction does (or does not) occur.

[87] G has '*currit*'; '*cucurrit*' in manuscript.

(*sunt duplices*); for this sentence can be said to be either compounded or divided[88] (*dici compositus vel divisus*).

If compounded, it must be pronounced with continuity (*continue proferri*), and the continuity of the subject with the predicate signifies that the supposition [of the subject] must be strictly indicated (*discerni*) by the predicate.[89] In that case 'man' [in 'a man has run'] supposits for past [men] and not for present [men] except insofar as they are past.[90]

If divided, it must be pronounced with discontinuity (as in 'a man has run'),[91] and the discontinuity of the expression signifies that the supposition [of the subject] is not strictly indicated by the predicate.[92]

---

[88] Distinctions between compounded and divided sentences or compounded and divided senses of sentences underlie the well-known fallacies of composition and division (see pp. 140–144) and occur in several different contexts in medieval logic. (See, e.g., Paul of Pergula (d. 1451), *Tractatus de sensu composito et diviso*, ed. Brown; Bocheński, *History*, pp 184–187.) Sherwood's use of such a distinction here may be characterized as an attempt to specify the scope of a tense operator. Thus the *compounded* sense of 'a man has run' might be analyzed into 'it has been the case that there is at least one individual such that it is a man and it is running,' while the *divided* sense might be analyzed into 'there is at least one individual such that it is a man and it has been the case that it is running.' In these analyzed versions the phrase 'it has been the case that . . .' serves as a tense operator, making explicit "the consignification of time" in the past-tense verb 'has run.' The distinction between compounded and divided senses and the associated notion of the scope of various operators is of primary importance in Sherwood's *Syncategoremata*. Cf. also p. 130 below.

[89] Evidently a difference in intonation patterns marks the difference between compounded and divided senses, and since a *continuous* pattern marks the *compounded* sense and a *discontinuous* pattern marks the *divided* sense (see next paragraph), there is some suggestion that the character of the pattern gives rise to the designation of the sense.

[90] What does it mean to pronounce 'a man has run' ('*homo cucurrit*') "with continuity"? It seems it must mean at least to pronounce it without any pause or unusual stress — i.e., in the ordinary way. Sherwood appears to be claiming that it ought then to be understood in this sense: 'something that was a man (regardless of whether or not it still is so) has run'; or, disregarding the anachronistic mode of analysis: 'it has been the case that there is at least one individual such that it is a man and it is running.' Such an account of the ordinary sense of 'a man has run' does seem substantially correct.

[91] G has '*currit*'; '*cucurrit*' in manuscript. Of course a mere reiteration of the original sentence cannot help to make the distinction clear. It seems likely that some indication of stress, probably on the verb — '*homo* cucurrit' — has been omitted.

[92] It is difficult to see what might be meant by a discontinuous pronunciation of 'a man has run' other than a pronunciation involving a slight pause after 'man' and an unusual stress on 'has' (or on the first syllable of '*cucurrit*,' the syllable distinguishing this past-tense form from the present-tense '*currit*'). Perhaps the example is not well chosen for this purpose, but it does not seem that such an intonation pattern (in English or in Latin) would convey the speaker's intention to have his utterance of the sentence understood in its divided sense. The divided sense, as

That is how [this] rule is to be understood. Thus this does not follow: 'something white was seen by Socrates; therefore Socrates has seen something white,' as, for example, if a shield is white now but was black when it was seen by Socrates. I maintain that it does not follow if the premiss (*antecedens*) is divided. It does follow, however, if the premiss is compounded.[93]

And [the portion of this rule] having to do with a future-tense verb is to be understood as follows: A common term [suppositing in connection with a future-tense verb] with reference to [things existing] before [the time of utterance] supposits for present or future things through composition and division, but with reference to [things existing] after [the time of utterance it supposits] only for future things (*Et sic intelligendum est de verbo de futuro scilicet quod terminus communis ex parte ante supponit pro presentibus vel futuribus per compositionem et divisionem, ex parte autem post solum pro futuris*).[94]

Sherwood might have expressed it, is evidently this: 'something that is now a man has run'; or, 'there is at least one individual such that it is a man and it has been the case that it is running.' On *this* analysis, as Sherwood remarks, the past tense of the verb does *not* restrict the supposition of the subject to past individuals bearing the form signified by the subject. On the analysis of the sentence as *compounded*, the past tense of the verb does have a restrictive effect, but even in that case present individuals are included among the supposita of the subject insofar as they have acted in the past.

[93] The different senses of the premiss may be presented in this way (see n. 88, this chapter). Compounded: 'it has been the case that there is at least one individual such that it is white and it is seen by Socrates'; divided: 'there is at least one individual such that it is white and it has been the case that it is seen by Socrates.' The divided sense as presented here follows Sherwood's illustration of the newly painted shield, but his point could have been made as well on this analysis of the divided sense: 'there is at least one individual such that it has been the case that it is white and it has been the case that it is seen by Socrates.' The two periods of past time indicated in this analysis need not, of course, coincide.

[94] Among the crucial difficulties in this very difficult passage are the phrases '*ex parte ante*' and '*ex parte post*.' The interpretations suggested for them stem from their use in such technical medieval phrases as '*infinitus ex parte ante*' ('infinite with respect to what went before' — i.e., without beginning) and '*infinitus ex parte post*' ('infinite with respect to what will come after' — i.e., without end). Consider the example 'a man will stand on the moon.' The analyzed versions of the two senses may be presented as follows. Divided: 'there is at least one individual such that it is a man and it will be the case that it is standing on the moon'; compounded: 'it will be the case that there is at least one individual such that it is a man and it is standing on the moon.' The *ex parte ante* case seems to be associated with the divided sense and the *ex parte post* case with the compounded sense, but there are difficulties with these apparent associations. For one thing, the phrase "through composition and division" seems totally out of place, and no plausible emendation suggests itself. For another, the supposition in the *ex parte ante* case should evidently be only for present things, not "for present or future things," and the suppo-

16.4. "That Has No Ampliating Force"

The reason for adding the phrase "that has no ampliating force" is that if the verb is an ampliating verb the subject can supposit for something that does not exist. 'A man is praised,' for example, is true for Caesar. An ampliating verb is one that signifies a condition that can occur in something that does not exist[95] (*cuius res potest inesse non enti*).

But [suppose someone says that] on the contrary a verb *restricts* the supposition of a term. Therefore it does so either through its signification or through its consignification. If through its signification, then, assuming that [at least] three men exist,[96] 'every man is running' is true, which is false (*ergo tribus hominibus existentibus hec est vera: omnis homo currit. Quod falsum est.*).[97] If through its consignification, [84] it will not be through any [consignification] other than its consignification of time. Therefore every present-tense verb restricts [the supposition of the subject] to present things. Therefore when I say 'a man is praised' the term 'man' supposits [only] for present things.

[In response to this] we must point out that a verb does not restrict exclusively through its signification or through its consignification but

---

sition in the *ex parte post* case should be extended to present things insofar as they are future (on the model of the discussion of the compounded sense on p. 127). On the other hand, those apparent associations suggest another interpretation (tempting but evidently farfetched) for the phrases '*ex parte ante*' and '*ex parte post*,' stemming from the different *positions* of the temporal operator in the analyses supplied in the notes (but not in the text) — i.e., the common term ('man') occurs *ex parte ante* when it occurs *before* the temporal operator ('it will be the case that . . .') in the analysis and *ex parte post* when it occurs *after*. The difficulties are no doubt partly the result of a corrupt text, but the choice among possible emendations is not a clear one.

[95] On ampliation see Peter of Spain, *Sum. log.*, Tr. IX, "On Ampliations" (ed. Bocheński, pp. 100–101); Kneale, *Development*, pp. 261–262; De Rijk, *Logica modernorum*, Vol. I, pp. 567–571.

[96] See p. 124.

[97] The response to this objection on p. 130 below suggests that a line has been omitted from the Latin, which probably should be emended to read: *ergo tribus hominibus existentibus hec est vera:* [*omnis homo est; tribus hominibus autem currentibus:*] *omnis homo currit, quod falsum est.* In that case the translation would read: "then assuming that [at least] three men exist ['every man exists' is true; but assuming that (at least) three men are running] 'every man is running' is false." The objection, however, seems to make some sense as it stands. The possibility that verbs restrict supposition through their signification is taken up here only to be dismissed, and it seems to be dismissed in the passage as it stands because of the absurd consequence that the present-tense verb 'is running' would then restrict the supposition of 'man' in 'every man is running' to *running* men, thereby rendering this statement and all other affirmative categoricals analytically true — 'every (running) man is running.'

through both. Therefore a present-tense verb forces (*cogit*) a term to supposit[98] for those things in which the condition it signifies (*sua res*) can occur [at present]. Thus, since the condition signified by the verb 'is praised' occurs at present in things that do not exist, the verb will ampliate to the extent of including [within the supposition of 'man'] something that does not exist. (The verb 'can' and others like it[99] are to be similarly treated.)

Thus it is clear why (assuming [at least] three men exist) 'every man exists' is true, but (assuming [at least] three men are running) 'every man is running' is false. It is because 'to exist' (*ly esse*) cannot occur at present in things that do not exist but is actually in all things that do exist, while 'to run' cannot occur at present in things that [do exist but] are not running.[100]

When all these conditions are observed the suppositum will be the same as the appellatum.[101]

Or, putting it another way, if we want to speak strictly we say that a term supposits on its own (*de se*) for present things and if it supposits for other things it will be because of what is adjoined to it — i.e., an ampliating verb or a past-tense or future-tense verb. And the ampliation will not be the result exclusively of the signification or of the consignification [of the verb] but will occur by virtue of both.

Thus when I say 'a man is running,' 'man' supposits on its own for present [men] and is not drawn away from that supposition by the predicate (*ad predicatum*). But if someone says 'a man is running or can run,' the supposition [of 'man'] is already drawn away in the sense of what I call composition to [men] that do not exist.[102]

Therefore, speaking strictly, we must say that the verb 'can' and others like it ampliate the supposition of a term while the verb 'is

---

[98] *G* has '*suppositione*'; '*supponere*' in manuscript.

[99] I.e., other modal operators. See pp. 130–131. Cf. Peter of Spain, *Sum. log.* (ed. Bocheński), pp. 100–101.

[100] See n. 97, this chapter.

[101] Although this sentence seems to announce the end of Sherwood's explication of the rule regarding supposition and appellation, the sentences immediately following seem to present some afterthoughts on the subject of ampliation.

[102] Divided: 'there is at least one individual such that it is a man and either it is running or it is possible that it is running.' Compounded: 'it is possible that there is at least one individual such that it is a man and either it is running or it is running' — i.e., 'it is possible that there is at least one individual such that it is a man and it is running.' In the *divided* sense the supposition of 'man' is presently existing men. In the *compounded* sense the supposition of 'man' is ampliated (by the modality) to include possible, nonexistent men — e.g., future men.

running' and others like it do not restrict [the supposition of] a term since a term supposits on its own for present things. And I say that the term 'man' does supposit on its own for present [men] because it signifies a form in relation to the things subordinate to the form; but that relation is preserved only in [men] that exist and, speaking strictly, it is for those [men] that exist that the term supposits on its own.

Let these remarks on the properties of terms suffice.

CHAPTER SIX *Sophistical Reasoning*

1. THE NATURE OF SOPHISTICAL REASONING[1]

As Aristotle says in *De sophisticis elenchis* I, there are four kinds of disputation: didactic (*doctrinale*) or demonstrative, dialectical, [85] probative (*temptative*), and sophistical.[2]

I maintain that the substance of disputation is nothing but syllogism.[3] Considered as an entity, therefore, disputation and syllogism are one and the same thing. It is called "syllogism," however, in virtue of the fact that it possesses power over its conclusion, "disputation," on the

---

[1] The heading of this chapter, *"De fallaciis,"* appears in the margin of the manuscript. A great deal of material valuable in the study of this chapter appears in De Rijk, *Logica modernorum*, Vol. I, "On the Twelfth Century Theories of Fallacy."

[2] *De sophisticis elenchis* (hereafter cited as *Soph. el.*), Ch. 2 (165a38–165b12): "Of arguments used in discussion there are four kinds, Didactic, Dialectical, Examination-arguments and Contentious arguments. Didactic arguments are those which reason from the principles appropriate to each branch of learning and not from the opinions of the respondent (for he who is learning must take things on trust). Dialectical arguments are those which, starting from generally accepted opinions, reason to establish a contradiction. Examination-arguments are those which are based on opinions held by the respondent and necessarily known to one who claims knowledge of the subject involved (in what manner, has been described elsewhere [*Topics*, 159a25ff]). Contentious arguments are those which reason or seem to reason from opinions which appear to be, but are not really, generally accepted. Demonstrative [i.e., "Didactic"] arguments have been treated in the *Analytics*, and dialectical arguments and examinations have been dealt with elsewhere [*Topics*, Bks. I–VIII]. Let us now deal with competitive and contentious arguments." See also *Soph. el.*, Chs. 10–11, for further discussion of these distinctions.

[3] 'Syllogism' is probably being used here in its broadest sense, in which it means any inference, acceptable or unacceptable, from one or more premises. See De Rijk, *Logica modernorum*, Vol. I, pp. 280–281; also n. 3, Chapter Four. Aristotle devotes Book VIII of the *Topics* to disputation, or "argument in dialogue-form." Formal disputation was the characteristic pedagogical method of the thirteenth-century universities. In theory it was "a syllogistic act between an opponent and a respondent to establish a point or proposition" (McKeon, "Glossary"). Peter of Spain introduces the study of logic generally as a basis for disputation (*Sum. log.*, ed. Bocheński, p. 1). Cf. Introduction, p. 15 above; also Prantl, *Geschichte*, 3.143. On the divisions of disputation in the twelfth century see De Rijk, *Logica modernorum*, Vol. I, pp. 91–92.

other hand, in virtue of the fact that a person can organize thought (*intellectum ordinare*) by means of it. And since this [organization of thought] can be accomplished (*contingat facere*) by means of more than one syllogism and not merely (*sufficienter*) by means of one, every disputation will be many syllogisms. Thus sophistical syllogism and sophistical disputation are one and the same.[4]

Now the end for which the sophist strives is apparent wisdom; sophistical disputation, therefore, is that by means of which a person can appear wise.[5] He does this when he apparently wins [an argument], and that happens when he apparently leads the respondent into some absurdity (*inconveniens*).

There are certain circumstances in discourse from which disputation derives a sophistical semblance of truth; these are called sophistical grounds[6] (*loci sophistici*). The absurdities for which the sophist strives are called the goals (*methe*).[7] Accordingly, in order to understand sophistical disputation we must understand the goal, which might be called its end, and the sophistical ground, which might be called its source (*principium*).

2. THE GOALS OF SOPHISTICAL DISPUTATION

The goal, then, as we have said, is the absurdity for which that kind of disputation strives; and it is called the goal because such disputation does not proceed beyond it.

There are five goals of this kind: Refutation (*redargutio*), Falsity (*falsum*), Paradox (*inopinabile*), Babbling (*nugatio*), Solecism (*soloecismus*).[8] Refutation is the denying of what was previously granted or

---

[4] The point of this paragraph seems to be that from a logician's point of view, disputation is simply inference (syllogism) employed in special circumstances (discussion) for special purposes (varying from one kind of disputation to another). But the purpose served by any given disputation could also have been served by some inference differing in one respect or another from the inference actually employed, and the inference actually employed may (usually) be broken up into several linked inferences. For these reasons "every disputation will be many syllogisms." Having taken note of these technical distinctions, Sherwood proposes to use 'sophistical syllogism' and 'sophistical disputation' interchangeably.

[5] See p. 69 above on sophistical syllogism; also *Soph. el.*, Ch. 1 (165a30ff).

[6] Cf. pp. 70–71 above on dialectical grounds. Cf. p. 134 below on the notion of a sophistical semblance of truth.

[7] The *methe* (or *metae*) are literally the limits or boundaries of the sophistical ground.

[8] See *Soph. el.*, Ch. 3 (165b12ff). In this chapter Sherwood considers only refutation.

the granting of what was previously denied. Falsity occurs in case thought is not adequated to reality (*Falsum autem est illud, cuius intellectus inequatur rei*). Paradox is what is contrary to the opinion of the many or of the wise. Babbling is pointless repetition of the same thing. Solecism, finally, is incongruity of discourse.

But [suppose someone says that] on the contrary refutation and falsity seem not to be opposed, since everyone who is [sophistically] refuted concedes what is false, although not vice versa. In response to this we must point out that the discomfiture of refutation is due not to conceding what is false, but to conceding incompossibles. Refutation and falsity, therefore, do differ as such.

3. REFUTATION

3.1. Verbal Grounds of Refutation

Refutation is the first of the goals, [and the one] for which the sophist chiefly strives. But there are two kinds of starting points for disputing towards this goal. One depends on discourse and is called a verbal ground (*locus in dictione*), and the other depends on reality and is called extra-verbal[9] (*extra dictionem*). They are, more particularly, named by means of a positive and a privative use of the word 'verbal' (*nominantur magis per positionem et privationem dictionis*), because even though reality as such (*res simpliciter*) is prior to words and discourse, the sophist aims at [treating them] the other way around.

Thus in every sophistical ground there must be the *Semblance* of some condition of a genuine syllogism together with its *Nonexistence*.[10] [86] Accordingly, all *verbal* grounds possess the Semblance as a result of sameness of discourse and the Nonexistence as a result of diversity of the [corresponding] reality.[11]

Now sameness of discourse is either of a linguistic whole (*totius sermonis*) or of an end — i.e., of a [grammatical] ending (*aut termini i.e.*

---

[9] Cf. *Soph. el.*, Ch. 4 (165b23–25).

[10] 'Semblance' (*apparentia*) and 'Nonexistence' (*non-existentia*) are important technical terms in Sherwood's treatment of sophistical reasoning, serving throughout the remainder of Chapter Six as abbreviations of, or allusions to, this explanation of the basis of all fallacy. The words will be capitalized in all their technical occurrences.

[11] Cf. *Soph. el.*, Ch. 4 (165b25ff): "Those ways of producing the false appearance of an argument which depend on language are six in number: . . . [for] this is the number of ways in which we might fail to mean the same thing by the same names or expressions."

terminationis). (Sameness of the beginning or middle [of a linguistic whole] cannot be the source of deception, as we shall see.[12]) Sameness in the case of a linguistic whole is either in the substance of the discourse alone or in the substance of the discourse together with its use (*cum suo actu*). (I speak of the use of discourse since in its use it is pronounced (*proferatur*).) This [last] sameness is either of a word alone or of an expression. If it is sameness of a word and there is diversity in the corresponding reality (*et illi correspondat diversitas in re*) it is called Equivocation;[13] if it is sameness of an expression it is called Amphibology.[14]

Sameness of discourse with respect to its substance alone is either sameness of an expression and called Composition or Division,[15] or it is sameness of a word and called Accent.[16]

On the other hand, sameness in the case of a grammatical ending (*terminationem sermonis*) insofar as it is a source of deception is in a word only and is called the Figure of a Word.[17]

(I am speaking of these samenesses [only] insofar as there is diversity on the part of the corresponding reality (*respondet diversitas ex parte rei*).)

3.1.1. Equivocation.[18] Equivocation is diverse signification on the part of one and the same word. This can occur in three ways. Either the word signifies [A] more than one thing on its own[19] (*de se*) or [B] as a result of its connection with something else; and there are two varieties of [A] — viz., it signifies [more than one thing] [A1] properly or [A2] transumptively.[20]

Example of [A1]: 'every dog runs, one of the heavenly constellations is a dog; therefore one of the heavenly constellations runs.' Here the word 'dog' properly signifies more than one thing. They must be reduced to this variety [of Equivocation] on the ground of diverse con-

---

[12] Pp. 146–150 below.

[13] Pp. 135–139 below.

[14] Pp. 139–140 below.

[15] Pp. 140–144 below.

[16] Pp. 144–146 below.

[17] Pp. 146–150 below; also p. 137 below.

[18] The heading *"De equivocatione et eius tribus modis"* appears in the margin of the manuscript. On Equivocation generally see *Soph. el.*, Ch. 4 (165b30ff).

[19] See p. 130 above.

[20] See n. 145, Chapter Four. Cf. *Soph. el.*, Ch. 4 (166a14ff); also De Rijk, *Logica modernorum*, Vol. I, pp. 135–139; p. 499.

signification[21] (*Ad hunc modum habent reduci per locum ex diversa consignificatione*); for in both instances there is a real diversity that corresponds properly rather than transumptively to the verbal unity[22] (*Utrobique enim unitati dictionis proprie respondet diversitas rei et non transumptive*). For example, 'the bishops are priests, these asses are the bishop's; therefore these asses are priests.'[23]

Example[s] of [A2]: 'whatever runs has feet, the Seine runs; therefore the Seine has feet';[24] 'whatever smiles has a mouth, there are smiling meadows; therefore there are meadows with mouths';[25] 'whatever is expedient (*expedit*) is good, an evil thing is expedient; therefore an evil thing is good.'[26] [These are examples of [A2]] because the terms 'runs,' 'smiles,' and 'expedient' signify one thing principally and are transumed to another thing by virtue of a certain resemblance. 'Expedient,' [for example,] is said properly of what is good and [in that use] is just the same as 'good' (*et est idem quod bonum simpliciter*); but then [its sense] is changed to [that of] 'useful' and it is predicated of an evil thing (*Tunc mutatur autem ad utile et dicitur de malo*).

Example of [B]: 'whoever was being cured is healthy, the sufferer was being cured; therefore the sufferer is healthy.' [87] [This is an example of [B]] because on its own the term 'the sufferer' (*laborans*) neither [properly] nor transumptively means anything other than what is at present (*nec de se nec transumptive dat intelligere nisi presens*), but as a result of its connection with the verb 'was being cured' it means what is past. But I am not claiming that it is thus in the past tense — rather that on its own it consignifies what is at present considered *as such*, while here [it consignifies] what is at present considered *in respect of the past* — i.e., insofar as the [present] thing is past[27] (*Nec tamen dico, quod sic sit preteriti temporis, sed quod de se consignificat presens simpliciter, hic autem presens respectu preteriti et hoc secundum rem preteritam est*). [In this case,] therefore, the diversity cor-

---

[21] On consignification in this context see, e.g., pp. 137 and 138.

[22] This sentence seems to belong *after* the second example of [A1] rather than immediately before it, as here (and in the original).

[23] The force of the example depends on the fact that '*episcopi*' is either the nominative plural — 'bishops' — or the genitive singular — 'bishop's' — and so only the *spoken* version of the English translation has the intended effect. On this example see also p. 137.

[24] Cf. De Rijk, *Logica modernorum*, Vol. I, Index C: "*curro.*"

[25] Cf. De Rijk, *Logica modernorum*, Vol. I, Index C: "*rideo.*"

[26] Cf. De Rijk, *Logica modernorum*, Vol. I, Index C: "*expedio.*"

[27] Cf. pp. 126–128.

responding to the unity of the utterance is the diversity between what is at present considered as such and what is at present considered in respect of the past.[28]

I am not claiming that these varieties of Equivocation differ essentially, for the diversity is connected solely with the Nonexistence [and not at all with the Semblance]. This is because the unity of the utterance is absolutely the same throughout [the three varieties], while the difference is connected with the significata.[29]

(Notice, by the way, that in one respect the second example of [A1] can be [a case of] the Figure of a Word — i.e., insofar as it is the sameness of the ending of the word 'bishops' [and that of the word 'bishop's'] rather than the sameness of the whole utterance that produces the apparent sameness of what is consignified.)[30]

The solution of paralogisms of this kind[31] consists in showing that the same term is taken in more than one way.

[Consider] the following [objections] against [B]. [In the first place,] a word is prior to any [complex] expression, and therefore [a word in a complex expression] retains the essence it had (*retinet ergo esse dictionis*) before becoming an ingredient in the expression. It has this essence, however, from its signification. Therefore it has its signification before it becomes an ingredient in an expression and not as a result of its being ordered in an expression.[32] Consequently, since "the sufferer" on its own (*ex se*) signifies one thing, it will not signify something else as a result of its being ordered together with other words.

In the second place, the deception resulting from the ordering of one

---

[28] The present participle '*laborans*' is like the English noun 'the sufferer' in that it may be used to refer to someone now suffering or to someone not now suffering but known to have suffered. See the objection to this example and Sherwood's reply on pp. 138 and 139 below. Cf. *Soph. el.*, Ch. 4 (166a2ff); also De Rijk, *Logica modernorum*, Vol. I, Index C: "*laborans*."

[29] The three varieties do not differ *essentially* because one of their two essential aspects — viz., the Semblance (of correct reasoning) — is the same in all three. They differ, then, only in the ways in which the Semblance turns out to be deceptive, only in the second of their two essential aspects — the Nonexistence of the sameness suggested by the discourse.

[30] See p. 136 above and n. 23. On the Figure of a Word see pp. 135 above and 146–150 below. What is consignified in this example is the grammatical case. There seems to be only one — the nominative plural — but there are really two — the nominative plural and the genitive singular.

[31] I.e., paralogisms (fallacies) of equivocation *generally*. On the solution of paralogisms of equivocation, see *Soph. el.*, Ch. 19 (177a9ff).

[32] Cf. p. 105.

137

word together with others is a result not of the word but of the expression. Thus this is not Equivocation.[33]

[In response to the first objection] we must point out that a word does necessarily have signification before [becoming an ingredient in] the expression and can acquire none from the expression. Nevertheless, the signification it has can undergo permutation as a result of what is adjoined to the word[34] (*Verumptamen significatio, quam habet ex adiuncto suo, poterit permutari*).[35] This applies not to every word but to a word whose signification or consignification is a single concept (*intentio*) participated in by what is more than one thing with respect to earlier and later (*participata a pluribus secundum prius et posterius*). On its own, that [kind of] word will signify that which first participates in the concept; alternatively it can as a result of adjunction signify that which participates in the concept later (*Et tunc illa dictio significabit de se illud, quod primo participat illam intentionem ex adiunctione aut potest significare illud, quod posterius eam participat*).[36] This is the case in our example, for the word 'sufferer' consignifies the present, which is first preserved in the present absolutely but later preserved incompletely in the present with reference to the past[37] (*quod primo salvatur in presenti simpliciter, per posterius autem et diminute in presenti de preterito*).

In response to the other objection we must point out that it is not the same for a word ordered [in an expression] to signify more than one thing as for the expression [as a whole to do so]; nor is deception resulting from an ordered word the same as deception resulting from the

---

[33] But rather Amphibology. See p. 135.

[34] Up to this point Sherwood's reply to this objection constitutes an exposition of the supposition of a term. See Chapter Five, especially pp. 123–124.

[35] Reading this passage without *G*'s commas.

[36] Reading '*aut ex adiunctione*' for '*ex adiunctione aut*.'

[37] The main point of Sherwood's response to this objection seems to be the same as Aristotle's point in his observations on a highly similar example: "For 'the sick man,' [who] does such and such a thing, or has such and such a thing done to him, does not signify one single thing. Sometimes it signifies a man who is now sick; sometimes it signifies a man who was formerly sick. Of course the man who was being cured was the sick man, who really was sick at that time; but he is healthy when he is not sick, and he *is* not the man who is now sick but the man who was formerly sick" (*Soph. el.*, Ch. 4 (166a1ff)). Sherwood's case is somewhat more complex because of the substantive use of the present active participle '*laborans*,' which, although serving as a noun, does consignify present time. The paragraph is further complicated by what appear to be implicit allusions to discussions in Chapter Five (see especially pp. 126–128).

expression (*nec deceptio ex illo i.e. dictione ordinata. Ex hoc i.e. in oratione est deceptio.*). In the former the Semblance is in the simple word, while in the latter it is in the expression [as a whole]. [88]

3.1.2. Amphibology.[38] Next, as to Amphibology. Amphibology is diversity of judgment (*sententie*) proceeding from unity of expression or from diverse signification on the part of an expression. The Semblance [in Amphibology] is the result of the unity of the expression while the Nonexistence is the result of the diversity of [its] signification. For just as in Equivocation the word is unified both in substance and in use (*actum*), and the diversity is in what is signified, so in Amphibology there is unity of the expression both in substance and in use, while the diversity is in what is signified.

As a result, deception occurs, and in three different ways: the expression signifies more than one thing [A1] principally, or [A2] not principally but as a result of translation;[39] or [B] it signifies one thing on its own but two things when connected with something else.[40]

Example of [A1]: 'if anyone did bread devour, bread did devour him; but the dog did bread devour; therefore bread did devour him'[41] (*quemcunque verum est panem comedere, panis comedit illum. Sed canem verum est panem comedere. Ergo panis comedit illum.*).

Example of [A2]: 'whoever plows the seashore moves sand, this man is plowing the seashore (indicating someone who is working in vain); therefore this man is moving[42] sand.'[43]

Example of [B]: 'if anyone the world did know, the world had knowledge of him; but this man the world did know (indicating someone having knowledge of the world); therefore the world had knowledge of him.'[44] Understand that the expressions 'if anyone the world did

---

[38] The heading "*Sequitur de amphibologia et eius tribus modis*" appears in the margin of the manuscript. On Amphibology generally see *Soph. el.*, Ch. 4 (166a-6ff).

[39] See n. 20, this chapter. "Principal" signification seems to be only a variant for the more usual "proper" signification, unless it marks a difference between the signification of a word and the derivative signification of an expression made up of words.

[40] Cf. *Soph. el.*, Ch. 4 (166a14–19).

[41] This is a version of a traditional example that suffers from a mistaken medieval emendation. The unemended form has 'the wolf' where this example has 'bread.' Cf. De Rijk, *Logica modernorum*, Vol. I, Index C: "canis."

[42] G has '*arat*'; '*movet*' in manuscript.

[43] "Plowing the seashore" as a metaphor for any labor in vain occurs in Ovid (*Tristia*, 5.4.48). Cf. De Rijk, *Logica modernorum*, Vol. I, Index C: "*litus*."

[44] Cf. De Rijk, *Logica modernorum*, Vol. I, Index C: "*scio*."

know' and 'this man the world did know' [are instances of] Amphibology of variety [A1]. On the other hand, 'the world did know' is an Amphibology of variety [B], since it does not signify more than one thing on its own but [only] when connected with something else.

These varieties do not differ essentially, since they do not differ because of the Semblance but solely because of the Nonexistence.[45] Nor is it true that every Amphibology results from diverse construction, as is clear in the example of [A2].

In paralogisms of this kind, therefore, we must break up the amphibologous expression by pointing out that it is taken now in one signification, now in the other.[46]

3.1.3. Composition and Division.[47] Next, as to Composition and Division. Composition is the connection of things that are more disposed to be compounded. Division, on the other hand, is the separation of things that are more disposed to be divided.[48] I am speaking here of connection and separation in the act of speaking[49] (*in actu proferendi*).

In Composition the cause of the Semblance is the fact that the expression compounded and the expression divided are the same with respect to the substance of discourse. The cause of the Nonexistence is their diversity in actual use, to which there corresponds a diversity in [89] reality. Of course an expression used in a syllogism must remain

---

[45] See p. 137.

[46] On the solution of paralogisms of Amphibology, see *Soph. el.*, Ch. 19 (177a-16ff).

[47] The heading *"De compositione et divisione"* appears in the margin of the manuscript. On Composition, see *Soph. el.*, Ch. 4 (166a23ff). On Division, see *Soph. el.* (166a33ff).

[48] The Latin here is *"Est enim compositio coniunctio aliquorum, que magis volunt componi. Divisio autem est separatio aliquorum, que magis volunt dividi."* Both the sense and the tradition seem to require reading '*dividi*' for '*componi*' and '*componi*' for '*dividi*.' (Cf., e.g., De Rijk, *Logica modernorum*, Vol. I, p. 142; Peter of Spain, *Sum. log.* (ed. Bocheński), pp. 74 and 76.) The use of this unusual version of the doctrine on p. 143 below, however, suggests that the unemended text is faithful to Sherwood's intentions.

[49] I.e., as in Aristotle's example of Division (*Soph. el.* (166a35ff)) — "I made you a slave once a free man" — the sense depends on whether the speaker *divides* the expression (by pausing and emphasizing) in this way: 'I made you — a slave once — a free man,' or *compounds* it in this way: 'I made you a slave, once a free man.' (Cf. the discussion of compounded and divided senses in Chapter Five, especially pp. 126–128 above.) The Aristotelian-medieval doctrine of the fallacies of Composition and Division is much broader than that found in textbooks of the modern period, which usually recognize only the difficulties associated with the compounded and divided senses of *generalizations*, such as 'all the interior angles of a triangle equal 180°.'

the same throughout, and since [Composition] violates this condition it violates the essence of syllogism.

In Division, on the other hand,[50] the Semblance is the sameness (with respect to the substance [of discourse]) of the expression divided and the expression compounded, while the cause of the Nonexistence is their diversity in actual use. And when I speak of that diversity I am at the same time speaking of diversity in the [corresponding] reality.

Understand that 'Composition' does not indicate (*dicit*) the cause of the Semblance [nor] 'Division' the cause of the Nonexistence.[51] Instead, 'Composition' indicates one act of discourse and 'Division' another, both acts, to be sure, being based on a single substance of utterance.[52]

The following is a paralogism of Composition: 'whatever is possible will be true, that a white thing is black is possible (*album esse nigrum est possibile*); therefore that a white thing is black will be[53] true.'[54] I maintain that the minor premiss is ambiguous, since these two — 'a white thing' and 'is black' — can be compounded in respect of 'possible,' in which case it is signified that the compounded dictum[55] is possible. In that case the [entire] expression is compounded.[56] Alternatively, 'a white thing' and 'is black' can be divided from each other [in respect of 'possible'], and then it is signified that the composition of the predicate 'is black' with the other, which then is 'a white thing' (*ad aliud, quod tunc est album*), is possible, since in that case 'a white thing' is divided from the predicate 'is [black],' which contains all time[57] (*quia*

---

[50] The only point of contrast between this paragraph on Division and the preceding paragraph on Composition is the order of the phrases 'the expression compounded' and 'the expression divided.'

[51] This is evidently an attempt to forestall any confusion of *compositio* with the sameness (*ydemptitas*) that has been described as the cause of the Semblance, and of *divisio* with the diversity (*diversitas*) that has been described as the cause of the Nonexistence.

[52] The substance of utterance (or of discourse) is the grammatically ordered string of words identifiable as a single expression. The acts of discourse known as Composition and Division are different ways of speaking (or reading) that string of words. See n. 49, 56, and 57, this chapter.

[53] Reading '*erit*' for '*est*.'

[54] Cf. De Rijk, *Logica modernorum*, Vol. I, Index C: "*possibilis*."

[55] See n. 71, Chapter One.

[56] To compound 'a white thing' and 'is black' in respect of 'possible' is to read the minor premiss as follows: 'it is possible that there is at least one individual such that it is (entirely) white and it is (entirely) black.'

[57] To divide 'a white thing' and 'is black' in respect of 'possible' is to read the minor premiss as follows: 'there is at least one individual such that it is (entirely) white and it is possible that it is (entirely) black.'

ly album eo quod dividitur ab hoc predicato: esse, quod habet tempus amplissimum). As a result, the word 'possible' does not draw the supposition of 'white thing' away from that [which it supposits on its own], so that it supposits for white things throughout all time; instead, it supposits for those things that are white now[58] (*Per hoc, quod dico possibile non trahit suam suppositionem ab illo, ut supponat pro albis illius temporis, sed supponit pro hiis, que nunc sunt alba*). Consequently, the minor premiss [taken as] divided is true; and since the same thing is [taken as] compounded [in the conclusion],[59] the compounded and the divided are one and the same with respect to the substance [of discourse] (*Est ergo minor vera propositio divisa et quia ipsa composita est, eadem illi secundum substantiam*). If anyone believes that they are absolutely the same and signify the same and that it would be a good syllogism if [the dictum] were taken as compounded [in both its occurrences], he also believes that it would be good if [the dictum] were taken as divided [in both its occurrences]. Accordingly, the expression 'that a white thing is black' is taken as divided in the minor and as compounded in the conclusion;[60] for otherwise the conclusion is not false. As a result, the condition of syllogism that an expression remain the same throughout is violated here. Nevertheless, it *seems* to remain the same, since the minor [premiss] compounded *seems* the same as [the minor premiss] divided.[61]

Again, 'whatever lives always exists, Socrates lives; therefore Socrates always exists.'[62] The expression 'always exists' is taken as divided in the major, as compounded in the conclusion,[63] and so this fails to be

---

[58] This is a reference to the doctrine developed at the end of Chapter Five. See pp. 130–131.

[59] It looks as if this may be a reference to the ambiguity of the minor premiss, which has been under discussion, but what follows makes it seem more probably a reference to the recurrence of the dictum in the conclusion.

[60] The compounding of the dictum in the conclusion is in respect of the future-tense verb, the result reading as follows: 'it will be the case that there is at least one individual such that it is (entirely) white and it is (entirely) black.' In its divided sense the conclusion reads as follows: 'there is at least one individual such that it is (entirely) white and it will be the case that it is (entirely) black.' Cf. the example of Socrates and the shield, p. 128.

[61] This difficult paragraph is somewhat clarified by Sherwood's discussion of modality on pp. 39–50 and by his discussion of compounded and divided senses of expressions on p. 127. Cf. also Bocheński, *History*, pp. 182–187.

[62] Cf. De Rijk, *Logica modernorum*, Vol. I, Index C: "*semper.*"

[63] I.e., the major and the conclusion are read as follows: 'for every individual, if it is always the case that it lives, then it exists'; 'for Socrates, it is always the case that he exists.'

a syllogism. It *seems* not to fail, however, since the expression *seems* to be taken as compounded in the major [also] [64] because of the sameness of the compounded and the divided [with respect to the substance of discourse].

One more example: 'whatever ceases now to exist will not exist hereafter (*Quicquid desinit nunc esse, de cetero non erit*), but God ceases now to exist; therefore God will not exist hereafter.'[65] The expression 'now [to exist]' is taken [90] as divided in the major, compounded in the minor.[66] Although the deception in this case can in one respect be attributed to Composition — since if ['now to exist'] were taken as compounded in the major it would be the same expression (and one may think this to be the case because of the unity of the compounded and the divided [with respect to the substance of discourse]) — still, in another respect the deception can be attributed to Division. For if ['now to exist'] were known to be divided in the minor this would be a good syllogism (and one may think that it is taken as divided because of the unity of the divided and the compounded [with respect to the substance of discourse]).

Thus in the first example the diversity of the expressions [with respect to their actual use] is in the minor [term], in the second in the major [term], in the third in the middle [term].[67]

But suppose someone asks why the expression 'God ceases now to exist' is said to be compounded by virtue of the composition of 'now' with the verb 'to exist' and divided by virtue of the division of 'now' from that verb rather than [compounded] by virtue of the composition of 'now' with the verb 'ceases' or [divided] by virtue of their division. I reply that, as Priscian says at the end of the treatise on the adverb,[68] adverbs more properly precede their verb; therefore the adverb 'now' is more disposed to determine the verb 'to exist' since it precedes that verb and does not precede the other. Moreover, we have said that Com-

---

[64] I.e., 'for every individual, if it lives, then it is always the case that it exists.'

[65] Cf. De Rijk, *Logica modernorum*, Vol. I, Index C: "*desino*"; also "*nunc.*"

[66] I.e., the major and the minor premisses are read as follows: 'for every individual, if at this time it ceases to exist, then it will be the case that it does not exist hereafter'; 'God ceases to exist at this time.' Taken as compounded the minor presents the claim that God (along with everything else) ceases to exist now (t_1), simply because of the passage of time, and begins to exist *now* (t_2).

[67] The terms in question are (1) 'that a white thing is black,' (2) 'always exists,' (3) 'to exist now.'

[68] *Inst. gram.*, 9.3.89.

position is the conjunction of things that are more disposed to be compounded.[69]

An example of Division: 'five are two and three; therefore five are both even and odd.' The expression 'two and three' is taken as compounded. If it were taken as divided the argument would hold.[70] [The expression] *seems* divided [71] because of the unity of the divided and the compounded [with respect to the substance of discourse], and the result is, as we have said,[72] the Semblance of Division.

Again, 'the greater is as much and more; therefore it is equal and unequal.' If the expression 'as much and more' were taken as divided, the argument would hold. It does *seem* to be so taken in one respect, however, because of the unity of the divided and the compounded [with respect to the substance of discourse]. This paralogism shows, then, that in Composition and Division the Semblance is not always one determination and two determinables, but only something that can be compounded and divided by itself, whether or not it is combined with anything else (*Patet ergo per hunc paralogismum, quod non semper apparet in compositione et divisione esse una determinatio et duo determinabilia, sed solum aliquod, quod possit componi et dividi ab illo sive cum alio componatur sive non*).[73]

3.1.4. Accent.[74] Next, as to Accent. Accent is the regular modulation

---

[69] See n. 48, this chapter.

[70] The premiss taken as compounded reads as follows (changing Sherwood's plural verb to singular): 'five is (the sum of) two and three.' As divided: 'five is two and (five is) three.' If the premiss were taken as divided the inference would be valid ("the argument would hold"), but of course the premiss would then be false. Both Sherwood's examples of Division are Aristotle's; see also De Rijk, *Logica modernorum*, Vol. I, Index C: "*quinque.*"

[71] G has '*diversa*'; '*divisa*' in manuscript.

[72] On p. 141.

[73] The main point of this difficult last sentence seems to be to distinguish Composition and Division from Amphibology. (Aristotle draws such a distinction in his chapter on the solution of paralogisms of Composition and Division, *Soph. el.*, Ch. 20 (177a33ff).) In each of the three examples of Composition there was one determination and two determinables — i.e., two occurrences of an expression that, for syllogistic purposes, had to be taken as determined in one single way, as compounded or as divided. Both these paralogisms of Division (singling out the last one alone seems mistaken) present instances in which there is only one determinable admitting of two determinations. In neither case, however, is there Amphibology, since these expressions admit of the two determinations — compounded and divided — regardless of any special grammatical context. (Much of this interpretation and even some points of the translation of this last sentence are uncertain.)

[74] The heading "*De accentu*" appears in the margin of the manuscript. On the paralogism of Accent see *Soph. el.*, Ch. 4 (166b1ff).

of the voice with respect to raising and lowering it. There are three kinds of accent: acute, grave, and circumflex. Acute starts [91] below and goes up, while grave is the other way around. Circumflex begins below, goes up, and then goes down again.[75]

The deception results, therefore, when an utterance signifies diverse things under diverse accents but there *seems* to be one signification and one word because of the sameness of the utterance in [its] substance. But the deception occurs sometimes because an utterance is governed first by one accent and then by another, sometimes because it is governed first by one and then by two, or vice versa.

For example: *'quicquid debet pendere debet suspendi, iustus debet pendere; ergo iustus debet suspendi.'*[76] Or: *'omnis populus est gens, populus est arbor; ergo arbor est gens.'*[77] Or: *'omnis quies est*[78] *requies, tu es qui es; ergo tu es requies.'*[79] Or: *'quod fit invite contra voluntatem, uva fit in vite; ergo uva fit contra voluntatem.'*[80] The way to solve these is to distinguish one name from another.[81]

I raise the following questions, however. [A] Composition and Division are to an expression as Accent is to a word;[82] therefore if there is more than one fallacy in the former case, so is there in this case. Al-

---

[75] These descriptions of variations of pitch corresponding to the Greek accent marks are correct (as regards their original use), but scarcely relevant to a discussion of examples in Latin, where the differences at issue concern the "quantity" of vowels and the degree of separation between words in speech. (For a more appropriate medieval account of Accent see the twelfth-century *Fallacie parvipontane* (in De Rijk, *Logica modernorum*, Vol. I), p. 583.)

[76] *'Pendere'* in the major premiss is the infinitive of *'pendo,'* and the second 'e' in it is short; *'pendere'* in the minor premiss is the infinitive of *'pendeo,'* and its second 'e' is long. Thus, 'anything that ought to be suspended (*pendere*) ought to be hung, a just man ought to be esteemed (*pendēre*); therefore a just man ought to be hung.' Cf. De Rijk, *Logica modernorum*, Vol. I, Index C: *"pendo."*

[77] *'Populus'* in the major premiss; *'pōpulus'* in the minor. Thus, 'every people (*populus*) is a nation, a [i.e., every] poplar (*pōpulus*) is a tree; therefore a [i.e, some] tree is a nation.'

[78] G has *'et'*; *'est'* in manuscript.

[79] *'Quiēs'* in the major premiss; *'qui es'* in the minor. Thus, 'every rest (*quiēs*) is a repose, you are who you are (*qui es*); therefore you are a repose.'

[80] *'Invitē'* in the major premiss; *'in vīte'* in the minor. Thus, 'whatever occurs unwillingly (*invitē*) occurs against one's will, a grape occurs on a vine (*in vīte*); therefore a grape occurs against one's will.' Cf. De Rijk, *Logica modernorum*, Vol. I, Index C: *"invitus."*

[81] What Sherwood means by this remark is clear enough despite its extreme brevity and the unexpected use of 'name' (*nomen*). Aristotle describes the solution of paralogisms of Accent in *Soph. el.*, Ch. 21 (177b35ff).

[82] G has *'divisionem'*; *'dictionem'* in manuscript.

ternatively, if there is [only] one in this case, so is there in the former case.

[B] It has been said[83] that in Equivocation and Amphibology the Semblance is the unity of the utterance with respect to [its] substance and use, while the unity of the utterance with respect to [its] substance [alone] is the source of the Semblance in Composition, Division, and Accent. But *this* division — viz., unity of utterance is either of a word or of an expression — seems to be based solely on *material* differences and this seems not to be divided essentially. Therefore we ought not to make an essential division between Equivocation and Amphibology, or between Composition and Division on the one hand and Accent on the other, for it seems they differ only materially.

In response to [A] I maintain that the act of Composition differs less from the act of Division than one accent differs from another. That is why Aristotle says it is of no use for dialecticians to construct a paralogism of Accent except in poetic discourse (*in sermonibus poematicis*), where accent is not expressly expressed.[84] For in every [other kind of] discourse a diversity of accent expresses a diversity of words. It is otherwise with Composition and Division, for Composition itself can be the source of the Semblance in respect of Division, and vice versa; but one accent is in no way [the source of the Semblance] in respect of another. In connection with Accent the sole source of the Semblance is in the unity of the utterance in [its] substance.

In response to [B] I maintain that that division is based not only on material but also on essential differences, for when I speak of [92] the unity of a word, I am speaking of a high degree of unity of utterance (*dico unitatem vocis magnam*); but when I speak [of the unity] of an expression, I am speaking of a lesser degree. Therefore it is as if I were to say that unity of utterance is either complete (in the case of a word) or incomplete (in the case of an expression).

3.1.5. The Figure of a Word.[85] Next, as to the Figure of a Word. A figure, properly so-called, consists in the termination of a quantity.[86]

---

[83] On p. 135.

[84] *Soph. el.*, Ch. 4 (166b1ff). Accent and breathing marks were still a novelty in the written Greek of Aristotle's day (see *Soph. el.*, Ch. 20 (177b5)), and in spoken poetry accent was subservient to meter.

[85] The heading *"De figura dictionis"* appears in the margin of the manuscript. On the paralogism of the Figure of a Word see *Soph. el.*, Ch. 4 (166b10ff).

[86] I.e., the boundary of an area or the surface of a solid.

Because of a resemblance to this the termination of a word is here called [its] figure.[87]

The deception [connected with the Figure of a Word] occurs because, as a result of the same ending for two different words (or for one word taken in different ways), people think they are to be predicated in one and the same way. The cause of the Semblance, therefore, is the sameness of words with respect to their endings, while the cause of the Nonexistence is diversity in the categories [to which the words belong] or in the way in which [the words] are to be predicated. For as a result of the fact that a word belonging to one category ends like one belonging to another, we use the one category instead of the other. For example: 'Sortes operatur; ergo patitur.'[88] People think the verb 'operatur' is passive, or in the category of passion, because of the passive ending; nevertheless it belongs to the category of action.

There is a question, however, as to [A] what the Semblance is in this paralogism: 'what you bought yesterday you ate today, but yesterday you bought something raw; [therefore today you ate something raw]'; or '. . . yesterday you bought something white; therefore today you ate something white.'[89] And I raise the further question, [B] What is the cause of the Nonexistence in that paralogism? If the claim is that there is a shift from the category of substance to the category of quality (since 'something white' (album) or 'something raw' (crudum) is taken under 'what'[90] (quicquid)), then by the same reasoning this would be a paralogism — 'what you saw yesterday you see today, yesterday you saw whiteness; therefore today you see [whiteness]' (Ergo hodie vides etc.) — which is false.

In reply to [A] we must point out that the word 'something white'

---

[87] G has 'facta'; 'figura' in manuscript. The phrase 'terminatio dictionis' is translated 'termination of a word' here for the sake of the analogy but will be translated 'ending of a word' in what follows.

[88] Operor: to operate, to be active; patior: to undergo, to be passive. Cf. De Rijk, Logica modernorum, Vol. I, Index C: "operor."

[89] Cf. De Rijk, Logica modernorum, Vol. I, Index C: "heri."

[90] Part of the Semblance in this paralogism is due to the fact that the Latin adjectives can also occur as substantives of a sort, which is why they are here translated as 'something white' and 'something raw' rather than merely as 'white' and 'raw.' The suggested explanation of the Semblance at this point (which Sherwood rejects) is that the effect of the 'quicquid' in the first premiss is to make us take 'crudum' or 'album' in the second premiss as a word belonging to the category of substance, while we take it in the conclusion as a word belonging to the category of quality. (We might represent this effect by writing 'something-raw' in the second premiss and 'something raw' in the conclusion.)

(*album*) or the word 'something raw' (*crudum*) under one and the same ending appellates a particular substance, and so appellates a *what*, and also signifies a *how* (*appellat hoc aliquid et sic quid et significat quale*). As a result, people believe it signifies a *what* just as it appellates a *what*.[91]

In reply to [B] we must point out that since there are ten ways in which genera are to be predicated,[92] the way in which to predicate the superior of the inferior in any genus is the same as the way in which to predicate with respect to *what* (*cum decem sint genera modi predicandi, modus predicandi superioris de inferiori in quolibet genere est modus predicandi in quid*), as if one were to say 'animal is substance,' 'line is quantity,' 'color is quality.' Accordingly, within its own genus anything is a *what*.[93] But if everything is considered in relation to primary substance, then only secondary substances[94] are predicated with respect to *what*, only qualities with respect to *how*, and so on. Therefore, the Nonexistence in the paralogism above is the result not of a transformation of a substance into a quality but of a transformation of a *what* into a *how*.[95] [93]

Notice also that sometimes [A] in one and the same genus a sort (*quale quid*) is transformed into a particular thing (*hoc aliquid*)[96] as a result of the same Semblance, while at other times [B] a *what* is trans-

---

[91] On the distinction between appellation and signification, see Chapter Five, e.g., pp. 105–106.

[92] I.e., the ten Aristotelian categories.

[93] A line or a color is never a substance, but within the genus *quantity* a line is a *what*, within the genus *quality* a color is a *what*.

[94] Primary substances are individuals; secondary substances are genera and species. Cf. *Cat.*, Ch. 5 (2a11–18).

[95] The transformation of a substance into a quality is impossible (see n. 93, this chapter), but the transformation of a *what* into a *how* requires only changes in interpretation. In the paralogism under discussion the first premiss — '*what* you bought yesterday you ate today' — warrants only the conclusion that the something raw you bought yesterday is *what* you ate today, not that *how* it was when you bought it is *how* it was when you ate it. The substantival use of interrogative pronouns associated with the various categories has its source in Aristotle (*Cat.*, Ch. 4 (1b25ff)).

[96] '*Quale quid*' and '*hoc aliquid*' are medieval technical terms corresponding to Aristotle's 'ποῖόν τι' and 'τόδε τι' respectively. (See, e.g., *Cat.*, Ch. 5 (3b10ff)). Cf. Sherwood's *Syncategoremata* (ed. O'Donnell), pp. 52–53: "When a term stands [i.e., supposits] for many immobilely it stands as a *quale quid*, and when it stands for many mobilely and for each one of those many it stands as a *hoc aliquid*." (On mobile and immobile supposition see pp. 108–109 above.) Cf. Ockham, *Expositio aurea*, II, 51v–52r (quoted in Ernest Addison Moody, *The Logic of William of Ockham*, p. 140, n. 1), on terms signifying *hoc aliquid* and *quale quid*.

formed into a *how* or a *how much*. An occurrence of [B] takes place either [1] under the Semblance described above — viz., because a single word ends in the same way (*similiter*) both when appellating and when [merely] signifying, or [2] because one word ends as does another word.

An example of [A]: suppose every man sees [only] himself and is running; then: 'for every man someone who sees him is running; therefore someone who sees every man is running' (*omnem hominem videns currit. Ergo videns omnem hominem currit*).[97] In the premiss[98] 'someone who sees' expresses a sort, for it supposits generally[99] for anyone who sees (*supponit enim pro vidente communiter*). In the conclusion, however, it stands for that which is a particular thing (*stat pro eo, quod hoc est aliquid*).[100]

An example of [B1]: 'what you bought you ate . . .';[101] or: 'whatever you did have and do not have you have got rid of, you did have ten and you do not have ten (supposing you have got rid of one); therefore you have got rid of ten.'[102] In this case a *what* is transformed into a *how much*. Alternatively: 'whatever you gave, you had, you gave only one; therefore you had only one.'[103] In this case a *what* is transformed into a particular thing (*in aliquid*). Alternatively: 'what you are drinking is wine, you are drinking a cup; therefore a cup is wine.'[104] In this case a *what* is changed[105] into a *where*, because to drink a cup is to drink from a *where*, the location of the wine. In all these examples the cause of the Semblance is the sameness of the ending in signifying and in appellating.

[An example of [B2]:] '*operatur; ergo patitur*';[106] or: 'he sees; there-

---

[97] Because he wants to use the same words in the premiss as in the conclusion Sherwood has some difficulty in expressing this paralogism. The translation sidesteps this difficulty.

[98] Reading '*in propositione*' for '*in prima propositione.*' '*Propositio*' in this context means the same as 'premiss,' and there is only one premiss.

[99] On suppositing "generally" see pp. 111–112.

[100] *G* has '*hoc est aliquid*'; '*est hoc aliquid*' in manuscript.

[101] An allusion to the paralogism on pp. 147–148 as an example of transforming a *what* into a *how*.

[102] Cf. De Rijk, *Logica modernorum*, Vol. I, Index C: "*amitto.*"

[103] Cf. De Rijk, *Logica modernorum*, Vol. I, Index C: "*do.*"

[104] Cf. De Rijk, *Logica modernorum*, Vol. I, Index C: "*bibo.*"

[105] The verb that has been translated 'is transformed' in this section is '*permutatur.*' The verb here is '*commutatur.*'

[106] An allusion to the paralogism on p. 147 above as an example of the case in which the source of the Semblance is the fact that one word ends as does another.

fore he acts'—for to see is to be passive.[107] Nevertheless people think that to see is to act, because of the active ending of 'sees.' In these and similar examples the Semblance is the sameness of the ending of one word and the ending of another.

In every case [of the Figure of a Word], therefore, the Semblance is sameness of an ending, or (what is the same thing), a like figure [of a word].

3.2. Extra-Verbal Grounds of Refutation [108]

3.2.1. Accident.[109] Next, as to extra-verbal sophistical grounds; and first, the sophistical ground associated with accident (*secundum accidens*). Aristotle says that paralogisms based on this ground occur whenever anything is attributed (*assignatum*) to a thing as subject and subsequently attributed to an accident [belonging to that thing].[110]

It is clear from this that there are three terms in these paralogisms —viz., the subject, the accident, and the attribute. These terms may be recognized in individual paralogisms in the following way. The term that is predicated (*dicitur inesse*) twice is the attribute, and this is the major extreme. In some paralogisms, however, its attribution is direct — i.e., effected through the nominative case — in others oblique — i.e., effected through an oblique case. Direct attribution occurs as follows: 'Socrates is esteemed by you, but Socrates is your father's murderer; [94] therefore your father's murderer is esteemed by you.'[111] The term 'is esteemed' (*diligitur*) is the attribute. Oblique attribution occurs as follows: 'Plato is something other than Socrates, Socrates is a man; therefore Plato is something other than a man'[112] (*a Sorte est Plato alter. Sortes est homo. Ergo ab homine est Plato alter*). That Plato is something other (*Hoc, quod dico Platonem esse alterum*) is what is attributed, but its attribution to Socrates and to man is effected obliquely.[113] In this way the attribute can be understood.

---

[107] In this case the active form of 'sees' (*videt*) misleads one into thinking that seeing is an activity, just as the passive form of '*operatur*' in the preceding example is supposed to mislead one into thinking that in operating one is passive rather than active. Cf. *Soph. el.*, Ch. 22 (178a4ff).

[108] See p. 134.

[109] The heading "*De fallacia accidentis*" appears in the margin of the manuscript. On the paralogism of Accident see *Soph. el.*, Ch. 5 (166b28ff).

[110] *Soph. el.*, Ch. 5 (166b28–30).

[111] Cf. De Rijk, *Logica modernorum*, Vol. I, Index C: "*interficio*."

[112] Cf. *Soph. el.*, Ch. 5 (166b32ff); also De Rijk, *Logica modernorum*, Vol. I, Index C: "*alter*."

[113] It is not clear just what is supposed to be attributed in this case. The attribute

In order to understand the other two terms it is important to notice what Aristotle says — viz., that this ground does not occur in connection with things that are the same in essence,[114] but in connection [only] with things that differ [in essence].[115] And this is to be understood in the following way. This ground does not occur unless the middle and minor terms differ; but this difference cannot be absolute (*secundum se*), because one of them is always truly predicated of the other. Instead, the difference is in respect of the third term, the attribute, which can be easily seen in the first paralogism [in the preceding paragraph]. Socrates and the murderer, although they are the same absolutely, are different in respect of the attribute 'is esteemed'; for 'murderer' adds a certain accident to Socrates, and it is under the concept of that accident that Socrates is regarded by the attribute in the conclusion (*ratione cuius respicitur in conclusione ab assignato*), for otherwise the conclusion would not be false.[116] It is clear, therefore, that the attribute does not regard the middle and the minor in the respect in which they are the same; thus they differ in respect of the attribute. This holds good in every case.

Since the middle and the minor are thus different and the difference is not with respect to the thing [they both stand for] (since in that case the one would not be truly predicated of the other), the difference will be either between the thing and a concept (*ratio*) [of it], as in the aforementioned example (for 'Socrates' expresses (*dicit*) a single thing and 'murderer' expresses a concept of difference from that thing (*dicit rationem differentie ab illa*)), or between a concept and a concept. For example: 'your friend is esteemed by you, but your friend is your father's murderer; therefore your father's murderer is esteemed by you.' 'Friend' expresses one concept [of the person], under which concept

---

is supposed to occur in the paralogism as the major extremity, and on that basis what is attributed would seem to be the "term" '*Plato alter*' (as the "term" '*diligitur*' is identified in the preceding paralogism as the attribute). But Sherwood seems to be suggesting something else here, perhaps that Plato's being something other (than) is what is being attributed. Both the predication of what is attributed and the occurrence of the oblique (ablative) case are discernible only in the Latin.

[114] Reading '*essentiam*' for '*substantiam*.'

[115] *Soph. el.*, Ch. 24 (179a35ff): "It is obvious that in all these instances it does not necessarily follow that the attribute that is true of the accident is true also of the subject. For it is only to things that are indistinguishable and one in essence that all the same attributes are generally said to belong."

[116] I.e., the conclusion must be taken as asserting that Socrates is esteemed by you in his (accidental) role as your father's murderer and not merely that the man (unknown to you) who murdered your father is esteemed by you.

[the person] is regarded by the attribute; 'murderer' expresses another. Thus in this case the diversity in respect of the attribute is between concepts.

Consequently, in cases where the diversity is between the thing and a concept [of it] the term denoting that which occurs as the thing (*denotans illud, quod est ut res*) is called the subject, while the term denoting the concept differing from the thing is called the accident; e.g., in the first example 'Socrates' is the subject, 'murderer' the accident. But in cases where the diversity is between a concept and a concept, the one that is subjected to the other is called the subject, the other its accident. And the universal principle by which we ought to recognize the subject is that the subject is that which possesses the concept of the thing to a greater extent than does the other (*subiectum est illud, quod magis habet rationem rei respectu alterius*). This is plain where the diversity is [95] between a concept and a thing; but where it is between a concept and a concept the one that is subjected to the other always occurs as the thing in respect of [the attribute], rather than vice versa. In this way [the subject and the accident] can be understood.

It is clear that the cause of the Semblance in these paralogisms is the sameness of the subject and the accident.[117] The cause of the Non-existence is, I maintain, their diversity in respect of the attribute. Since the Semblance results from the condition of a thing (*ex conditione rei*) and not [from the condition] of a word or sign, this is an extra-verbal ground. Now Accident is one and the same thing alienated [from itself] or one and the same thing divided (*idem extraneum vel idem divisum*); in saying "one and the same thing" I indicate the Semblance, while in saying "alienated" and "divided" I indicate the Nonexistence. Paralogisms of this kind are, therefore, said to be associated with Accident.

The way to solve paralogisms of this kind is to show this diversity in the middle and the minor in respect of the major, or attribute.[118] Example: 'you know Coriscus; it is Coriscus who is approaching (*Coriscus est veniens*); therefore you know who is approaching.'[119] That you know [him] (*Te cognoscere*) is attributed first to Coriscus and after-

---

[117] In the extra-verbal grounds the "sameness" is of course not verbal. E.g., 'Socrates' (the subject) and 'your father's murderer' (the accident) both refer to the same person.

[118] On the solution of paralogisms of Accident see *Soph. el.*, Ch. 24 (179a26ff).

[119] Cf. *Soph. el.*, Ch. 24 (179b1ff); also De Rijk, *Logica modernorum*, Vol. I, Index C: "*cognosco*" and "*venio*."

wards to the person approaching. 'Coriscus' is the subject and 'who is approaching' is the accident, for it adds an accident to Coriscus, and it is under the concept of that added accident that he is regarded by the attribute [in the conclusion], for otherwise the conclusion would not be false. As a result, 'Coriscus' and 'who is approaching' are diverse in respect of the attribute. Since in this case the diversity is between a concept and a thing, 'Coriscus' is called the subject because it occurs as the thing, while 'who is approaching' occurs as the accident.

Understand that it is not [an instance of] Accident if I say 'you are hitting Coriscus, and he is approaching; therefore you are hitting the person approaching.' The person approaching is not regarded in the conclusion in respect of an accident that 'approaching' adds to the subject [in the second premiss] but only under the concept of a substance.[120] Consequently 'Coriscus' [the subject] and 'the person approaching' [the accident] are one and the same in respect of this attribute.

3.2.2. In a Certain Respect as Well as Absolutely.[121] Next, as to the sophistical ground [of using a locution] in a certain respect as well as absolutely (*secundum quid et simpliciter*). Aristotle says that paralogisms based on this ground occur when some [locution] is used in a certain respect and not strictly (*proprie*), and a conclusion is drawn [as if it had been used] absolutely.[122]

Understand that a respect is the same as a determination[123] (*quod quid idem est quod determinatio*). There are two kinds of determination, one of which is strict — i.e., the kind in which what is determined is [thereby] contracted into something less general[124] (*que trahit de-*

---

[120] I.e., as regarded by the attribute of being hit by you, Coriscus is simply a physical object.

[121] The heading *"De fallacia secundum quid et simpliciter"* appears in the margin of the manuscript. On the paralogism of using a locution in a certain respect as well as absolutely, see *Soph. el.*, Ch. 5 (166b36ff).

[122] *Soph. el.*, Ch. 5 (166b37ff).

[123] Cf. De Rijk, *Logica modernorum*, Vol. I, p. 216. On determination cf. p. 14 above.

[124] On this distinction between kinds of determination cf. De Rijk, *Logica modernorum*, Vol. I, pp. 130–131, 372–373, 528–529. Examples of inferences involving strict determination: 'he is a white man; therefore he is a man'; 'it is white over its entire surface; therefore it is white.' Four or more kinds of unstrict determination are distinguished in twelfth-century texts (see De Rijk, *loc. cit.*) — e.g., (a) determination with respect to a cause: 'I want to sell everything I have in order to get out of jail'; (b) with respect to a part: 'an Ethiopian is white as regards his teeth'; (c) with respect to place: 'monks eat in a refectory'; (d) with respect to time: 'monks sleep at night'; (e) miscellaneous (*alia determinatio*): 'a chimera is thinkable,' 'Homer is a poet' (from which, it was supposed, one might be deceived into infer-

terminatum ad minus commune). That kind is strict, and the other kind is not. No deception occurs in connection with the first kind, [96] but [deception does occur] in connection with the second kind, and it is for that reason that 'not strictly' is joined to 'in a certain respect.'

The cause of the Semblance in these paralogisms is the closeness (*propinquitas*) of some [locution] used in a certain respect to that same [locution] used absolutely. I am speaking of closeness in connection with a word, and I do not mean a word [considered as] an action, which is an utterance, but a word [considered as] a passion — i. e., the significatum of an utterance, which is a concept (*intellectus*); for a concept is what is primarily (*primo*) signified by an utterance.[125] Thus it is clear that this is an extra-verbal ground, because its Semblance has to do with (*est ex parte*) the significatum and not with the sign.

The cause of the Nonexistence, on the other hand, is the diversity between [a locution used in a certain respect and that same locution used absolutely] (*diversitas eorundem*).

Unstrict [determination] is of two sorts, however.[126] It is either alienating (*distrahens*), in case the determination is in opposition to what is determined (as in 'dead man'), or not alienating but lessening (*diminuens*) (as in 'white of foot' (*albus pedem*)).

Accordingly, paralogisms [of this sort] occur in two ways. For example: 'Socrates is a dead man; therefore he is a man.' Or: 'Socrates is white of foot; therefore he is white.' Nevertheless, this holds: 'he is curly headed (*Est crispus capud*); therefore he is curly,' since 'curly' denominates only under the concept of this part [of the body], and as a result this part is a strict respect[127] (*quia hoc, quod dico crispus, solum denominat ratione huius partis et propterea hec pars est quid proprium*).

Aristotle says that these paralogisms should be solved by considering the conclusion in relation to its contradiction.[128] What this means is that we are to extract the contradiction of the conclusion from the conclu-

---

ring 'a chimera is,' or 'Homer is'), 'he is a good thief' (from which, with the premiss 'a thief is a man,' one might be deceived into inferring 'he is a good man'). Cf. Sherwood's division of unstrict determination on p. 154 below.

[125] See p. 105 above.

[126] Cf. n. 124, this chapter.

[127] I.e., since the only respect in which a man *can* be said to be curly is in respect of his head of hair, this respect, or determination, is strict. On the other hand, there are many respects in which a man can be white other than in respect of his foot, and so the example immediately preceding is a paralogism. It involves unstrict determination.

[128] *Soph. el.*, Ch. 25 (180a24ff).

sion and then see if this contradiction can stand together with the premisses. If that is possible it is clear that the conclusion does not follow and that the respect [in which the locution was used in the premiss] was not a strict respect (*Sed istud quid fuit quid non proprium*).

3.2.3. *Ignorance Regarding Refutation.*[129] The next thing to be discussed is Ignorance Regarding Refutation (*ignorantia elenchi*);[130] but first we need to know what a refutation is. Aristotle defines it as follows: [131] A refutation is a contradiction of one and the same [predicate], not of the name alone but of the thing together with the name, and not of a synonym but of the very same name, on the basis of the stated [premisses] and [following] necessarily from them (without including in them what was in the original point to be proved) — [A] in the same respect, [B] in the same relation, [C] in the same way, and [D] at the same time.

Now paralogisms occur in connection with Ignorance Regarding Refutation insofar as some but not all of those parts [of a refutation] are omitted — but of these four parts only: [A] in the same respect, [B] in the same relation, etc. This raises the question why [97] paralogisms of Ignorance Regarding Refutation are assigned to these four parts rather than to the others. In reply we must point out that these four parts are especially associated with (*appropriantur*) contradiction, while the others are not but are common to both syllogism and contradiction (since [except for contradiction] syllogism falls under the concept of refutation (*in ratione elenchi cadit*)).[132] A refutation is either a syllogism with the contradiction of the [original] conclusion or two syllogisms leading to contradictory opposites (*inferentes contradictione opposita*).

There are then four paralogisms depending on the omission of these four parts. In connection with [A] as follows: '*a* is twice as great as *b*

---

[129] The heading "*De ignorantia elenchi*" appears in the margin of the manuscript. On the paralogism of Ignorance Regarding Refutation see *Soph. el.*, Ch. 5 (167a21ff).

[130] '*Elenchus*' is a transliteration of Aristotle's word for refutation — 'ἔλεγχος.' The corresponding Latin word used throughout Boethius's translation of Aristotle is '*redargutio*,' used by Sherwood in earlier sections of this chapter; e.g., p. 133.

[131] The following passage differs only in minor detail (such as replacing '*redargutio*' with '*elenchus*') from the wording of Boethius's translation of *Soph. el.*, Ch. 5 (167a24ff).

[132] Sherwood is using 'syllogism' here in the broad sense of proof. For the relation between proof and refutation cf. *Soph. el.*, Ch. 6 (168a35ff).

in length and is not twice as great as *b* in width; therefore it is both twice as great and not twice as great.' In connection with [B] as follows: '*a* is twice as great as *b* and is not twice as great as *c*; therefore it is both twice as great and not twice as great.'[133] In connection with [C] as follows: 'Socrates is naturally pious but he is not absolutely pious; therefore he is both pious and not pious.' In connection with [D] as follows: 'Socrates is running at [time] *a* (*currit in a*) and he is not running at [time] *b*; therefore he is both running and not running.'[134] There is Ignorance Regarding Refutation in these four paralogisms because [in each of them] a contradiction seems to be concluded but is not [really] concluded, for [in each of them] one of those four parts is missing.

There is some doubt here, however, because each of these paralogisms seems to be [a case of using a locution] In a Certain Respect as Well as Absolutely, because of the omission of a determination. [It is] as if one were to say 'it is not twice as great in length; therefore it is not twice as great'; 'he is naturally pious; therefore he is pious'; and so on with respect to the others.

In reply we must point out that there is nothing in those paralogisms preventing them from being [considered] cases of erring [as a result of using a locution] In a Certain Respect as Well as Absolutely. But that is not the main issue (*causa principalis*). The difference between Ignorance Regarding Refutation and [using a locution] In a Certain Respect as Well as Absolutely is that the latter does not aim at concluding a contradiction, as was shown earlier, although in solving it it is necessary to consider the conclusion in relation to its contradiction.[135] In Ignorance Regarding Refutation, even though some determination is involved, still the aim is to conclude a contradiction absolutely. In that way these paralogisms differ from those that are [based on using a locution] In a Certain Respect as Well as Absolutely.

[The source of] the Semblance of paralogisms of this kind is our ignorance, because we are ignorant regarding contradiction. Since there are so many little parts to a contradiction we believe that the

---

[133] For both [A] and [B] cf. De Rijk, *Logica modernorum*, Vol. I, Index C: "*duplus.*"

[134] These four paralogisms of *ignorantia elenchi* correspond to four of the five fallacies discussed by Boethius in his *Introductio ad syllogismos categoricos* (P.L., 64.778B–780A). Cf. De Rijk, *Logica modernorum*, Vol. I, pp. 39–43.

[135] See pp. 154–155.

omission of one little part does not impair the whole contradiction. Thus the difference between the Semblance of this ground and the Semblance of [the extra-verbal grounds] preceding it is obvious: the Semblance of the preceding [extra-verbal grounds] has to do either with a thing or with a concept, while the Semblance of this one has to do with us, because [98] it results from our ignorance. Nevertheless, *some* of the Semblance has to do with a thing, as was said above.[136]

3.2.4. Begging the Original Issue.[137] Next, as to paralogisms that occur in connection with Begging the Original Issue (*petitio principii*). Aristotle says that such paralogisms occur in as many ways as it is possible to beg the original issue.[138]

The original issue is begged in five ways:

In one way, when, in order to prove something, that very thing is assumed, differing neither in utterance nor in concept — e.g., 'a man is running; therefore a man is running.'[139]

In another way, when, in order to prove a particular, we assume the universal in which that particular is — e.g., 'the knowledge of opposites is one and the same; therefore [so is the knowledge] of all contraries.'

In a third way, when one has to prove a universal and begs it in its parts, as if one were required to show this — 'the knowledge of all opposites is one and the same' — and begged this — 'the knowledge of all contraries, and of all privative opposites . . . (and so on of the others) . . . is one and the same,' concluding that the knowledge of all opposites is one and the same.[140]

---

[136] Perhaps an allusion to Aristotle's stipulation that in refutation the predicate must be contradicted of the thing and not just of the name.

[137] The heading *"De fallacia petitionis principii"* appears in the margin of the manuscript. On the paralogism of Begging the Original Issue see *Soph. el.*, Ch. 5 (167a36ff).

[138] *Soph. el.*, loc. cit. Cf. *Topics*, Bk. 8, Ch. 13 (162b34–163a13).

[139] Cf. Peter of Spain (*Sum. log.*, ed. Bocheński, pp. 85–86), who specifically rejects this example as "ridiculous." He claims that the paralogism does not genuinely occur unless what is assumed is "in" the original issue rather than identical to it. Thus his example of this first way is 'a man is running; therefore a mortal rational animal is running.'

[140] As Sherwood puts it, this third way of Begging the Original Issue seems to be the same as an induction by exhaustive enumeration. Aristotle's description of it does not give this impression: "A third way is if anyone were to beg in particular cases what he undertakes to show universally: e.g., if he undertakes to show that the knowledge of contraries is always one, and begged it of certain pairs of contraries: for he also is generally considered to be begging independently and by itself what, together with a number of other things, he ought to have shown" (*Topics*, Bk. 8, Ch. 13 (163a4ff)).

a conversion is effected as follows: 'it is an animal; therefore it is a man.' In this connection it is customary to point out several varieties — as when one proceeds by way of negation from an inferior to a superior ('it is not a man; therefore it is not an animal'), and by way of affirmation from a superior to an inferior ('it is an animal; therefore it is a man') (*ut cum sit processus ab inferiori ad superius negando et a superiori ad inferius affirmando ut hic: non est homo. Ergo non est animal. Similiter: est homo. Ergo est animal*).[145] And it is also [a paralogism of] the Consequent when one syllogizes using affirmative premises in the second figure [146] — e.g., 'a man is an animal, an ass is an animal; therefore an ass is a man.'

But we must consider how it is that people believe that a consequence is converted in instances when it is not converted. [The answer is that] since a consequence from a superior to an inferior by way of negation is acceptable (*vera*), people believe it [can] be converted to a consequence from an inferior to a superior by way of negation; and since [100] a consequence from an inferior to a superior by way of affirmation is acceptable, people believe it [can] be converted to a consequence from a superior to an inferior by way of affirmation.

When, on the other hand, one syllogizes in the second figure that an ass is a man since it is an animal, it is only because one believes that *animal* can be converted with *man*. As a result one believes that 'every man is an animal' is absolutely converted — 'therefore every animal is a man' — and in this way one believes that the inference is acceptable. Deception of this kind occurs especially in cases having to do with sense perception (*que sunt secundum sensum*).[147] For example: 'honey is ruddy, gall is ruddy; therefore gall is honey.'[148]

It occurs likewise in rhetorical inferences — 'he is elegantly dressed; therefore he is an adulterer'; 'he wanders about at night; therefore he is a thief.' The reason is that this does follow: 'he is a thief; therefore he wanders about at night,' and so this is thought to be convertible although it is not. Similarly, this follows: 'if he is an adulterer, he is ele-

---

[145] *G* has '*negando*'; '*affirmando*' in manuscript. The last example evidently should be "*Similiter: est animal. Ergo est homo.*" This emendation is confirmed by the final clause in the paragraph immediately following.

[146] Cf. De Rijk, *Logica modernorum*, Vol. I, pp. 150 and 604.

[147] Cf. *Soph. el.*, Ch. 5 (167b4ff).

[148] Cf. De Rijk, *Logica modernorum*, Vol. I, Index C: "*mel.*"

gantly dressed'; as a result people believe it [can] be converted: 'if he is elegantly dressed, he is an adulterer.'[149]

On the basis of these [examples] it is obvious that in every case of a paralogism of the Consequent there will be a double consequence, one acceptable (*vera*) and the other unacceptable (*falsa*).[150] In some of these paralogisms, however, not both consequences are actually expressed; instead, the acceptable one is supplied in thought (*utraque consequentia non exprimitur ut in entibus, sed vera subintelligitur*).

Thus it is clear what the Nonexistence is in this [kind of] paralogism. In pointing out the Nonexistence associated with it, however, Aristotle says that Consequent is part of Accident.[151] A doubt exists, however, regarding the respect in which it is a part, whether it is an integral or a subjective part.[152]

That it is not an integral part is clear from the fact that the author goes on to say that the consequent occurs as an accident (*consequens accidit*).[153] If that predication is the reason why [he says that] the predicate [or accident] is a whole in relation to the subject [or consequent], then it will not be every [sort of] part but rather a subjective part, which must be granted (*Si enim hec predicatio est causa, quare predicatum sit totum ad subiectum, non erit pars quelibet, sed pars subiectiva. Quod concedendum est.*).

Nevertheless, Accident and Consequent are not one and the same ground. There is no *part* of Accident that is a sophistical ground, but there is a part of Accident that is common to Accident and Consequent. And this is what he next gives one to understand, when he points out that the difference between Accident and Consequent is that Accident

---

[149] Cf. *Soph. el.*, Ch. 5 (167b9ff); also De Rijk, *Logica modernorum*, Vol. I, Index C: "*adulter*," "*errabundus*."

[150] Cf. *Soph. el.*, Ch. 28 (181a21ff).

[151] *Soph. el.*, Ch. 6 (168b27); Ch. 7 (169b6).

[152] I.e., whether it is a part of Accident in the sense in which a wall is (an integral) part of a house, or in the sense in which the species *man* is (a subjective) part of the genus *animal*. (See pp. 26–27 above.) An integral part can exist on its own, in the absence of the whole of which it is a part; a subjective part cannot do so.

[153] *Soph. el.*, Ch. 6 (168b27ff): "Those of the Consequent form part of Accident. for the consequent occurs as an accident. Consequent differs from Accident, however, in that an admission of Accident can be secured in the case of a single thing — e.g., honey and something yellow are one and the same, also a swan and something white. Consequent, on the other hand, always involves more than one thing, for we claim that things that are the same as one and the same thing are the same as each other, and this is how refutation proceeds based on the Consequent."

is secured (*sumere*) in the case of a single thing but Consequent in more than one, which is clearly true. An accident is an extrinsic middle that is not in both extremes from a single point of view, but [first] from one [point of view] and [then] from another (*sed secundum alteram et alteram*). That is why he says it is in a single thing, meaning that it is in one from one point of view and in the other from another. In [a paralogism of] the Consequent, on the other hand, when one and the same thing is predicated of [101] more than one — as *animal* of *man* and of *ass* — it is not predicated of them from different points of view but from one and the same point of view. And that is why he says that a consequent is in more than one. Still, because it is in more than one, [it is] an accident. It is not an accident, however, in the sense of an extraneous middle (*Sed non sic accidens sicut medium extraneum*), and therefore it is not called (*appellatur*) an accident in that sense.[154]

There is a single Semblance in paralogisms of the Consequent — viz., that the consequent is inseparable from the antecedent; and for that reason people believe the reverse — that the antecedent is inseparable from the consequent.[155]

3.2.6. Treating What Is Not a Cause as a Cause.[156] Next, as to paralogisms dependent on treating what is not a cause as a cause (*secundum non causam ut causam*). Paralogisms of this kind properly occur in connection with syllogisms leading to an impossibility (as Aristotle points out in the second book of the *Prior Analytics*).[157] Syllogisms of this kind occur when, because something impossible follows, one of the premises is demolished on the grounds that it seems to be the cause of the impossibility (although it is not).[158] This is also a method of

---

[154] See pp. 150–153.

[155] Cf. *Soph. el.*, Ch. 7 (169b6ff); also Sherwood's discussion of separable and inseparable accidents on p. 56 above.

[156] The heading "*De fallaciis secundum non causam ut causam*" appears in the margin of the manuscript. On the paralogism of treating what is not a cause as a cause see *Soph. el.*, Ch. 5 (167b21ff).

[157] See *An. pr.*, Bk. II, Ch. 17 (65a38ff). Although Sherwood's reference is quite pertinent, much of his discussion here is actually closer to *Soph. el.*, Ch. 5 (167b20ff). See n. 160, this chapter.

[158] Because of the opening clause 'Syllogisms of this kind occur' ('*fiunt enim sillogismi huiusmodi*') this sentence appears to be an account of syllogisms leading to an impossibility rather than of the occurrence of the paralogism of mistaken cause in connection with such syllogisms. In all probability the opening clause should be deleted and the remainder of this sentence should be appended to the preceding sentence.

proving something *per impossibile*.[159] For example, if someone wants to prove that soul and life are not one and the same (*non sunt eadem sive idem*) [he might argue as follows:] 'death and life are contraries, generation and corruption are contraries, to die is to be corrupted; therefore to live is to be generated. But that is impossible. Therefore the first — viz., that soul and life are one and the same — is impossible. Therefore life is an opposite of soul.'[160] The deception in this case is due to the fact that the proposition 'soul and life are one and the same' seems to be a cause of the conclusion and is not, although it seems impossible that [the conclusion] follows and [that proposition] is not [a cause of it] (*videtur esse tamen impossibile, quod sequitur et non est*).

Deception of this sort occurs only in syllogisms leading to an impossibility;[161] for a single proposition is not the cause of the conclusion, although the falsity of one proposition is the cause of the falsity of the conclusion. Therefore, treating what is not a cause as a cause will occur only in syllogisms with false conclusions, and not in every such syllogism; for if an ostensive syllogism[162] has a false conclusion we do not care which of the premisses is the cause of the falsity, but [only] that one of the premisses is false. When, however, we care to demolish one of the premisses because of the impossibility of the conclusion, then we do care which of the premisses was the cause of it,

---

[159] A syllogism *ad impossibile*, better known as a *reductio ad impossibile* (or *ad absurdum*), is a means of proving a proposition *per impossibile*, the proved proposition being the contradictory of what is reduced to an impossibility.

[160] Cf. Aristotle's version of this same example, used by him in the same connection (*Soph. el.*, Ch. 5 (167b24ff)): "If, then, what is not a cause is counted among the questions that are necessary to establish the resulting impossibility [in an argument *ad impossibile*], it will often seem that the refutation depends on it, e.g., in the proof that the soul and life are not one and the same: for if coming-to-be is contrary to perishing, then a particular form of perishing will have a particular form of coming-to-be as its contrary: now death is a particular form of perishing and is contrary to life: life, therefore, is a coming-to-be, and to live is to come-to-be. But this is impossible: accordingly, the soul and life are not one and the same. Now this is not proved: for the impossibility results all the same, even if one does not say that life is the same as the soul, but says merely that life is contrary to death, which is a form of perishing, and that perishing has coming-to-be as its contrary." (Cf. also De Rijk, *Logica modernorum*, Vol. I, Index C: "*anima.*") The use of the notion of cause in this connection stems from the Aristotelian doctrine that in demonstrative syllogism "the premisses must be the causes of the conclusion" (*An. post.*, Bk. I, Ch. 2 (71b29ff)).

[161] Cf. *An. pr.*, Bk. II, Ch. 17 (65b9ff).

[162] On the difference between ostensive syllogism and syllogism *ad impossibile* see *An. pr.*, Bk. II, Ch. 14 (62b29ff).

and then [that one] is demolished. So deception of this sort occurs only in syllogisms leading to an impossibility.

It is clear, then, that those who introduce an example such as the following in connection with this ground are mistaken (*mentiuntur*): 'every animal [102] is a substance, every man is an animal, the sun is in Cancer; therefore every man is a substance.'[163] Moreover, in respect of the diminution of one of the premisses this is not a case of treating what is not a cause as a cause[164] (*Nec etiam est non causa ut causa in diminutione alterius premissarum*), as some have said. For Aristotle says that inferences of this sort are not absolutely syllogistic.[165] They are syllogistic to the extent to which they lead to an impossibility. The impossible is truly concluded, but [only] to the extent to which the premisses[166] are set out syllogistically (*Impossibile enim vere concluditur, sed quantum ad propositum in sillogizante sunt*), for it is not the case that one or another of the premisses is truly demolished as a result of that kind of impossible.[167]

The Semblance in paralogisms of this sort is the fact that the proposition that is not a cause has some continuity (*habet continuationem*)

---

[163] For example, the anonymous twelfth-century *Fallacie Vindobonenses* introduces the following inference as an instance of a second kind of paralogism of treating what is not a cause as a cause: "'every man is an animal, but everything risible is a man, and the sun is in Aries; therefore everything risible is an animal.' This does not follow, because it is a paralogism dependent on treating what is not a cause as a cause, since the proposition 'the sun is in Aries' is not a cause of the conclusion although it is treated as a cause, for when it is deleted the conclusion will follow from the [remaining] premisses no less" (ed. De Rijk, *Logica modernorum*, Vol. I, p. 539). Examples containing premisses that are merely logically superfluous were probably introduced following the suggestion of *Soph. el.*, Ch. 29 (181a31ff), which purports to provide a method of solving paralogisms of mistaken cause but seems to be alluding to a much broader category of paralogism than that originally described in *Soph. el.*, Ch. 5 (167b21ff). Peter of Spain agrees with Sherwood in dismissing such cases: "From the foregoing remarks it is clear that this fallacy does not occur in an ostensive syllogism such as 'every man is running, Socrates is a man, and the sun is in Cancer; therefore Socrates is running.' This is not a fallacy dependent on treating what is not a cause as a cause since the proposition 'the sun is in Cancer' neither is nor *seems* to be a cause, and since this is not a syllogism leading to an impossibility" (*Sum. log.*, ed. Bocheński, p. 88).

[164] Apparently diminution here is the same as the demolishing of one of the premisses, and the claim is that the example is mistaken not only because it does not have a false conclusion but also because there is no inference back to the denial of one of the premisses.

[165] Probably a reference to the beginning of *An. pr.*, Bk. II, Ch. 14 (62b29ff), where "demonstration *per impossibile*" is distinguished from "ostensive proof," the latter being absolutely syllogistic. Cf. *An. pr.*, Bk. I, Ch. 23 (especially 41a20ff).

[166] Reading '*proposita*' for '*propositum*.'

[167] The conclusion of this paragraph, beginning with the reference to Aristotle,

with the propositions that are causes, and with the conclusion, and with the impossibility that follows; and it is for that reason that it is treated as a cause (*et propterea est ut causa*). If a proposition were proposed that had no point of agreement (*non haberet convenientiam*) with the impossibility it would not be a cause, but neither would it be treated as if it were a cause (*sed non ut causa*), as Aristotle shows in the second book of the *Prior Analytics*.[168]

3.2.7. *Treating More Than One Question as One.*[169] Next, as to paralogisms that occur in connection with treating more than one question as one (*secundum plures interrogationes ut unam*). It should be noted that a question and a proposition are one and the same thing here, except that it is a question when it is asked prior to [the construction of] a syllogism, and it is a proposition when it is ordered in a syllogism.

The deception comes about because a proposition that is more than one seems to be one, and one responds to it with a single response. For example: 'Are Socrates and Plato at home?' (when the one has gone out and the other has not). If one says 'yes,' then Socrates, who is not at home, is at home. If one says 'no,' then Plato, who is at home, is not at home.

Similarly, suppose that two things are pointed to, one of which is good, the other bad. 'Are these things good or not good?' If one takes the affirmative (*si concedat*), one is necessarily refuted, for it follows that what is not good is good. But if one takes the negative (*neget*), refutation seems to follow although it does not follow; for this does not follow: 'they are not good; therefore this one of them is not good.'[170]

---

is obscure. For one thing, it is not clear whether "inferences of this sort" are inferences of the sort exemplified immediately above or inferences leading to an impossibility. Moreover, what is said about the inferences seems confused on either interpretation.

[168] Apparently a reference to *An. pr.*, Bk. II, Ch. 17 (especially 65b9ff). Aristotle's example: "This is to treat what is not a cause as a cause; as if someone wishing to prove that the diagonal of a square is incommensurable [with the side] were to try to prove Zeno's theorem that motion is impossible and so establish a *reductio ad impossibile*; for there is no connection between Zeno's false theorem and the original assertion." Ch. also *Topics*, Bk. VIII, Ch. 11 (162a24ff), on superfluous premisses. In this paragraph, however, Sherwood seems to be presenting a reason for *dismissing* the inference in the preceding paragraph as an example of treating what is not a cause as a cause.

[169] The heading *"De fallaciis secundum plures interrogationes ut unam"* appears in the margin of the manuscript. On the paralogism of treating more than one question as one see *Soph. el.*, Ch. 5 (167b37ff).

[170] Sherwood's distinction between the two answers is a significant variation on

That is why Aristotle says that if someone puts forward a proposition that holds for more than one in the same way as for one (*similiter est in pluralibus sicut in singulari*), then it does follow necessarily.[171] It is true to say of one thing 'this is not good; therefore it is bad.' So if it holds in the same way [103] for more than one, then this follows: 'these are not good; therefore they are bad.' The solution in this case is that it does not hold in the same way in the singular and in the plural, for the negation of it in the plural can be taken in two ways: either for the whole plurality (*aut gratia totius multitudinis*) and not for every part under the plurality, in which case [the inference] does not follow; or for every part under the plurality, in which case it does follow.

To a proposition that is more than one, one must respond with more than one response.

It seems, however, that this ground does not differ from Equivocation. Aristotle says in *De interpretatione* that the proposition 'a cloak is white' is more than one when 'cloak' is equivocal.[172]

In response to this we must point out that the proposition 'a cloak is white' [in Aristotle's example] does signify more than one thing; nevertheless, in putting it in the form of a question one does not ask more than one question but only one, because having imposed the name [only] once we do not use it equivocally (*nomine semel posito non utimur equivoce*).[173] Accordingly, the question ['is a cloak white?'] is not more than one although the proposition ['a cloak is white'] is more than one.

Aristotle's similar example (*Soph. el.*, Ch. 5 (168a7ff)): "Or again, where part is good and part bad, 'is the whole good or bad?' For whichever he says, it is possible that he might be thought to expose himself to an apparent refutation or to make an apparently false statement: for to say that something is good which is not good, or not good which is good, is to make a false statement."

[171] See *Soph. el.*, Ch. 30 (181a35ff).

[172] *De int.*, Ch. 8 (18a18ff): "But if one name is given to two things which do not make up one thing, there is not a single affirmation. Suppose, for example, that one gave the name 'cloak' to horse and man; 'a cloak is white' would not be a single affirmation. For to say this is no different from saying 'a horse and a man is white,' and this is no different from saying 'a horse is white and a man is white.' So if this last signifies more than one thing and is more than one affirmation, clearly the first also signifies either more than one thing or nothing (because no man is a horse). . . ."

[173] Perhaps he means that although someone may have done the weird thing described in Aristotle's example, so that the name 'cloak' really is (albeit on a small scale) equivocal, nevertheless we, who have attached the name 'cloak' only to a kind of garment, ask only one question when we ask 'is a cloak white?'

In paralogisms of this kind the Semblance is a result of the way in which the question is raised, for questioning in [the form of] a single question is the way in which a *single* question is raised. In order to ask one question we use one interrogation mark, and in order to ask more than one we use more than one. Thus if someone asks 'is Socrates at home?' 'is Plato at home?' there is no Semblance of a single question. But when one asks this under a single interrogation mark there does appear to be a single question.

Let these remarks suffice regarding paralogisms that occur in connection with sophistical grounds [of refutation], verbal as well as extra-verbal. [104]

BIBLIOGRAPHY AND INDEX

Bibliography

The many works of Aristotle and Boethius cited in the notes are sufficiently identified there and are not included in this bibliography.

Abelard, Peter. *Abaelardiana inedita*, ed. L. Minio-Paluello, *Twelfth Century Logic: Texts and Studies*, II. Rome: Edizioni di Storia e Letteratura, 1958.

——. *Dialectica*, ed. L. M. De Rijk. Assen: Van Gorcum, 1956.

——. *Peter Abaelards Philosophische Schriften*, ed. B. Geyer, *Beiträge zur Geschichte der Philosophie und Theologie des Mittelalters*, Vol. XXI. Münster i.W.: Aschendorff, 1919–1933.

Adam of Balsham. *Ars disserendi*, ed. L. Minio-Paluello, *Twelfth Century Logic: Texts and Studies*, I. Rome: Edizioni di Storia e Letteratura, 1956.

Anselm. *De grammatico*, S. *Anselmi cantuariensis archiepiscopi opera omnia*, I, 141–168. Edinburgh: Nelson, 1938.

Anstey, Henry, ed. *Munimenta academica; or, Documents Illustrative of Academical Life and Studies at Oxford*. Rolls Series, Vol. 50 [1–2]. London: Longmans, 1868.

Bacon, Roger. *Compendium studii philosophiae*, ed. J. S. Brewer, *Fr. Rogeri Bacon opera quaedam hactenus inedita*, I. London: Longmans, 1859.

——. *Compendium studii theologiae*, ed. H. Rashdall, *British Society of Franciscan Studies*, III. Aberdeen: University Press, 1911.

——. *Opus majus*, ed. J. H. Bridges, 3 vols. Oxford: Clarendon, 1897–1900.

——. *Opus tertium*, ed. J. S. Brewer, *Fr. Rogeri Bacon opera quaedam hactenus inedita*, I. London: Longmans, 1859.

——. *Summa de sophismatibus et distinctionibus*, ed. R. Steele, *Opera hactenus inedita Rogeri Baconi*, XIV. Oxford: Clarendon, 1937.

——. *Sumule dialectices*, ed. R. Steele, *Opera hactenus inedita Rogeri Baconi*, XV. Oxford: Clarendon, 1940.

Baudry, Léon. *Lexique philosophique de Guillaume d'Ockham*. Paris: P. Lethielleux, 1958.

Blomefield, Francis. *An Essay Towards a Topographical History of the County of Norfolk*. 5 vols. 1st ed., 1739–1775. 2nd ed.; London: W. Miller, 1805–1810.

Bocheński, Innocentius M. *A History of Formal Logic*, tr. I. Thomas. Notre Dame, Ind.: University Press, 1961.

——. "Introductio" to his edition of Peter of Spain's *Summulae logicales, q.v.*

Boehner, Philotheus. *Medieval Logic: An Outline of Its Development from 1250–c.1400*. Manchester: University Press, 1952.

——. "A Medieval Theory of Supposition," in *Franciscan Studies*, XVIII (1958), 240–289.

Brewer, J. S. "Preface" to his edition of Roger Bacon's *Opus tertium, q.v.*

Burleigh, Walter. *De puritate artis logicae tractatus longior*, ed. P. Boehner, *Franciscan Institute Publications*, Text Series, No. 9. St. Bonaventure, N.Y.: Franciscan Institute, 1955.

Calendar of Entries in the Papal Registers Relating to Great Britain and Ireland, I (A.D. 1198–1304). London: H.M. Stationery Office, 1893.

Calendar of the Patent Rolls Preserved in the Public Record Office, vols. for A.D. 1247–1258 and A.D. 1313–1317. London: H.M. Stationery Office, 1908 and 1898.

Callus, D. A., ed. *Robert Grosseteste, Scholar and Bishop: Essays in Commemoration of the Seventh Centenary of His Death.* Oxford: Clarendon, 1955.

Chenu, M.-D. "Notes de lexicographie médiévale — ANTIQUI, MODERNI." *Revue des sciences philosophiques et théologiques,* XVII (1928), 82–94.

Crombie, A. C. *Robert Grosseteste and the Origins of Experimental Science, 1100–1700.* Oxford: Clarendon, 1953.

Davis, F. N., ed. *Rotuli Ricardi Gravesend, episcopi Lincolniensis* A.D. *MCCLVIII–MCCLXXIX. The Publications of the Lincoln Record Society,* XX. Hereford: Lincoln Record Society, 1925.

Deferrari, Roy Joseph. *A Lexicon of St. Thomas Aquinas.* 5 vols. Washington, D.C.: Catholic University of America Press, 1948–1949.

Delisle, Leopold Victor. *Inventaire général et méthodique des manuscrits français de la Bibliothèque nationale.* 2 vols. Paris: H. Champion, 1876–1878.

De Rijk, Lambertus Maria. "Introduction" to his edition of Abelard's *Dialectica, q.v.*

―――. "Introduction" to his edition of Garland's *Dialectica, q.v.*

―――. *Logica modernorum: A Contribution to the History of Early Terminist Logic,* Vol. I. *On the Twelfth Century Theories of Fallacy.* Assen: Van Gorcum, 1962.

Dugdale, William. *Monasticon anglicanum.* 3 vols. London: Richard Hodginson, 1655–1673.

Dürr, Karl. *The Propositional Logic of Boethius. Studies in Logic and the Foundations of Mathematics.* Amsterdam: North-Holland, 1951.

Edwards, Kathleen. *The English Secular Cathedrals in the Middle Ages.* Manchester: University Press, 1949.

Foster, Charles W., and Kathleen Major, eds. *The Registrum antiquissimum of the Cathedral Church of Lincoln. The Publications of the Lincoln Record Society,* XXVII, XXIX, XXXII, XXXIV, XLI, XLII, XLVI. Hereford: Lincoln Record Society, 1931–1953.

Garlandus Compotista. *Dialectica,* ed. L. M. De Rijk. Assen: Van Gorcum, 1959.

Geach, Peter. *Reference and Generality; An Examination of Some Medieval and Modern Theories.* Ithaca, N.Y.: Cornell University Press, 1962.

Gilson, Étienne. *History of Christian Philosophy in the Middle Ages.* New York: Random House, 1955.

Grabmann, Martin. "Aristoteles im zwölften Jahrhundert." *Medieval Studies,* XII, 123–162. Toronto: Pontifical Institute of Medieval Studies, 1950.

―――. "Bearbeitungen und Auslegungen der aristotelischen Logik aus der Zeit von Peter Abaelard bis Petrus Hispanus . . ." *Abhandlungen der Preussischen Akademie der Wissenschaften,* Jahrgang 1937, Philosophisch-historische Klasse, nr. 5. Berlin: Akademie der Wissenschaften, 1937.

―――. "Einleitung" to his edition of William of Sherwood's *Introductiones in logicam, q.v.*

―――. "Die Entwicklung der mittelalterlichen Sprachlogik" in his *Mittelalterliches Geistesleben.* I, 104–146. Munich: Hueber, 1926.

―――. "Forschungen über die lateinischen Aristotelesübersetzungen des XIII. Jahrhunderts." *Beiträge zur Geschichte der Philosophie und Theologie des Mittelalters,* Bd. XVII, H. 5–6. Münster i.W.: Aschendorff, 1916.

―――. "Kommentare zur aristotelischen Logik aus dem 12. und 13. Jahrhundert . . ." *Abhandlungen der Preussischen Akademie der Wissenschaften,* Jahrgang 1938, Philosophisch-historische Klasse, nr. 18. Berlin: Akademie der Wissenschaften, 1938.

―――. "Die Sophismatenliteratur des 12. und 13. Jahrhunderts . . ." *Beiträge zur Geschichte der Philosophie und Theologie des Mittelalters,* Bd. XXXVI, H. 1. Münster i.W.: Aschendorff, 1940.

John of Salisbury. *The Metalogicon of John of Salisbury,* tr. D. D. McGarry. Berkeley and Los Angeles: University of California Press, 1955.

BIBLIOGRAPHY

Joseph, Horace William Brindley. *An Introduction to Logic*. Oxford: Clarendon, 1906.

Kingsford, C. L. "Shirwood, William of," in *Dictionary of National Biography*.

Kneale, William, and Martha Kneale. *The Development of Logic*. Oxford: Clarendon, 1962.

Kretzmann, Norman. "Semantics, History of," in Paul Edwards, ed., *Encyclopedia of Philosophy*.

Leland, John. *Commentarii de scriptoribus Britannicis*, ed. Hall. 2 vols. Oxford: Sheldonian Theatre, 1709.

———. *De rebus Britannicis collectanea*, 2nd ed. 6 vols. London: W. and J. Richardson, 1770–1774.

Le Neve, John. *Fasti ecclesiae anglicanae*, not 1st ed. 3 vols. Oxford: University Press, 1854.

Lilje, Gerald W. "Signification and Supposition in the Logic of William of Sherwood." M.A. thesis, University of Illinois, 1964.

Łukasiewicz, Jan. *Aristotle's Syllogistic*. Oxford: Clarendon, 1951.

McKeon, Richard. "Glossary" in his *Selections from Medieval Philosophers*, II. New York: Scribner, 1930.

Michalski, Konstantyn. "Le criticisme et le scepticisme dans la philosophie du XIV⁰ siècle." *Bulletin internationale de l'académie Polonaise des sciences et des lettres*, Classe d'histoire et de philosophie, l'année 1925, pt. 1, no. 11, pp. 41–122. Cracow, 1926.

Minio-Paluello, L. *Twelfth Century Logic: Texts and Studies*. 2 vols. Rome: Edizioni di Storia e Letteratura, 1956–1958.

Moody, Ernest Addison. *The Logic of William of Ockham*. London: Sheed and Ward, 1935.

———. *Truth and Consequence in Medieval Logic. Studies in Logic and the Foundations of Mathematics*. Amsterdam: North-Holland, 1953.

Mullally, Joseph Patrick, ed. and tr. *The Summulae Logicales of Peter of Spain* (A practical edition and a translation of Tractatus VII with an introduction and bibliographies). *Notre Dame Publications in Medieval Studies*, VIII. Notre Dame, Ind.: University Press, 1945.

Ockham, William. *Philosophical Writings: A Selection*, ed. and tr. P. Boehner. Edinburgh: Nelson, 1957.

———. *Summa logicae*, ed. P. Boehner. 3 vols. (Vol. III in preparation.) *Franciscan Institute Publications*, Text Series, No. 2. St. Bonaventure, N.Y.: Franciscan Institute, 1951–.

Paetow, Louis John. *The Arts Course at Medieval Universities with Special Reference to Grammar and Rhetoric*. Champaign, Ill.: University of Illinois Press, 1910.

Page, William, ed. *The Victoria County History of the County of Buckingham*. 4 vols. London: A. Constable, 1905–1927.

Paris, Matthew. *Chronica maiora*, ed. H. R. Luard. 7 vols. London: Longman, 1872–1883.

Paul of Pergula. *Logica and Tractatus de sensu composito et diviso*, ed. Sister Mary Anthony Brown. *Franciscan Institute Publications*, Text Series, No. 13. St. Bonaventure, N.Y.: Franciscan Institute, 1961.

Pegge, Samuel. *The Life of Robert Grosseteste*. London: John Nichols, 1793.

Peter of Spain. *Summulae logicales*, ed. I. M. Bocheński. Turin: Marietti, 1947.

———. *Tractatus syncategorematum*, tr. J. P. Mullally (with an introduction by J. P. Mullally and R. Houde). Milwaukee, Wis.: Marquette University Press, 1964.

Prantl, Carl. *Geschichte der Logik im Abendlande*. 4 vols. in 2. Leipzig: Gustav Fock, 1927 ("Manualdruck der Originalausgabe, 1855").

Priscian. *Institutionum grammaticarum libri XVIII*, ed. M. Hertz. Leipzig: Teubner, 1855.

Rashdall, Hastings. *The Universities of Europe in the Middle Ages*, 2nd ed., ed. F. M. Powicke and A. B. Emden. 3 vols. Oxford: Clarendon, 1936.

Russell, Josiah Cox. *Dictionary of Writers of Thirteenth Century England. Special Supplement No. 3 to the Bulletin of the Institute of Historical Research*. London: Longmans, 1936.

Steele, Robert. "Introduction" to his edition of Roger Bacon's *Sumule dialectices*, *q.v.*

Steenberghen, Fernand van. *Aristotle in the West: The Origins of Latin Aristotelianism*, tr. L. Johnston. Louvain: E. Nauwelaerts, 1955.

Stevenson, Francis Seymour. *Robert Grosseteste, Bishop of Lincoln*. London: Macmillan, 1899.

Tanner, Thomas. *Bibliotheca britannico-hibernica*, ed. D. Wilkins. London, 1748.

Thompson, A. Hamilton. *The English Clergy and Their Organisation in the Later Middle Ages*. Oxford: Clarendon, 1947.

Thomson, S. Harrison. *The Writings of Robert Grosseteste*. Cambridge: University Press, 1940.

Watts, Isaac. *Logic: or The Right Use of Reason in the Enquiry after Truth*, 7th ed. London: Hett & Brackstone, 1740.

Whately, Richard. *Elements of Logic*, 7th ed. London: B. Fellowes, 1840.

William of Sherwood. *Introductiones in logicam*, ed. M. Grabmann. *Sitzungsberichte der Bayerischen Akademie der Wissenschaften*, Philosophisch-historische Abteilung, Jahrgang 1937, H. 10. Munich, 1937.

———. *Syncategoremata*, ed. J. R. O'Donnell. *Medieval Studies*, III, 46–93. Toronto: Pontifical Institute of Medieval Studies, 1941.

Wood, Anthony à. *Historia et antiquitates universitatis oxoniensis, duobus voluminibus comprehensae*. 2 vols. in 1. Oxford: Sheldonian Theatre, 1674.

———. *The History and Antiquities of the University of Oxford*, ed. J. Gutch. 3 vols. Oxford: University Press, 1792–1796.

Index

Listings for "William of Sherwood" are confined to the Introduction. Except in cases (very rare) of exceptional interest, words and names occurring in Sherwood's examples are not indexed.

175